PINGOUIN
CLASSIC KNITS
FOR ALL THE FAMILY

PINGOUIN
CLASSIC
KNITS
FOR ALL THE FAMILY

SALLY HARDING

PAVILION

First published in Great Britain in 1994 by Pavilion Books Limited,
26 Upper Ground, London SE1 9PD

Text copyright © Pingouin 1994
Photography copyright © Pingouin 1994

Design and typesetting by Ian Muggeridge

A CIP catalogue record for this book is available from the
British Library

ISBN 1 85793 241 2

Printed and bound in Italy by New Interlitho

2 4 6 8 10 9 7 5 3 1

This book may be ordered by post direct from the publisher.
Please contact the Marketing Department.
But try your bookshop first.

CONTENTS

INTRODUCTION
Page 6

ELEGANT ROMANTICS
Page 8

CITY CHIC
Page 40

EVERYDAY CASUALS
Page 68

BRIGHT MODERNS
Page 96

COUNTRY CLASSICS
Page 118

INTRODUCTION

What a treat it was to be asked to select a collection of designs from Pingouin's extensive knitting pattern archive. I have such fond memories of Pingouin yarns and friendly, inviting Pingouin yarn shops. When I first started working on knitting books in the late seventies, Pingouin stood out like a beacon for aspiring designers. They were producing some of the best quality yarns around, as well as undoubtedly the best and most stylish knitting patterns. Those involved in the beginning of the great knitting 'renaissance' at this time will probably, like me, have a soft spot for Pingouin. They played an important role in showing the potential for beautiful handknits and helped to plant the idea that knitwear could find a place in high fashion.

As I was making the selection for this book, I discovered an aspect of Pingouin history that I wasn't familiar with. I was amazed to find that Pingouin had been successful and prominent since the late 1920s. I knew they had a well-deserved worldwide reputation, but I had no idea how long they had been established in the hearts of French knitters, and how influential they had been in the yarn industry. As early as 1929, Pingouin began establishing their own yarn shops and started designing their stylish knitwear.

The Pingouin name and logo have an interesting origin. They were inspired by Alain Saint Ogan, the father of the French comic strip. Saint Ogan's popular characters Zig and Puce were, by all accounts, a French institution in the 1920s. In their capers Zig and Puce were accompanied by their inseparable, much-loved companion Alfred, an amiable *pingouin*. Alfred's popularity led to the stylized animal that became Pingouin's logo – now familiar to knitters all over the world.

Over sixty-five years have passed since Pingouin started producing their sensitively coloured and finely textured yarns and they now have an impressive archive of over 10,000 knitting pattern designs. The admiration I have long had for Pingouin designers was confirmed as

I sifted through designs from the last four years. It wasn't easy to choose a limited number from such an impressive collection. Certainly a whole book could have been devoted to the baby layette designs alone. To my mind, no other yarn manufacturer has ever been able to match Pingouin's ability to design consistently delightful baby knitwear. Perusing catalogues full of these tiny creations made me think what a shame it is that the time-honoured tradition of knitting for newborns has declined over the past 40 years. How quick it is to knit these miniature sweaters and what treasured gifts they are!

Perhaps the three baby outfits included in this book will spur you on to knitting for a baby. Although I have placed the emphasis on knits for women, you will find, apart from the baby knits, several sweaters for men and for children. For the five men's sweaters I have chosen three intricately cabled designs and two very versatile simple ribbed garments. The seven children's sweaters are true classics which will appeal to a wide range of tastes.

While many of the garments are worked either in plain stocking (stockinette) stitch or in simple textures, you will see that cabled surfaces are well represented throughout the book. I am convinced that most knitters love cables as much as I do. They may make the knitting a little slower, but their sculptural quality is spellbinding. One never tires of looking at them and their feel is incredibly comfortable.

The designs included in the book use a range of yarn types: smooth wool yarns, cottons and Pingouin's lovely mohairs. Many of the smooth yarns, and of course the cottons, are machine washable, which is especially convenient for the baby and children knits.

One is always tempted to knit a sweater in the same colour as it appears in the photo, because that is the colour which first catches the eye. But my advice is to be adventurous. Don't stick slavishly to the specified colour. Instead, choose a colour which appeals even more to you, or which matches your wardrobe better. The range of Pingouin colours is not vast, but the colours they do have are stunning. Their soft traditional Shetland-type shades are lovely, and their gentle pastels have a pleasing warmth. Pingouin's range of intense jewel colours are most impressive. They illustrate how strong colours need not look acidic and jarring like many yarns today, but can instead approach the richness of stained-glass colours. Detailed information about the specific Pingouin yarns used is given on page 143. For yarn care you should always refer to the yarn label.

All of the knitting patterns are graded according to how easy or difficult they are (see page 142 for explanation). Only three of the sweaters are a real challenge, nine are for experienced knitters, ten even a moderately average knitter will whizz through, and ten are easy knits. Because the sweaters are graded in this way, you can decide before embarking on a design whether you have chosen an easy project or one which will require a little more time and concentration. If you are like me, you will sometimes be in the mood for knitting something that has an heirloom quality, and at other times you will want to make a sweater to wear within a few weeks.

I hope you enjoy this enticing collection of classic Pingouin designs for all the family and that my selection gives a flavour of all the stunning knitwear designs and gorgeous yarns with which Pingouin has been delighting knitters for many years.

Sally Harding, 1994

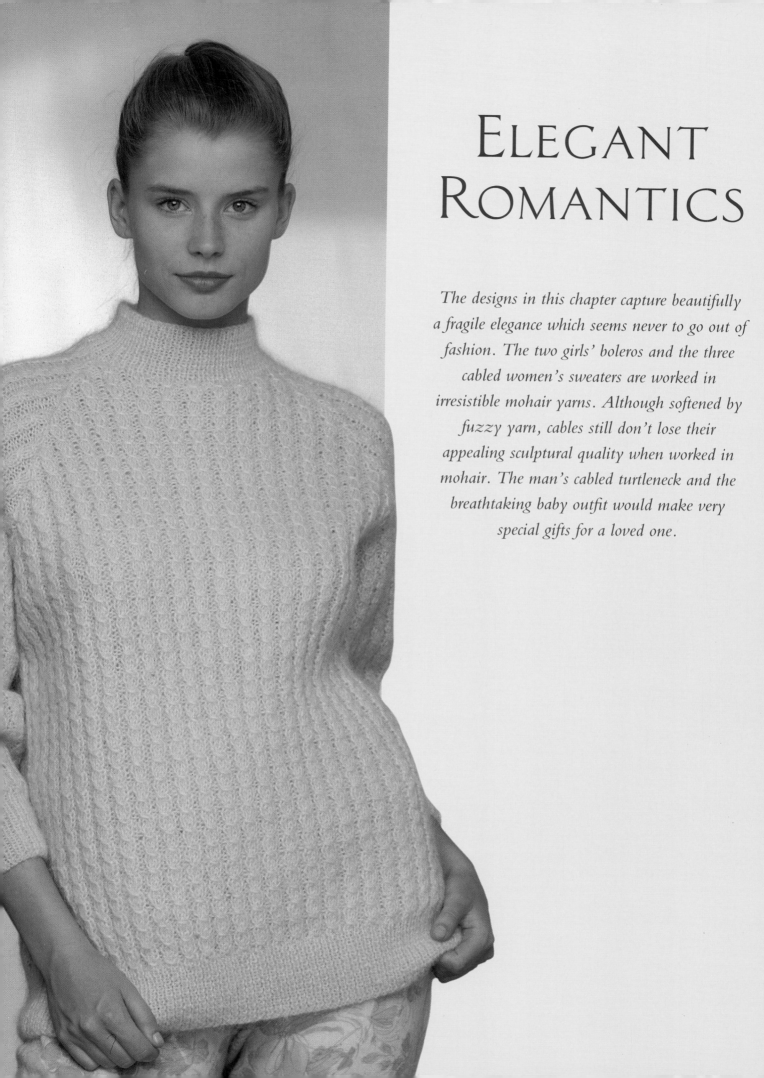

ELEGANT ROMANTICS

The designs in this chapter capture beautifully a fragile elegance which seems never to go out of fashion. The two girls' boleros and the three cabled women's sweaters are worked in irresistible mohair yarns. Although softened by fuzzy yarn, cables still don't lose their appealing sculptural quality when worked in mohair. The man's cabled turtleneck and the breathtaking baby outfit would make very special gifts for a loved one.

Zigzag Cable Cardigan

in Soft'Hair

✳✳✳

Sizes

To fit 81–86 [91: 96: 102]cm/32–34 [36: 38: 40]in bust
Actual width around bust (buttoned) 104 [110: 114.5: 121.5]cm/41¼ [43¾: 46: 48½]in
Directions for larger sizes are in brackets [ ]; if there is only one set of figures it applies to all sizes.

Materials

Pingouin Soft'Hair:
11 [12: 13: 14] balls Amande No. 28
Pair each of 3¾mm and 4½mm (US sizes 5 and 7) needles
Cable needle (cn)
7 buttons

Tension (Gauge)

Worked with 4½mm (US size 7) needles.
Rev st st: 18 sts and 24 rows to 10cm/4in over rev st st; work a sample on 26 sts.
Panel patt: measures 10cm/4in in width; work a sample on 29 sts, working 2 sts in rev st st at each end of row.

Stitches used

Special abbreviations

cable 3 back – slip next 2 sts onto cn and hold at back of work, k1, then k2 from cn.
C5R (cross 5 right) – slip next st onto cn and hold at back of work, k4, then p1 from cn.
C5Rk – work as for C5R, but k1 from cn instead of p1.
C5L (cross 5 left) – slip next 4 sts onto cn and hold at front of work, p1, then k4 from cn.
C5Lk – work as for C5L, but k first st (st which passes behind cn).

Panel pattern

Work panel patt over 25 sts as foll:
1st row (RS) K11, cable 3 back, k11.
2nd row P25.
3rd row K6, C5R, cable 3 back, C5L, k6.
4th row P10, k1, p3, k1, p10.
5th row K5, C5R, p1, cable 3 back, p1, C5L, k5.
6th row P9, k2, p3, k2, p9.
7th row K4, C5R, p2, cable 3 back, p2, C5L, k4.
8th row P8, k3, p3, k3, p8.
9th row K3, C5R, p3, cable 3 back, p3, C5L, k3.
10th row P7, k4, p3, k4, p7.
11th row K2, C5R, p4, cable 3 back, p4, C5L, k2.
12th row P6, k5, p3, k5, p6.
13th row K1, C5R, p5, cable 3 back, p5, C5L, k1.
14th row P5, k6, p3, k6, p5.
15th row C5R, p6, cable 3 back, p6, C5L.
16th row P4, k7, p3, k7, p4.
17th row C5Lk, p6, cable 3 back, p6, C5Rk.
18th row As 14th row.
19th row K1, C5Lk, p5, cable 3 back, p5, C5Rk, k1.
20th row As 12th row.
21st row K2, C5Lk, p4, cable 3 back, p4, C5Rk, k2.
22nd row As 10th row.
23rd row K3, C5Lk, p3, cable 3 back, p3, C5Rk, k3.
24th row As 8th row.
25th row K4, C5Lk, p2, cable 3 back, p2, C5Rk, k4.
26th row As 6th row.
27th row K5, C5Lk, p1, cable 3 back, p1, C5Rk, k5.
28th row As 4th row.
29th row K6, C5Lk, cable 3 back, C5Rk, k6.
30th row P25.
Rep 3rd–30th rows inclusive to form patt (first and 2nd rows are foundation rows and are not worked again).

Instructions

Back

With 3¾mm (US size 5) needles, cast on 101 [105: 109: 113] sts and beg rib as foll:
★★1st rib row (RS) P1, *k1, p1; rep from * to end.
2nd rib row K1, *p1, k1; rep from * to end.
Rep these 2 rows until work measures 5cm/2in from beg, ending with a 2nd rib row.★★
Inc row (RS) Keeping rib correct, rib 5 [5: 4: 4], (work into front and back of next st,

rib 4) 18 [19: 20: 21] times, work into front and back of next st, rib 5 [4: 4: 3]. 120 [125: 130: 135] sts.

Change to 4½mm (US size 7) needles.

Next row (WS) K4 [5: 6: 7], *p25, k4 [5: 6: 7]; rep from * 3 times more.

Beg patt on next row as foll:

1st patt row (RS) P4 [5: 6: 7], *work first row of panel patt over next 25 sts (see Stitches Used), p4 [5: 6: 7]; rep from * 3 times more.

2nd patt row K4 [5: 6: 7], *work 2nd row of panel patt over next 25 sts, k4 [5: 6: 7]; rep from * 3 times more.

Cont working 4 panels across back (working rev st st between panels and at each end of each row as set) until back measures 41 [42: 43: 44]cm/16 [16½: 17: 17¼]in from beg, ending with a WS row.

Armhole shaping

Keeping patt correct as set throughout, cast (bind) off 4 sts at beg of next 2 rows, 3 sts at beg of next 2 rows and 2 sts at beg of next 4 rows.

Dec one st at each end of next 2 [2: 3: 3] alt rows. 94 [99: 102: 107] sts.

Work in patt without shaping (keeping 2 [3: 3: 4] sts at each end of row in rev st st beyond the cable 3 back) until back measures 63 [65: 67: 69]cm/24¾ [25½: 26½: 27]in

from beg, ending with a WS row.

Shoulder and neck shaping

Cast (bind) off 9 [10: 10: 11] sts at beg of next 2 rows.

Next row (RS) Cast (bind) off 9 [10: 10: 11] sts, work in patt until there are 14 sts on RH needle and slip these sts onto a spare needle, cast (bind) off next 30 [31: 34: 35] sts, work in patt to end.

Cont with rem 23 [24: 24: 25] sts only, for left back.

Cast (bind) off 9 [10: 10: 11] sts at beg of next row and 4 sts at neck edge on foll row.

Cast (bind) off rem 10 sts to complete shoulder shaping.

With WS facing, rejoin yarn to neck edge of right back sts and cast (bind) off first 4 sts, then work in patt to end.

Cast (bind) off rem 10 sts.

Right front

With 3¾mm (US size 5) needles, cast on 51 [53: 55: 57] sts and work as for back ribbing from ** to **.

Inc row (RS) Keeping rib correct, rib 5 [4: 5: 3], (work into front and back of next st, rib 4) 8 [9: 9: 10] times, work into front and back of next st, rib 5 [3: 4: 3].
60 [63: 65: 68] sts.

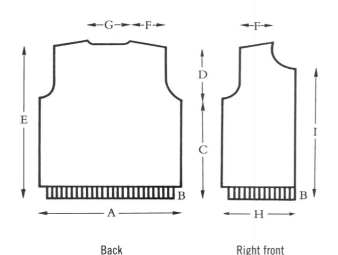

Back

Right front

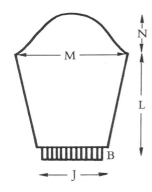

Sleeve

Key

A	51 [54: 56.5: 59.5]cm 20½ [21½: 22¾: 23¾]in	F	12 [13: 13: 14]cm 4¾ [5: 5: 5½]in
B	5cm 2in	G	16.5 [17: 18: 18.5]cm 6½ [6¾: 7: 7¼]in
C	41 [42: 43: 44]cm 16 [16½: 17: 17¼]in	H	25.5 [27: 28: 30]cm 10¼ [10¾: 11¼: 12]in
D	22 [23: 24: 25]cm 8¾ [9: 9½: 9¾]in	I	55 [57: 58: 60]cm 21¾ [22½: 23: 23½]in
E	63 [65: 67: 69]cm 24¾ [25½: 26½: 27]in	J	27.5 [28: 30: 31.5]cm 11 [11¼: 12: 12½]in

L	45 [46: 47: 48]cm 17¾ [18: 18½: 19]in
M	44 [45.5: 47: 48]cm 17¼ [18: 18½: 19]in
N	15 [16: 16.5: 17.5]cm 6 [6¼: 6½: 7]in

Change to 4½mm (US size 7) needles.★★★
Next row (WS) ★K4 [5: 6: 7], p25; rep from ★ once more, k2 [3: 3: 4].
Beg patt on next row as foll:
1st patt row (RS) P2 [3: 3: 4], ★work first row of panel patt over next 25 sts, p4 [5: 6: 7]; rep from ★ once more.
2nd patt row ★K4 [5: 6: 7], work 2nd row of panel patt over next 25 sts; rep from ★ once more, k2 [3: 3: 4].
Cont working 2 panels across front (working rev st st between panels and at each end of each row as set) until front is same length as back to beg of armhole shaping, but ending at armhole edge after a RS row.
Armhole shaping
Keeping patt correct as set throughout, cast (bind) off 4 sts at beg of next row (armhole edge), 3 sts at same edge on next alt row and 2 sts at beg of next 2 alt rows.
Dec one st at armhole edge on next 2 [2: 3: 3] alt rows. 47 [50: 51: 54] sts.
Work in patt without shaping until front measures 55 [57: 58: 60]cm/21¾ [22½: 23: 23½]in from beg, ending at straight centre front edge.
Neck and shoulder shaping
Cast (bind) off 7 [8: 8: 9] sts at beg of next row (neck edge), 3 sts at same edge on next alt row and 2 sts at beg of next 3 alt rows.
Dec one st at neck edge on next 3 [3: 4: 4] alt rows. 28 [30: 30: 32] sts.
Work without shaping until front is same length as back to beg of shoulder shaping, ending at armhole edge.
Cast (bind) off 9 [10: 10: 11] sts at beg of next row and next alt row.
Work one row without shaping.
Cast (bind) off rem 10 sts.

Left front

Work as for right front to ★★★.
Next row (WS) K2 [3: 3: 4], ★p25, k4 [5: 6: 7]; rep from ★ once more.
Beg patt on next row as foll:
1st patt row (RS) ★P4 [5: 6: 7], work first row of panel patt over next 25 sts; rep from ★ once more, p2 [3: 3: 4].
2nd patt row K2 [3: 3: 4], ★work 2nd row of panel patt over next 25 sts, k4 [5: 6: 7]; rep from ★ once more.
Cont in patt as now set and complete as for right front, but reversing all shaping.

Sleeves

With 3¾mm (US size 5) needles, cast on 51 [53: 55: 57] sts and work as for back ribbing from ★★ to ★★.
Inc row (RS) Keeping rib correct, rib 1 [4: 3: 2], (work into front and back of next st, rib 3) 12 [11: 12: 13] times, work into front

and back of next st, rib 1 [4: 3: 2]. 64 [65: 68: 71] sts.
Change to 4½mm (US size 7) needles.
Next row (WS) P1 [0: 0: 0], ★k4 [5: 6: 7], p25; rep from ★ once more, k4 [5: 6: 7], p1 [0: 0: 0].
Beg patt on next row as foll:
1st patt row (RS) For first size only k1 forming part of a panel patt, then ★p4 [5: 6: 7], work first row of panel patt over next 25 sts; rep from ★ once more, p4 [5: 6: 7], then for first size only k1.
Cont in patt as now set for 3 rows more.
Work in patt, inc one st at each end of next row, then on every foll 6th row 5 [4: 5: 6] times, then on every foll 4th row 13 [15: 14: 13] times, working extra sts into patt. 102 [105: 108: 111] sts.
Work in patt without shaping until sleeve measures 45 [46: 47: 48]cm/17¾ [18: 18½: 19]in from beg, ending with a WS row.
Top of sleeve shaping
Keeping patt correct throughout, cast (bind) off 4 sts at beg of next 2 rows, 3 sts at beg of 2 next rows and 2 sts at beg of next 4 rows.
Dec one st at each end of next 3 [4: 5: 6] alt rows.
Cast (bind) off 2 sts at beg of next 14 rows, 3 sts at beg of next 4 rows and 4 sts at beg of next 4 rows.
Cast (bind) off rem 18 [19: 20: 21] sts.

Finishing and borders

Do not press. Join shoulder seams, matching panel patt.
Neckband
With RS facing and 3¾mm (US size 5) needles, pick up and k26 [27: 29: 30] sts evenly along right front neck edge, 35 [37: 39: 41] sts across back neck and 26 [27: 29: 30] sts along left front neck.
87 [9l: 97: 101] sts.
Beg with 2nd rib row, work in kl, pl rib for 6 rows, then cast (bind) off loosely in rib.
Button band
With 3¾mm (US size 5) needles, cast on 11 sts for button band and work in k1, p1 rib until band, when slightly stretched, fits along front edge of left front to top of neckband.
Cast (bind) off in rib.
Sew button band to left front.
Mark positions of buttons on button band, the first to come 1.5cm/½in from lower edge, the last 2cm/¾in from top edge and the rem 5 evenly spaced between.
Buttonhole band
Work buttonhole band as for button band, but working buttonholes over 2 rows when reached as foll:
1st buttonhole row (RS) Keeping rib correct, rib 4, cast (bind) off 2, rib to end.

2nd buttonhole row Rib as set, casting on 2 sts over those cast (bound) off in last row.
Sew in sleeves, then join side and sleeve seams.
Sew buttonhole band to right front.
Sew on the buttons to correspond with the buttonholes.

GIRL'S SLEEVELESS BOLERO

IN SWEET'HAIR

Sizes

To fit ages 2 [4: 6: 8: 10] years or 53 [58: 63: 68: 72]cm/21 [23: 25: 27: 28½]in chest
Actual width around chest (fastened) 73 [78: 83: 86.5: 91.5]cm/29¼ [31: 33: 34½: 36½]in
Directions for larger sizes are in brackets [ ]; if there is only one set of figures it applies to all sizes.

Materials

PINGOUIN Sweet'Hair:
3 [4: 4: 5: 5] balls Rose No. 04
Pair each of 3¼mm and 3¾mm (US sizes 3 and 5) needles

Tension (Gauge)

Worked with 3¾mm (US size 5) needles.
Moss (seed) st: 21 sts and 38 rows to 10cm/4in over moss (seed) st; work a sample on 31 sts.

Stitches used

The bolero is worked in simple moss (seed) st with k1, p1 ribbing. The directions for these stitches are given in the instructions.

Instructions

Body

Body of bolero is worked in one piece until armholes are reached.
With 3¼mm (US size 3) needles, cast on 151 [161: 171: 179: 189] sts and beg rib as foll:
1st rib row (RS) P1, *k1, p1; rep from * to end.
2nd rib row K1, *p1, k1; rep from * to end.
Rep these 2 rows once more.
Change to 3¾mm (US size 5) needles.

Beg moss (seed) st patt on next row as foll:
1st patt row (RS) K1, *p1, k1; rep from * to end.
Last row is repeated to form moss (seed) st patt. Mark first row as RS of work and cont in moss (seed) st until body measures 10 [12: 13: 14: 15]cm/4 [4¾: 5: 5½: 6]in from beg, ending with a WS row.

Divide for armholes

Keeping moss (seed) st correct throughout, divide for armholes on next row as foll:
Next row (RS) Work first 38 [41: 43: 45: 48] sts in moss (seed) st for right front, then turn leaving rem sts on a spare needle.

Right front

Cont on these sts only for right front and keeping moss (seed) st correct throughout (for first and 5th sizes WS rows will now beg with p1), **work in patt until front measures 16 [19: 21: 23: 24]cm/6¼ [7½: 8¼: 9: 9½]in from beg, ending at centre front edge after a WS row.

Neck shaping

Cast (bind) off 5 [7: 7: 8: 9] sts at beg of next row (neck edge), then 2 sts at same edge on next 2 alt rows.
Work one row without shaping.
Dec one st at neck edge on next and every foll alt row 3 times in all, then dec one st at same edge on every foll 4th row 3 [3: 3: 3: 4] times. 23 [24: 26: 27: 28] sts.
Work without shaping until front measures 24 [27: 29: 31: 33]cm/9½ [10¾: 11¼: 12½: 13]in from beg, ending at armhole edge.

Shoulder shaping

Cast (bind) off 6 sts at beg of next row and next alt row, then 6 [6: 7: 7: 7] sts at same edge on next alt row.
Work one row without shaping.
Cast (bind) off rem 5 [6: 7: 8: 9] sts.

Back

With RS facing, rejoin yarn to sts left unworked at armhole opening and beg with k1 [p1: p1: p1: k1], work 75 [79: 85: 89: 93] sts in moss (seed) st for back, then turn leaving rem 38 [41: 43: 45: 48] sts of left front on a spare needle.
Cont on these sts only for back, work in patt until back measures 24 [27: 29: 31: 33]cm/9½ [10¾: 11¼: 12½: 13]in from beg, ending with a WS row.

Shoulder and neck shaping

Cast (bind) off 6 sts at beg of next 4 rows.
Next row (RS) Cast (bind) off 6 [6: 7: 7: 7] sts, work in patt until moss (seed) st until there are 8 [9: 10: 11: 12] sts on RH needle and slip these sts onto a spare needle, cast (bind) off next 23 [25: 27: 29: 31] sts, work in moss (seed) st to end.
Cont with rem 14 [15: 17: 18: 19] sts only, for left back.
Cast (bind) off 6 [6: 7: 7: 7] sts at beg of next row and 3 sts at neck edge on foll row.

Cast (bind) off rem 5 [6: 7: 8: 9] sts to complete shoulder shaping.
With WS facing, rejoin yarn to neck edge of right back sts and cast (bind) off 3 sts, then work in moss (seed) st to end.
Cast (bind) off rem 5 [6: 7: 8: 9] sts.

Left front
With RS facing, rejoin yarn to left front sts and beg with p1 [k1: k1: k1: p1], work in moss (seed) st to end.
Complete as for right front from ★★ to end, but reversing all shapings.

Finishing and borders

Do not press moss (seed) st.
Armbands
With RS facing and 3¼mm (US size 3) needles, pick up and k34 [36: 39: 41: 43] sts evenly down right front armhole edge, one st at base of armhole opening and 34 [36: 39: 41: 43] sts up right back armhole edge. 69 [73: 79: 83: 87] sts.
Beg with 2nd rib row, work 4 rows in rib as given on lower border.
Cast (bind) off loosely in rib.
Work left armband in same way, but beg pick up down back armhole edge.
Join shoulder seams and ends of armbands.
Neckband
With RS facing and 3¼mm (US size 3) needles, pick up and k28 [30: 30: 31: 34] sts evenly along right front neck edge, 33 [35: 37: 39: 41] sts across back neck and 28 [30: 30: 31: 34] sts along left front neck. 89 [95: 97: 101: 109] sts. Work ribbing as for armbands.

Front bands
With RS facing and 3¼mm (US size 3) needles, pick up and k41 [49: 53: 57: 59] sts evenly up front edge of right front including edge of neckband. Work ribbing as for armbands.
Work band on left front as for band on right front, but picking up sts beg at neck edge.
Tie strips
With 3¼mm (US size 3) needles, cast on 5 sts to beg tie strip.
1st row (RS) K2, p1, k2.
2nd row (K1, p1) twice, k1.
Rep these 2 rows until strip measures 16cm/6¼in from beg.
Cast (bind) off in patt.
Make 5 more strips in same way.
Sew cast-on edge of each strip underneath front bands, placing one strip at lower edge on each front, another at neck edge and a 3rd evenly spaced between.

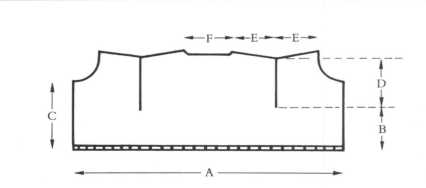

Key

A 72 [76.5: 81.5: 85: 90]cm
   28¾ [30½: 32½: 34: 36]in
B 10 [12: 13: 14: 15]cm
   4 [4¾: 5: 5½: 6]in
C 16 [19: 21: 23: 24]cm
   6¼ [7½: 8¼: 9: 9½]in

D 14 [15: 16: 17: 18]cm
   5½ [6: 6¼: 6¾: 7]in
E 11 [11.5: 12: 12.5: 13]cm
   4¼ [4½: 4¾: 5: 5¼]in
F 13.5 [14.5: 15.5: 16.5: 17.5]cm
   5¼ [5¾: 6: 6½: 6¾]in

MAN'S CABLED TURTLENECK

IN STAR +

✳✳✳✳

Sizes

One size only to fit 102 to 107cm/40 to 42in chest
Actual width around chest when completed 122cm/48½in

Materials

PINGOUIN Star +:
20 balls Ecru No. 17
Pair each of 3¼mm 3¾mm and 4mm
(US sizes 3, 5 and 6) needles
2 cable needles (cn)

Tension (Gauge)

Worked with 4mm (US size 6) needles.
Rev st st: 19 sts and 27 rows to 10cm/4in over rev st st; work a sample on 25 sts.
Panel patt No. 1: 28 sts and 27 rows to 10cm/4in over panel patt No. 1 worked at beg of back and front; work a sample on 36 sts, beg sample with foundation row worked as foll: k3, p4, k6, p4, k2, p4, k6, p4, k3 – then work panel patt No. 1 at centre, keeping 2 sts in rev st st at each end of row.
Main cable patt: 24 sts and 27 rows to 10cm/4in over main cable patt worked on back and front; it is not necessary to work a sample of this patt provided the other tensions (gauges) are correct.

Stitches used

Special abbreviations

kfb – knit into front and back of next st.
pfb – purl into front and back of next st.
C5L (cross 5 left) – slip next 4 sts onto cn and hold at front of work, p1, then k4 from cn.

C5Lk – work as for C5L, but k first st (st which passes behind cn).
C5R (cross 5 right) – slip next st onto cn and hold at back of work, k4, then p1 from cn.
C5Rk – work as for C5R, but k1 from cn instead of p1.
cable 8 front – slip next 4 sts onto cn and hold at front of work, k4, then k4 from cn.
cross 8 – slip next 3 sts onto first cn and hold at front of work, slip next st onto 2nd cn and hold at back of work, p next st, now k3 from first cn, k next 3 sts, then p1 from 2nd cn.
cross 6 – slip next 2 sts onto first cn and hold at front of work, slip next st onto 2nd cn and hold at back of work, p next st, now k2 from first cn, k next 2 sts, then p1 from 2nd cn.
C2L (cross 2 left) – pass RH needle behind first st on LH needle and p into back of 2nd st leaving it on LH needle, then k into front of first st and slip both sts off LH needle.
C2R (cross 2 right) – pass RH needle in front of first st on LH needle and lift up 2nd st and k it leaving it on LH needle, then p first st and slip both sts off LH needle at the same time.

Panel pattern No. 1

Work panel patt No. 1 (for beg of back and front) over 32 sts as foll:
1st row (RS) P1, C5L, p4, C5R, p2, C5L, p4, C5R, p1.
2nd row K2, (p4, k4) 3 times, p4, k2.
3rd row P2, C5L, p2, C5R, p4, C5L, p2, C5R, p2.
4th row K3, p4, k2, p4, k6, p4, k2, p4, k3.
5th row P3, C5L, C5R, p6, C5L, C5R, p3.
6th row K4, p8, k8, p8, k4.
7th row P4, cable 8 front, p8, cable 8 front, p4.
8th row As 6th row.
9th row P3, C5R, C5L, p6, C5R, C5L, p3.
10th row As 4th row.
11th row P2, C5R, p2, C5L, p4, C5R, p2, C5L, p2.
12th row As 2nd row.
13th row P1, C5R, p4, C5L, p2, C5R, p4, C5L, p1.
14th row K1, p4, k6, p4, k2, p4, k6, p4, k1.
15th row (C5R, p6, C5L) twice.
16th row P4, k8, p8, k8, p4.
17th row K4, p8, cable 8 front, p8, k4.
18th row As 16th row.
19th row K4, p8, k8, p8, k4.
20th–25th rows Rep rows 18 and 19 three times.
26th row As 16th row.
27th row As 17th row.
28th row As 16th row.
29th row (C5L, p6, C5R) twice.
30th row As 14th row.
31st–43rd rows Rep first–13th rows.
This completes panel patt No. 1.

Panel pattern No. 2

Work panel patt No. 2 over 34 sts (on sleeves) as foll:
1st row (RS) K9, C5Lk, p6, C5Rk, k9.
2nd row P14, k6, p14.
3rd row K10, C5Lk, p4, C5Rk, k10.
4th row P15, k4, p15.
5th row K11, C5Lk, p2, C5Rk, k11.
6th row P16, k2, p16.
7th row K12, C5Lk, C5Rk, k12.
8th row P34.
9th row K13, cable 8 front, k13.
10th row As 8th row.
11th row K12, C5R, C5L, k12.
12th row As 6th row.
13th row K11, C5R, p2, C5L, k11.
14th row As 4th row.
15th row K10, C5R, p4, C5L, k10.
16th row As 2nd row.
17th row K9, C5R, p6, C5L, k9.
18th row P13, k8, p13.
Cont in this way, moving the k4 ribs one st outwards on every RS row and keeping all sts at centre in rev st st, until 35th row has been worked and no sts rem at sides.
36th row P4, k26, p4.
37th row C5Lk, p24, C5Rk.
38th row P5, k24, p5.
39th row K1, C5Lk, p22, C5Rk, k1.
40th row P6, k22, p6.
41st row K2, C5Lk, p20, C5Rk, k2.
Cont in this way, moving the k4 ribs one st towards the centre on every RS row and keeping all sts at sides in st st, until 53rd row has been worked and there are 8 sts in rev st st at centre of panel.
54th row P12, k8, p12.
55th–72nd row Rep first–18th rows.
This completes panel patt No. 2.

Instructions

Back

With 3¼mm (US size 3) needles, cast on 111 sts and beg rib as foll:
1st rib row (RS) P1, *k1, p1; rep from * to end.
2nd rib row K1, *p1, k1; rep from * to end.
Rep these 2 rows until work measures 8cm/3in from beg, ending with a 2nd rib row.
Inc row (RS) P1, *p1, kfb twice, p2, pfb, p2, kfb twice, pfb, kfb twice, p2, pfb, p2, kfb twice, p1,* pfb;** rep from * to ** 3 times more, then rep from * to *, p1. 170 sts.
Change to 4mm (US size 6) needles.
Work foundation row for panel patt No. 1 on next row as foll:
Foundation row (WS) K1, *k1, p4, k6, p4, k2, p4, k6, p4, k1,* k2;** rep from * to ** 3 times more, then rep from * to *, k1.

Beg panel patt No. 1 on next row as foll:
1st row (RS) P1, ★work first row of panel patt No. 1 over next 32 sts, p2;★ rep from ★ to ★ 3 times more, work first row of panel patt No. 1 over next 32 sts, p1.

Cont as now set, working 5 panels across back (with 2 sts in rev st st between the panels and one st at each side) until 43rd row of panel patt No. 1 has been worked, so ending with a RS row.

Dec row (WS) K1, ★k1, p2tog twice, k2, k2tog, k2, p2tog twice, k2tog, p2tog twice, k2, k2 tog, k2, p2tog twice, k1,★ k2tog;★★ rep from ★ to ★★ 3 times more, then rep from ★ to ★, k1. 111 sts.

K one row (RS).

Beg with a K row, work 3 rows in rev st st, so ending with a WS (k) row.

Inc row (RS) (K3, kfb) twice, k4, ★kfb twice, (p2, pfb) 4 times, p2, kfb twice;★ k4, kfb, k4, kfb twice, p4, pfb, p4, kfb twice, k3, kfb, k3, kfb twice, p4, pfb, p4, kfb twice, k4, kfb, k4; rep from ★ to ★, k4, (kfb, k3) twice. 144 sts.

Work foundation row for main cable patt on next row as foll:

Foundation row (WS) P18, k18, p18, k10, p16, k10, p18, k18, p18.

Beg main cable patt on next row as foll:
1st row (RS) K14, C5Lk, p16, C5Rk, k9, C5R, p9, C5Rk, k8, C5Lk, p9, C5L, k9, C5Lk, p16, C5Rk, k14.

2nd row P19, k16, (p18, k10) twice, p18, k16, p19.

3rd row K15, C5Lk, p14, C5Rk, k9, C5R, p9, C5Rk, k10, C5Lk, p9, C5L, k9, C5Lk, p14, C5Rk, k15.

4th row P20, k14, p18, k10, p20, k10, p18, k14, p20.

5th row K16, C5Lk, p12, C5Rk, k9, C5R, p9, C5Rk, k12, C5Lk, p9, C5L, k9, C5Lk, p12, C5Rk, k16.

Cont in this way, moving the k4 ribs in the same directions on every RS row and working sts at sides in st st, until 17th row has been worked (beg and ending with k22).

18th row P45, k10, p34, k10, p45.

19th row K23, cable 8 front, k14, p10, k34, p10, k14, cable 8 front, k23.

20th row As 18th row.

21st row K22, C5R, C5L, k9, C5L, p9, C5L, k24, C5R, p9, C5R, k9, C5R, C5L, k22.

22nd row P26, k2, p18, k10, p32, k10, p18, k2, p26.

23rd row K21, C5R, p2, C5L, k9, C5L, p9, C5L, k22, C5R, p9, C5R, k9, C5R, k2, C5L, k21.

24th row P25, k4, p18, k10, p30, k10, p18, k4, p25.

25th row K20, C5R, p4, C5L, k9, C5L, p9, C5L, k20, C5R, p9, C5R, k9, C5R, p4, C5L, k20.

Cont in this way, moving the ribs in the same directions on every RS row until 35th row has been worked (beg and ending with k15).

Work 36th row in patt as set.

Armhole shaping

Keeping patt correct as set, cast (bind) off 7 sts at beg of next 2 rows. 130 sts.

Cont as set, moving the ribs as before, until 45th row has been worked (beg and ending with k3).

Work 46th patt row as set.

47th row K7, p26, k14, C5Lk, p9, cross 8, p9, C5Rk, k14, p26, k7.

48th row P7, k26, p19, k10, p6, k10, p19, k26, p7.

49th row K3, C5Lk, p24, C5Rk, k11, C5Lk, p9, cross 6, p9, C5Rk, k11, C5Lk, p24, C5Rk, k3.

50th row P8, k24, p21, k10, p4, k10, p21, k24, p8.

51st row K4, C5Lk, p22, C5Rk, k13, C5Lk, p9, C2L, C2R, p9, C5Rk, k13, C5Lk, p22, C5Rk, k4.

52nd row P9, (k22, p23) twice, k22, p9.

53rd row K5, ★C5Lk, p20, C5Rk, k15;★ rep from ★ to ★ once more, C5Lk, p20, C5Rk, k5.

Cont in this way, moving the ribs in the same directions on every RS row and keeping sts in centre in rev st st, until 73rd row has been worked (beg and ending with k15).

74th row Purl all sts.

75th row K16, (cable 8 front, k37) twice, cable 8 front, k16.

76th row Purl.

77th row P15, (C5R, C5L, k35) twice, C5R, C5L, p15.

78th row K19, (p2, k43) twice, p2, k19.

79th row P14, (C5R, p2, C5L, k33) twice, C5R, p2, C5L, p14.

Cont in this way, moving the ribs in these directions, until 106th row has been worked.

Shoulder and neck shaping

During foll rows keep patt correct and cast (bind) off tightly over the k4 ribs.

Next row (RS) Cast (bind) off 13 sts, work in patt until there are 33 sts on RH needle and slip these sts onto a spare needle, cast (bind) off next 38 sts, work in patt to end.

Cont with rem 46 sts only, for left back.

★★★Cast (bind) off 13 sts at beg of next row and 4 sts at neck edge on foll row.★★★

Rep from ★★★ to ★★★ once more.

Cast (bind) off rem 12 sts to complete shoulder shaping.

With WS facing, rejoin yarn to neck edge of right back sts and cast (bind) off first 4 sts, then work in patt to end.

Cast (bind) off 13 sts at beg of next row and 4 sts at neck edge on foll row.

Cast (bind) off rem 12 sts.

Front

Work as given for back until there are 20 rows fewer than on back to beg of shoulder shaping, so ending with a WS row.

Neck and shoulder shaping

Keeping patt correct, divide for neck on next row as foll:

Next row (RS) Work first 57 sts in patt and slip these sts onto a spare needle, cast (bind) off next 16 sts, work in patt to end.

Cont with rem 57 sts only, for right front.

Work one row without shaping.

★★★★Cast (bind) off 4 sts at beg of next row (neck edge) and next alt row, then 2 sts at same edge on next 3 alt rows.

Work one row without shaping.

Dec one st at neck edge on next row and every foll alt row 5 times in all. 38 sts.

Keeping neck edge straight, cast (bind) off 13 sts at beg of next row (armhole edge) and next alt row.

Work one row without shaping.

Cast (bind) off rem 12 sts.

With WS facing, rejoin yarn to neck edge of left front sts and complete as for right front from ★★★★ to end.

Sleeves

With 3¼mm (US size 3) needles, cast on 51 sts and work rib as on back for 8cm (3in), ending with a 2nd rib row.

Inc row (RS) P2, pfb, p1, rep from ★ to ★★ in the first inc row above back ribbing, then rep from ★ to ★, p1, pfb, p2. 76 sts.

Change to 4mm (US size 6) needles.

Work foundation row for panel patt No. 1 on next row as foll:

Foundation row (WS) K5, rep from ★ to ★★ in foundation row given above back ribbing (for panel patt No. 1), then rep from ★ to ★, k5.

Beg panel patt No. 1 on next row as foll:

1st row (RS) P5, work first row of panel patt No. 1 over next 32 sts, p2, work first row of panel patt No. 1 over next 32 sts, p5.

Cont as now set, working 2 panels across sleeve (with sts at sides in rev st st) until 4 rows more have been worked.

Cont in patt as set, inc one st at each end of next row, then on every foll 4th row 9 times, keeping these extra sts in rev st st.

Work one row on these 96 sts to complete patt No. 1.

Dec row (WS) K15, rep from ★ to ★★ in corresponding row of back, then rep from ★ to ★, k15. 73 sts.

K one row (RS).

Beg with a k row, work 3 rows in rev st st, so ending with a WS row.

Inc row (RS) K31, kfb twice, p3, pfb, p3, kfb twice, k31. 78 sts.

Work foundation row for panel patt No. 2 on next row as foll:

Foundation row (WS) P35, k8, p35.

Beg panel patt No. 2 on next row as foll:

1st row (RS) K22, work first row of panel patt No. 2 over next 34 sts, k22.

Work 2 rows more in panel patt No. 2 as now set (with sts at sides in st st) without shaping.

Cont in patt as set, inc one st at each end of next row, then on every foll 4th row 13 times more, keeping these extra sts in st st.

Cont in patt on these 106 sts until panel patt No. 2 has been completed.

Cast (bind) off all sts.

Do not press. Join right shoulder seam, matching patt.

Collar

With RS facing and 3¼mm (US size 3) needles, pick up and k67 sts evenly around front neck edge and 50 sts across back neck. 117 sts.

Beg with first rib row as on back, work in k1, p1 rib for 9cm/3½in.

Change to 3¾mm (US size 5) needles and cont in rib as set, work 8cm/3in more.

Cast (bind) off loosely in rib.

Join left shoulder seam, cont seam along sides of collar for 6cm/2¼in, then join remainder of seam on reverse side.

Sew cast (bound) off edge of sleeves to sides of armholes and sew armhole cast (bind) off to last 10 rows on sides of sleeves.

Join side and sleeve seams.

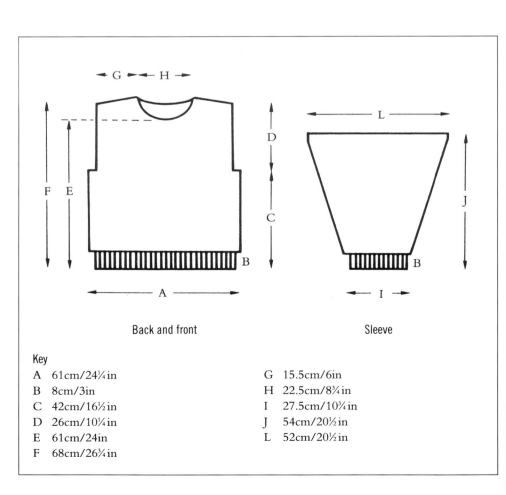

Back and front

Sleeve

Key

A	61cm/24¼in		G	15.5cm/6in
B	8cm/3in		H	22.5cm/8¾in
C	42cm/16½in		I	27.5cm/10¾in
D	26cm/10¼in		J	54cm/20½in
E	61cm/24in		L	52cm/20½in
F	68cm/26¾in			

V-NECK CABLED CARDIGAN

IN SOFT'HAIR

✳✳✳

Sizes

To fit 81 [86 to 91: 96 to 102]cm/32 [34 to 36: 38 to 40]in bust
Actual width around bust (buttoned) 94 [101: 114.5: 122.5]cm/37¾ [40½: 46: 49]in
Directions for larger sizes are in brackets [ ]; if there is only one set of figures it applies to all sizes.

Materials

PINGOUIN Soft'Hair:
10 [11: 12: 13] balls Ecru No. 21
Pair each of 3¾mm and 4½mm (US sizes 5 and 7) needles
Cable needle (cn) and 5 buttons

Tension (Gauge)

Worked with 4½mm (US size 7) needles.
Rev st st: 18 sts and 24 rows to 10cm/4in over rev st st; work a sample on 26 sts.
Panel patt: measures 4.5cm/1¾in in width; work a sample on 18 sts, working 3 sts in rev st st at each end of row.
Overall patt: 24 sts and 24 rows to 10cm/4in over overall patt.

Stitches used

Special abbreviations

pfb – purl into front and back of next st.
C4L (cross 4 left) – slip next st onto cn and hold at front of work, p3, then k1 from cn.
C4R (cross 4 right) – slip next 3 sts onto cn and hold at back of work, k1, then p3 from cn.

Panel pattern

Work panel patt over 12 sts as foll:
1st row (RS) K3, p6, k3.

2nd row P3, k6, p3.
3rd and 4th rows As first and 2nd rows.
5th row K2, C4L, C4R, k2.
6th row (P2, k3) twice, p2.
7th row K1, C4L, k2, C4R, k1.
8th row P1, k3, p4, k3, p1.
9th row C4L, k4, C4R.
10th row K3, p6, k3.
11th row P3, k6, p3.
12th row As 10th row.
13th row C4R, k4, C4L.
14th row As 8th row.
15th row K1, C4R, k2, C4L, k1.
16th row As 6th row.
17th row K2, C4R, C4L, k2.
18th row As 2nd row.
19th and 20th rows As first and 2nd rows.
These last 20 rows form one patt repeat of the panel pattern.

Instructions

Back

With 3¾mm (US size 5) needles, cast on 95 [101: 113: 121] sts and beg rib as foll:
★★1st rib row (RS) P1, ★k1, p1; rep from ★ to end.
2nd rib row K1, ★p1, k1; rep from ★ to end.
Rep these 2 rows until work measures 4cm/1½in from beg, ending with a first rib row.★★
Inc row (WS) P5 [5: 4: 5], (pfb, p5 [5: 4: 4]) 14 [15: 21: 22] times, pfb, p5 [5: 3: 5]. 110 [117: 135: 144] sts.
Change to 4½mm (US size 7) needles.
Beg patt on next row as foll:
1st patt row (RS) P4 [5: 2: 3], ★work first row of panel patt over next 12 sts (see Stitches Used), p6 [7: 5: 6];★ rep from ★ to ★ 4 [4: 6: 6] times more, work first row of panel patt over next 12 sts, p4 [5: 2: 3].
2nd patt row K4 [5: 2: 3], work 2nd row of panel patt over next 12 sts, ★k6 [7: 5: 6], work 2nd row of panel patt over next 12 sts;★ rep from ★ to ★ 4 [4: 6: 6] times more, k4 [5: 2: 3].
Cont working 6 [6: 8: 8] panels across back (working rev st st between panels and at each end of each row as set) until back measures 38 [39: 40: 41]cm/15 [15¼: 15¾: 16]in from beg, ending with a WS row.
Armhole shaping
Keeping patt correct as set throughout, cast (bind) off 4 sts at beg of next 2 rows, 3 sts at beg of next 2 [2: 4: 4] rows and 2 sts at beg of next 4 [6: 6: 6] rows.
Work one row without shaping.
Dec one st at each end of next row and every foll alt row 3 [2: 2: 3] times in all. 82 [87: 99: 106] sts.
Work in patt without shaping (keeping 8 [9: 1: 2] sts at each end of row in rev st st)

until back measures 59 [61: 63: 65]cm/23¼ [23¾: 24¾: 25½]in from beg, ending with a WS row.
Shoulder and neck shaping
Cast (bind) off 7 [8: 10: 11] sts at beg of next 2 rows.
Next row (RS) Cast (bind) off 7 [8: 10: 11] sts, work in patt until there are 12 [12: 13: 14] sts on RH needle and slip these sts onto a spare needle, cast (bind) off next 30 [31: 33: 34] sts, work in patt to end.
Cont with rem 19 [20: 23: 25] sts only, for left back.
Cast (bind) off 7 [8: 10: 11] sts at beg of next row and 4 sts at neck edge on foll row.
Cast (bind) off rem 8 [8: 9: 10] sts to complete shoulder shaping.
With WS facing, rejoin yarn to neck edge of right back sts and cast (bind) off first 4 sts, then work in patt to end.
Cast (bind) off rem 8 [8: 9: 10] sts.

Right front

With 3¾mm (US size 5) needles, cast on 49 [53: 57: 61] sts and work as for back ribbing from ★★ to ★★.
Inc row (WS) (P5 [6: 4: 4], pfb) 7 [7: 10: 11] times, p rem 7 [4: 7: 6] sts. 56 [60: 67: 72] sts.
Change to 4½mm (US size 7) needles.
Beg patt on next row as foll:
1st patt row (RS) P4 [5: 2: 3], rep from ★ to ★ in first patt row of back 2 [2: 3: 3] times, work first row of panel patt over next 12 sts, p4 [5: 2: 3].
Cont working 3 [3: 4: 4] panels across front (working rev st st between panels and at each end of each row as set) until front measures 27 [29: 31: 33]cm/10½ [11: 12: 12¾]in from beg, ending at centre front edge after a WS row.
Front and armhole shaping
Keeping patt correct as set throughout, dec one st at beg of next row (centre front edge) and every foll alt row 5 [7: 5: 7] times in all, then dec at same edge on every foll 4th row 15 [14: 15: 14] times, **and at the same time** when front is same length as back to beg of armhole shaping and ending at armhole edge, cast (bind) off 4 sts at beg of next row (armhole edge) 3 sts at same edge on next 1 [1: 2: 2] alt rows and 2 sts on next 2 [3: 3: 3] alt rows, then dec one st at armhole edge on next 3 [2: 2: 3] alt rows.
When all decs are completed, work without shaping on rem 22 [24: 29: 32] sts until front is same length as back to beg of shoulder shaping, ending at armhole edge.
Shoulder shaping
Cast (bind) off 7 [8: 10: 11] sts at beg of next row and foll alt row.
Work one row without shaping.
Cast (bind) off rem 8 [8: 9: 10] sts.

Left front

Work as for right front, arranging patt in same way but reversing all shapings.

Sleeves

With 3¾mm (US size 5) needles, cast on 49 [51: 55: 57] sts and work as for back ribbing from ** to **.

Inc row (WS) P4 [1: 5: 4], (pfb, p3) 10 [12: 11: 12] times, pfb, p4 [1: 5: 4]. 60 [64: 67: 70] sts.

Change to 4½mm (US size 7) needles.
Beg patt on next row as foll:

1st patt row (RS) P6 [7: 2: 2], rep from * to * in first patt row of back 2 [2: 3: 3] times, work first row of panel patt over next 12 sts, p6 [7: 2: 2].

Cont in patt as now set for 4 rows more. Work in patt, inc one st at each end of next row, then on every foll 6th row 10 [9: 10: 7] times, then on every foll 4th row 5 [7: 6: 11] times, working extra sts into patt. 92 [98: 101: 108] sts.

Work in patt without shaping until sleeve measures 43 [44: 45: 46]cm/17 [17¼: 17¾: 18]in from beg or desired length to underarm, ending with a WS row (and ending with same patt row as back to

beginning of armhole if possible).

Top of sleeve shaping

Keeping patt correct throughout, cast (bind) off 4 sts at beg of next 2 rows, 3 sts at beg of next 2 [2: 4: 4] rows and 2 sts at beg of next 4 [6: 6: 6] rows.

Work one row without shaping.
Dec one st at each end of next row and every foll alt row 5 [5: 6: 5] times in all.
Cast (bind) off 2 sts at beg of next 14 [14: 12: 16] rows and 4 sts at beg of next 4 rows.
Cast (bind) off rem 16 [18: 17: 18] sts.

Finishing and front bands

Do not press. Join shoulder seams, matching panel patt.

Button band

With 3¾mm (US size 5) needles, cast on 13 sts for button band and work in rib as foll:

1st row (RS) K2, (p1, k1) 5 times, k1.
2nd row (K1, p1) 6 times, k1.
Rep these 2 rows until band, when slightly stretched, fits along front edge of left front to centre back neck.
Cast (bind) off in rib.
Sew button band to left front.
Mark positions of buttons on button band, the first to come 2cm/¾in from lower edge,

the last at beg of V-neck shaping and the rem 3 evenly spaced between.

Buttonhole band

Work buttonhole band as for button band, but when positions of buttonholes are reached (ending with a RS row facing for next row) work buttonholes over 2 rows as foll:

1st buttonhole row (RS) K2, p1, k1, p1, cast (bind) off 3, work in patt to end.
2nd buttonhole row (K1, p1) twice, k1, cast on 3 sts onto RH needle, (k1, p1) twice, k1.
Sew buttonhole band to right front and join front bands at centre back neck.
Sew in sleeves, then join side and sleeve seams.
Sew on the buttons to correspond with the buttonholes.

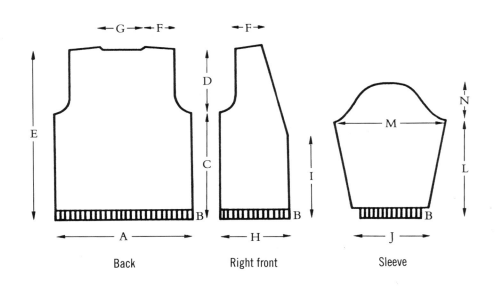

Back   Right front   Sleeve

Key

A	45.5 [48.5: 56: 60]cm	
	18¼ [19½: 22½: 24]in	
B	4cm	
	1½in	
C	38 [39: 40: 41]cm	
	15 [15¼: 15¾: 16]in	
D	21 [22: 23: 24]cm	
	8¼ [8½: 9: 9½]in	
E	59 [61: 63: 65]cm	
	23¼ [23¾: 24¾: 25½]in	

F	9 [10: 12: 13]cm	
	3½ [4: 4¾: 5¼]in	
G	15.5 [16: 17: 17.5]cm	
	6¼ [6½: 6¾: 7]in	
H	23 [25: 28: 30]cm	
	9¼ [10: 11¼: 12]in	
I	27 [29: 31: 33]cm	
	10½ [11: 12: 12¾]in	
J	25 [26.5: 28: 29]cm	
	10 [10½: 11: 11½]in	

L	43 [44: 45: 46]cm	
	17 [17¼: 17¾: 18]in	
M	38 [40.5: 42: 45]cm	
	15¼ [16¼: 16¾: 18]in	
N	15 [15.5: 16.5: 17.5]cm	
	6 [6¼: 6½: 7]in	

MOCK CABLE RAGLAN PULLOVER

IN SOFT'HAIR

**

Sizes

To fit 86 to 91 [96 to 102]cm/34 to 36 [38 to 40]in bust
Actual width around bust when completed 110 [118]cm/44 [47]in
Directions for larger size are in brackets [ ]; if there is only one set of figures it applies to both sizes.

Materials

PINGOUIN Soft'Hair:
12 [13] balls Aurore No. 04
Pair each of 3¾ mm and 4½ mm (US sizes 5 and 7) needles

Tension (Gauge)

Worked with 4½ mm (US size 7) needles.
Mock cable patt: 24 sts and 24 rows to 10cm/4in over mock cable patt; work a sample on 32 sts, flattening work slightly when measuring width.

Stitches used

Special abbreviations

yo (yarn over) – take yarn to front of work between two needles, then take yarn from front to back over top of RH needle to make a new loop on RH needle.
k loop – insert LH needle from front to back under horizontal loop between needles, then k through back of it.

Mock cable pattern

Work mock cable patt over a multiple of 5 sts plus 2 extra sts as foll:
1st row (RS) P2, *k3, p2;* rep from * to *.
2nd row *K2, p3;* rep from * to *, ending row with k2.

3rd row P2, *slip next st knitwise, k2, yo, pass slipped st over the 2 k sts and the yo and off the RH needle, p2;* rep from * to *.
4th row As 2nd row.
These 4 rows form one patt repeat.

Instructions

Back

With 3¾ mm (US size 5) needles, cast on 105 [113] sts and beg rib as foll:
1st rib row (RS) P1, *k1, p1; rep from * to end.
2nd rib row K1, *p1, k1; rep from * to end.
Rep these 2 rows until work measures 7cm/2¾ in from beg, ending with a first rib row.
Inc row (WS) Keeping rib correct, k1, k loop, (rib 3, k loop, k1) 26 [28] times. 132 [142] sts.
Change to 4½ mm (US size 7) needles.
Work in mock cable patt (see Stitches Used) until back measures 38 [40]cm/15 [15¾]in from beg, ending with a WS row.
Raglan armhole shaping
Keeping patt correct throughout, cast (bind) off 3 sts at beg of next 2 rows.
Work one row without shaping, then dec one st at each end of next 3 rows; rep these last 4 rows 12 [13] times more, so ending with a WS row.******
Work one row without shaping.
Dec one st at each end of next row and every foll alt row 7 [8] times in all.
Cast (bind) off rem 34 [36] sts for back neck.

Front

Work as for back to ******, then for 2nd size only dec one st at each end of next alt row, so ending with a WS row for both sizes. 48 [50] sts.
Neck shaping
Next row (RS) Work first 14 sts in patt and slip these sts onto a spare needle, cast (bind) off next 20 [22] sts, work in patt to end.
Cont with rem 14 sts only, for right front.
Dec one st at each end of next row, then dec at neck edge only on foll row; rep these last 2 rows twice more.
Dec one st at each end of next row.
Cast (bind) off rem 3 sts.
With WS facing, rejoin yarn to neck edge of left front sts and complete as for right front, but reversing shapings.

Left sleeve

With 3¾ mm (US size 5) needles, cast on 47 [49] sts and work in rib as on back for 7cm/2¾ in, ending with a first rib row.
Inc row (WS) Keeping rib correct, rib 4 [2],

(work into front and back of next st, rib 2) 13 [15] times, work into front and back of next st, rib 3 [1]. 61 [65] sts.

Change to 4½mm (US size 7) needles.

Beg mock cable patt on next row as foll:

1st row (RS) K2 [0], p2 [1], *k3, p2;* rep from * to *, ending k2 [3], p0 [1].

Cont in patt as now set for 2 rows more.

Work in patt, inc one st at each end of next row, then on every foll 4th row 10 [9] times, then on every alt row 12 [16] times, working extra sts into patt. 107 [117] sts.

Work in patt without shaping until sleeve measures 38 [40]cm/15 [15¾]in from beg, ending with a WS row.

Raglan shaping

Keeping patt correct throughout, cast (bind) off 3 sts at beg of next 2 rows.

Work one row without shaping, then dec one st at each end of next 3 rows; rep these last 4 rows 12 [13] times more, so ending with a WS row.

Work one row without shaping.

Dec one st at each end of next row and every foll alt row 4 [5] times in all. 15 [17] sts.★★★

Work one row without shaping, then cast (bind) off 3 [4] sts at beg of next row and dec one st at end of same row; rep these last 2 rows twice more.

Cast (bind) off rem 3 [2] sts.

Right sleeve

Work as for left sleeve to ★★★.

Cast (bind) off 3 [4] sts at beg of next row, then dec one st at beg of next row; rep these last 2 rows twice more.

Cast (bind) off rem 3 [2] sts.

Finishing and neckband

Do not press. Join front raglan seams and right back raglan seam, matching patt along shaped edges and ensuring that shorter edge of each sleeve is joined to front.

Neckband

With RS facing and 3¾mm (US size 5) needles, pick up and k10 [11] sts evenly across top edge of left sleeve, 44 [46] sts around front neck edge, 10 [11] sts across top of right sleeve and 31 [33] sts across back neck. 95 [101] sts.

Beg with 2nd rib row, work in rib as on back for 6cm/2¼in.

Cast (bind) off loosely in rib.

Join left back raglan seam and neckband seam. Join side and sleeve seams.

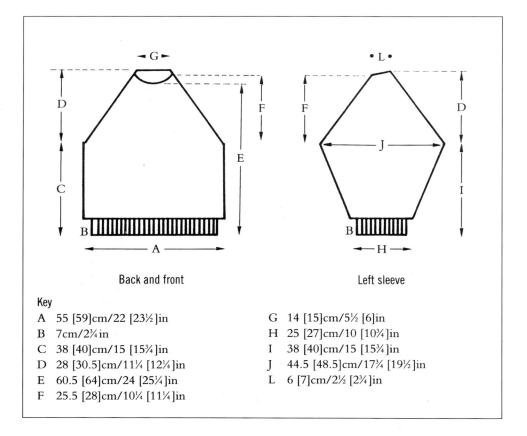

Back and front

Left sleeve

Key

A 55 [59]cm/22 [23½]in

B 7cm/2¾in

C 38 [40]cm/15 [15¾]in

D 28 [30.5]cm/11¼ [12¼]in

E 60.5 [64]cm/24 [25¼]in

F 25.5 [28]cm/10¼ [11¼]in

G 14 [15]cm/5½ [6]in

H 25 [27]cm/10 [10¾]in

I 38 [40]cm/15 [15¾]in

J 44.5 [48.5]cm/17¾ [19½]in

L 6 [7]cm/2½ [2¾]in

BABY'S CABLED OUTFIT

IN PINGOLAINE

✳✳

WRAP-AROUND TOP

The baby's cabled wrap-around top overlaps and buttons at the back. The borders along the the front and at the lower edge of the sleeves are worked in white in plain stocking (stockinette) stitch and embroidered in cross st later (see charts on page 31). Any name can be worked on the front.

Sizes

To fit newborn [3 months: 6 months]
Actual width around chest (buttoned) 50 [52: 54]cm/20 [21: 21½]in
Directions for larger sizes are in brackets [ ]; if there is only one set of figures it applies to all sizes.

Materials

PINGOUIN Pingolaine:
2 [2: 3] balls Tilleul No. 102 (A)
1 ball Blanc No. 01 (B)
Small amounts of Citron No. 58 (C), Rosette No. 02 (D) and Melon No. 110 (E)
Pair each of 2¾mm and 3mm (US sizes 2 and 3) needles
Cable needle (cn)
2 small buttons

Tension (Gauge)

Worked with 3mm (US size 3) needles.
St st: 28 sts and 38 rows to 10cm/4in over st st; work a sample on 42 sts.
Cable and rib patt: 39 sts and 38 rows to 10cm/4in over cable and rib patt; work a sample on 48 sts, working from ★ to ★ 4 times on each row of patt.

Stitches used

Special abbreviations

pbf – purl into front and back of next st.
cable 4 back – slip next 2 sts onto cn and hold at back of work, k2, then k2 from cn.
yo (yarn over) – take yarn to front of work between two needles, then take yarn from front to back over top of RH needle to make a new loop on RH needle.

Cable and rib pattern

Work cable and rib patt over a multiple of 12 sts as foll:
1st row (RS) ★P2, k4 (for the base of a cable), p2, k4;★ rep from ★ to ★.
2nd row ★P4, k2, p4, k2;★ rep from ★ to ★.
3rd row ★P2, cable 4 back, p2, k4;★ rep from ★ to ★.
4th row As 2nd row.
5th and 6th rows Rep first and 2nd rows.
These 6 rows form one patt repeat.

Instructions

Front

With 2¾mm (US size 2) needles and yarn A, cast on 69 [73: 77] sts and beg rib as foll:
1st rib row (RS) P1, ★k1, p1; rep from ★ to end.
2nd rib row K1, ★p1, k1; rep from ★ to end.
Rep these 2 rows once more, then rep first row again.
Inc row (WS) (P9 [10: 10], pfb) 6 times, p rem 9 [7: 11] sts. 75 [79: 83] sts.
Change to 3mm (US size 3) needles and yarn B.
Beg with a k row, work 23 rows in st st, so ending with a RS row. (Embroidery will be worked in this section later.)
Break off yarn B and change back to yarn A.
Inc row (WS) P4 [6: 8], (pfb, p2) 22 times, pfb, p4 [6: 8]. 98 [102: 106] sts.
Beg cable and rib patt on next row as foll:
1st patt row (RS) P0 [1: 3], k3 [4: 4] and keep these sts in st st, rep from ★ to ★ in first row of cable and rib patt 7 times, p2, k4 (for the base of a cable), p2, k3 [4: 4] and keep these sts in st st, p0 [1: 3].
2nd patt row K0 [1: 3], p3 [4: 4], k2, p4, k2, rep from ★ to ★ in 2nd row of cable and rib patt 7 times, p3 [4: 4], k0 [1: 3].
Cont in cable and rib patt as now set until front measures 11 [13: 14]cm/4¼ [5: 5½]in from beg, ending with a WS row.
Armhole shaping
Keeping patt correct as set throughout, cast (bind) off 4 sts at beg of next 2 rows. 90 [94: 98] sts.
Work without shaping until front measures

17 [20: 22]cm/6½ [7¾: 8½]in from beg, ending with a WS row.
Neck shaping
Next row (RS) Work first 38 [40: 41] sts in patt and slip these st onto a spare needle, cast (bind) off next 14 [14: 16] sts, work in patt to end.
Cont with rem 38 [40: 41] sts only, for right front.
Work one row without shaping.
★★Cast (bind) off 4 sts at beg of next row (neck edge) and next alt row, then 2 sts at same edge on next 2 alt rows.
Work one row without shaping.
Dec one st at neck edge on next row and every foll alt row 3 times in all.
23 [25: 26] sts.
Work 2 rows without shaping, so ending at armhole edge.
Shoulder shaping
Cast (bind) off 11 [12: 13] sts at beg of next row.
Work one row without shaping.
Cast (bind) off rem 12 [13: 13] sts.
With WS facing, rejoin yarn to neck edge of left front sts and complete as for right front from ★★ to end.

Right back

With 2¾mm (US size 2) needles and yarn A, cast on 49 [51: 53] sts and work 5 rows in rib as on front, so ending with a RS row.
Inc row (WS) P3 [4: 5], (pfb, p2) 14 times, pfb, p3 [4: 5]. 64 [66: 68] sts.★★★
Change to 3mm (US size 3) needles.
Still using yarn A (there is no embroidery on back sections), beg cable and rib patt on next row as foll:
1st patt row (RS) P0 [1: 3], k3 [4: 4], rep from ★ to ★ in first row of cable and rib patt 5 times, p1.
Cont in cable and rib patt as now set until back measures 11 [13: 14]cm/4¼ [5: 5½]in from beg, ending with a WS row.
Armhole shaping
Keeping patt correct as set throughout, cast (bind) off 4 sts at beg of next row.
60 [62: 64] sts.
Work without shaping until back measures 19 [22: 24]cm/7½ [8½: 9½]in from beg, ending with a WS row.
Neck and shoulder shaping
Next row (RS) Work first 53 [55: 57] sts in patt, turn leaving rem 7 sts on a st holder.
Cast (bind) off 16 [16: 17] sts at beg of next row.
Work one row without shaping.
Cast (bind) off 7 sts at beg of next row (neck edge), 11 [12: 13] sts at beg of next row (armhole edge) and 7 sts at beg of next row.
Cast (bind) off rem 12 [13: 13] sts to complete shoulder shaping.

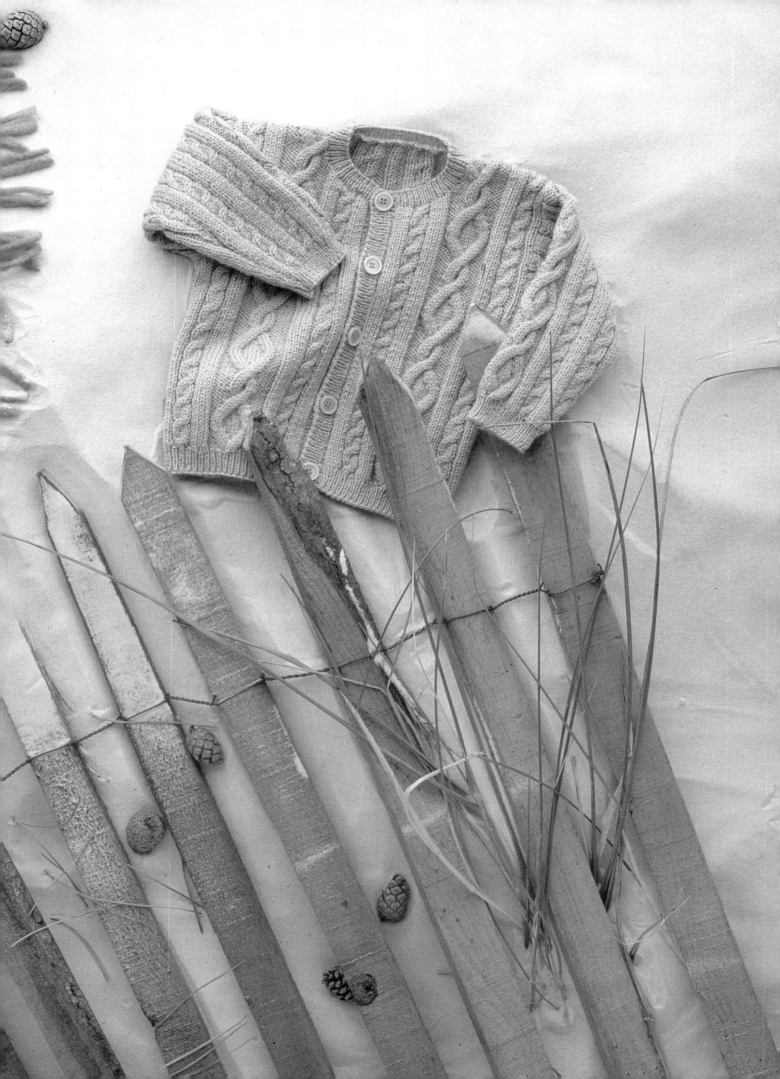

With RS facing, rejoin yarn to rem 7 sts and cast (bind) off first 4 sts, then work in patt to end.
Cast (bind) off rem 3 sts.

Left back

Work exactly as given for right back to ★★★.
Change to 3mm (US size 3) needles.
Beg cable and rib patt on next row as foll:
1st patt row (RS) P1, k4 and keep these sts in st st, rep from ★ to ★ in first row of cable and rib patt 4 times, p2, k4 (for the base of a cable), p2, k3 [4: 4] and keep these sts in st st, p0 [1: 3].
Cont in cable and rib patt as now set and complete left back as for right back, but reversing all shapings.

Sleeves

With 2¾mm (US size 2) needles and yarn A, cast on 41 [43: 45] sts and work 5 rows in rib as on front, so ending with a RS row.
Inc row (WS) P3 [4: 5], (pfb, p6) 5 times, pfb, p2 [3: 4]. 47 [49: 51] sts.
Change to 3mm (US size 3) needles and yarn B.
Beg with a k row, work 5 rows in st st, so ending with a RS row.
Work next row in st st, inc one st at each end of row. 49 [51: 53] sts.
Work 3 rows more in st st without shaping, so ending with a RS row.
Break off yarn B and change back to yarn A.
First size only:
Inc row (WS) P4, (pfb, p2) 15 times. 64 sts.
2nd size only:
Inc row (WS) P1, (pfb, p2) 16 times, pfb, p1. 68 sts.

3rd size only:
Inc row (WS) (P1, pfb) 3 times, (p2, pfb) 14 times, (p1, pfb) twice, p1. 72 sts.
All sizes:
Beg cable and rib patt on next row as foll:
1st patt row (RS) K0 [0: 2], p0 [2: 2], k4 and keep these sts in st st, rep from ★ to ★ in first row of cable and rib patt 5 times, p0 [2: 2], k0 [0: 2].
Cont in cable and rib patt as now set for 4 rows more.
Work in patt, inc one st at each end of next row, then on every foll 6th row 2 [4: 4] times, then on every foll 4th row 2 [2: 4] times, working extra sts into patt. 74 [82: 90] sts.
Work 8 rows in patt without shaping.
Cast (bind) off in patt.

Finishing and borders

First work embroidery in cross stitch, using a single strand of yarn in specified colour and a tapestry needle.
Beg on 5th row of the st st panel on front and working from Chart No. 1, miss first 1 [2: 3] sts, work Panel No. 1 on next 25 sts, miss next 1 [2: 3] sts, work Panel No. 2 on next 31 sts, miss next 1 [2: 3] sts, work Panel No. 3 on next 15 sts, thus leaving 1 [2: 3] sts at side edge.
On sleeves work from Chart No. 2; beg on 2nd row of st st panel, miss first 1 [2: 3] sts, ★then using yarn E, work a cross st on next 3 sts, miss next 3 sts;★ rep from ★ to ★ along row, ending with 3 sts in yarn E, miss rem 1 [2: 3] sts. Now work the diagonal lines in A as shown on chart and work remainder of embroidery.

Neckband

Do not press ribbing or cables.
Join shoulder seams, matching patt.
With RS facing, 2¾mm (US size 2) needles and yarn A, pick up and k41 [41: 42] sts evenly along shaped edges of left back neck, 49 [49: 51] sts around front neck and 41 [41: 42] sts on right back neck. 131 [131: 135] sts.
Beg with 2nd rib row, work 4 rows in rib as on front.
Cast (bind) off loosely in rib.
Back borders
With RS facing, 2¾mm (US size 2) needles and yarn A, pick up and k67 [77: 85] sts evenly along straight edge of right back, including edge of neckband.
Work 2nd rib row as on front.
Make a buttonhole on next row as foll:
Buttonhole row (RS) Keeping rib correct and beg at neck edge, p1, k1, yo, k2tog, work in rib to end.
Work 2 rows more in rib.
Cast (bind) off loosely in rib.
Pick up same number of sts on left back and work 2nd rib row.
Make a buttonhole on next row as foll:
Buttonhole row (RS) Keeping rib correct and beg at lower edge, work in rib to last 4 sts, k2tog, yo, k1, p1.
Work 2 rows more in rib.
Cast (bind) off loosely in rib.
Sew cast (bound) off edge of sleeves to sides of armholes, stretching sleeves slightly to fit.
Sew armhole cast (bind) off to last 4 rows on sides of sleeves.
Join side and sleeve seams.
Lap right back over left for 10 [10: 11]cm/4 [4: 4¼]in and sew on buttons to correspond with buttonholes, one on RS of left back and the other on WS of right back.

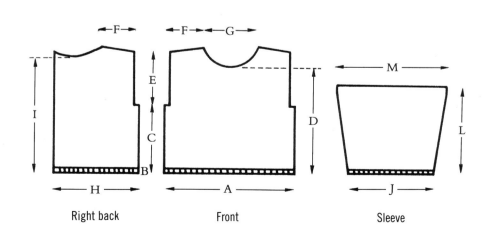

Right back   Front   Sleeve

Key

A	25 [26: 27]cm/10 [10½: 10¾]in	E	10 [11: 12]cm/4 [4¼: 4¾]in	I	19 [22: 24]cm/7½ [8½: 9½]in
B	1cm/½in	F	5.5 [6: 6.5]cm/2¼ [2½: 2¾]in	J	16.5 [17.5: 18]cm/6½ [7: 7¼]in
C	11 [13: 14]cm/4¼ [5: 5½]in	G	11 [11: 12]cm/4¼ [4¼: 4¾]in	L	13 [16: 18]cm/5 [6¼: 7]in
D	17 [20: 22]cm/6½ [7¾: 8½]in	H	16 [16.5: 17]cm/6½ [6¾: 7]in		

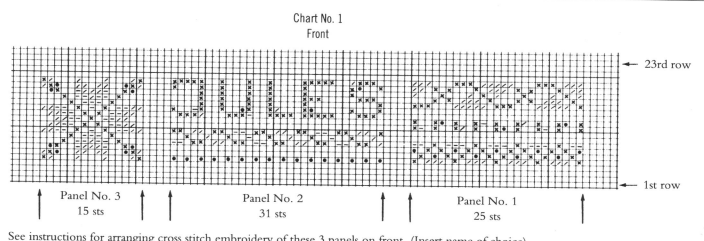

Chart No. 1
Front

← 23rd row

← 1st row

Panel No. 3
15 sts

Panel No. 2
31 sts

Panel No. 1
25 sts

See instructions for arranging cross stitch embroidery of these 3 panels on front. (Insert name of choice)
Background is in B   X = A   ● = C   − = D   / = E

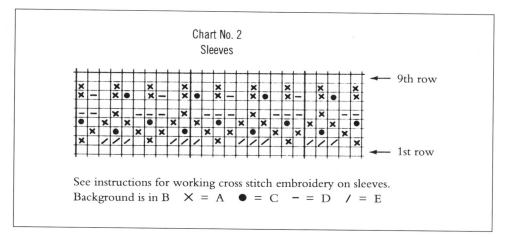

Chart No. 2
Sleeves

← 9th row

← 1st row

See instructions for working cross stitch embroidery on sleeves.
Background is in B   X = A   ● = C   − = D   / = E

BABY'S TROUSERS

The baby's cabled trousers are designed
in order to fit loosely over other clothes.
The waistband is doubled to enclose a length
of elastic.

Sizes

To fit 3 months [6 months: 12 months]
Actual width around hips when completed
62 [66: 70]cm/25 [26: 28]in
*Directions for larger sizes are in brackets [ ]; if
there is only one set of figures it applies to all sizes.*

Materials

PINGOUIN Pingolaine:
3 [3: 4] balls Tilleul No. 102
Pair each of 2¾ mm and 3mm (US sizes 2
and 3) needles
Cable needle (cn)
2cm/¾in wide elastic for waistband

Tension (Gauge)

Worked with 3mm (US size 3) needles.
Cable and rib patt: 39 sts and 38 rows to
10cm/4in over cable and rib patt; work a
sample on 48 sts, working from ★ to ★ 4
times on each row of patt.

Stitches used

Special abbreviations

pbf – purl into front and back of next st.
cable 4 back – slip next 2 sts onto cn and
hold at back of work, k2, then k2 from cn.

Cable and rib pattern

Work cable and rib patt over a multiple of
12 sts as foll:
1st row (RS) ★P2, k4 (for the base of a
cable), p2, k4;★ rep from ★ to ★.
2nd row ★P4, k2, p4, k2;★ rep from ★ to ★.
3rd row ★P2, cable 4 back, p2, k4;★ rep
from ★ to ★.

4th row As 2nd row.
5th and 6th rows Rep first and 2nd rows.
These 6 rows form one patt repeat.

Instructions

Back

Back of trousers is begun at lower edge of
legs. The two legs are worked separately to
the crutch (crotch), then joined.
First leg
With 2¾mm (US size 2) needles, cast on 39
[41: 45] sts and beg rib as foll:
1st rib row (RS) P1, ★k1, p1; rep from ★
to end.
2nd rib row K1, ★p1, k1; rep from ★ to end.
Rep these 2 rows twice more, then rep first
row again.
Inc row (WS) P3 [2: 2], (pfb, p1) 16 [18: 20]
times, pfb, p3 [2: 2]. 56 [60: 66] sts.
Change to 3mm (US size·3) needles.
First size only:
Beg cable and rib patt on next row as foll:
1st patt row (RS) Rep from ★ to ★ in first
row of cable and rib patt 4 times, p2, k4

(for the base of a cable), p2.
2nd patt row K2, p4, k2, rep from ★ to ★ in 2nd row of cable and rib patt 4 times.

2nd size only:
Beg cable and rib patt on next row as foll:
1st patt row (RS) K2, rep from ★ to ★ in first row of cable and rib patt 4 times, p2, k4 (for the base of a cable), p2, k2.
2nd patt row P2, k2, p4, k2, rep from ★ to ★ in 2nd row of cable and rib patt 4 times, p2.

3rd size only:
Beg cable and rib patt on next row as foll:
1st patt row (RS) P1, k4, rep from ★ to ★ in first row of cable and rib patt 5 times, p1.
2nd patt row K1, rep from ★ to ★ in 2nd row of cable and rib patt 5 times, p4, k1.

All sizes:
Cont in cable and rib patt as now set, work 2 [4: 6] rows more, so ending with a WS row.

Leg shaping
The leg is shaped at both side edges; because the shapings at the two sides are worked on different rows the instructions should be followed carefully. (These incs are worked on RS rows only.)

First size only:
Working all extra sts into patt, shape inner leg by inc one st at end of next row (inner edge), then on every foll 6th row 3 times and then on every foll 4th row 5 times (thus adding 9 sts to inner edge), **and at the same time** keep outer leg edge straight until 10 rows have been worked in patt, then inc one st at beg of next row (outer edge), then at the same edge on every foll 10th row 3 times more (thus adding 4 sts to outer edge). 69 sts.

2nd size only:
Working all extra sts into patt, shape inner leg by inc one st at end of next row (inner edge) and then on every foll 6th row 8 times (thus adding 9 sts to inner edge), **and at the same time** keep outer leg edge straight until 10 rows have been worked in patt, then inc one st at beg of next row (outer edge), then at the same edge on every foll 10th row 4 times more (thus adding 5 sts to outer edge). 74 sts.

3rd size only:
Working all extra sts into patt, shape inner leg by inc one st at end of next row (inner edge), then on every foll 8th row 4 times and then on every foll 6th row 4 times (thus adding 9 sts to inner edge), **and at the same time** keep outer leg edge straight until 10 rows have been worked in patt, then inc one st at beg of next row (outer edge), then at the same edge on every foll 10th row 5 times more (thus adding 6 sts to outer edge). 81 sts.

All sizes:
Work in patt on these 69 [74: 81] sts until leg measures 15 [18: 21]cm/6 [7: 8¼]in, ending at inner leg edge after working a RS row.★★

Crutch (crotch) shaping
Keeping patt correct throughout, cast (bind) off 3 sts at beg of next row and 2 sts at same edge on next 1 [2: 3] alt rows, then dec one st at same edge on next 2 [2: 3] alt rows. 62 [65: 69] sts.
Work one row without shaping, so ending at inner leg edge after working a RS row.
Break off yarn and leave sts on a spare needle.

Second leg
Work second leg in same way as first, but reversing shapings by working inner leg shapings at *beg* and outer leg shapings at *end* of corresponding rows.
After all incs have been worked, work without shaping on these 69 [74: 81] sts until there is one row more than on first leg to ★★, thus ending with a WS row instead of a RS row.
Work crutch (crotch) shaping as on first leg, ending at outer leg edge after last dec row. (Do not break off yarn.)

Join legs
Next row (WS) Work in patt across sts of second leg, then work in patt across sts of first leg. 124 [130: 138] sts.
Cont in patt until trousers measure 31 [36: 40]cm/12¼ [14: 15¾]in from beg, ending with a RS row.
Dec row (WS) P4 [4: 2], (p2tog, p1) 38 [40: 44] times, p2tog, p4 [4: 2]. 85 [89: 93] sts.
Change to 2¾mm (US size 2) needles.
Rep first and 2nd rib rows 10 times.
Cast (bind) off loosely in rib.

Front

Work front of trousers exactly as given for back of trousers.

Finishing

Do not press. Join short centre front and back seams along crutch (crotch) shapings, then join side and inner leg seams.
Cut elastic to baby's waist measurement, overlap ends forming a ring and sew ends securely tog.
Fold waistband in half to WS over elastic, and slip stitch cast (bound) off edge in place.

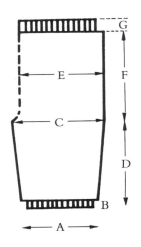

Right half back or Left half front

Key
A 14 [15: 17]cm/5¾ [6: 6¾]in
B 1.5cm/½in
C 17.5 [19: 20.5]cm/7 [7½: 8¼]in
D 15 [18: 21]cm/6 [7: 8¼]in
E 15.5 [16.5: 17.5]cm/6¼ [6½: 7]in
F 16 [18: 19]cm/6¼ [7: 7½]in
G 5cm/2in

BABY'S AND CHILD'S CARDIGAN

The cabled cardigan can be worked to go with the cabled trousers as an alternative to the wrap-around top. It can also be worked on its own for an 18 month or 2 year old boy or girl.

Sizes

To fit 3 months [6 months: 12 months: 18 months: 2 years]
Actual width around chest (buttoned) 52 [55: 59: 62: 65]cm/20½ [21½: 23: 24½: 25½]in
Directions for larger sizes are in brackets [ ]; if there is only one set of figures it applies to all sizes.

Materials

PINGOUIN Pingolaine:
2 [3: 4: 4: 5] balls Tilleul No. 102
Pair each of 2¾mm and 3mm (US sizes 2 and 3) needles
Cable needle (cn)
5 [5: 5: 6: 6] small buttons

Tension (Gauge)

Worked with 3mm (US size 3) needles.
Main cable patt: 39 sts and 38 rows to 10cm/4in over main cable patt; work a sample on 48 sts, working from ★ to ★ 4 times on each row of patt. It is essential to work this sample in order to become familiar with the patt.
Diamond cable panel: measures 4.5cm/1¾in wide.

Stitches used

Special abbreviations

cable 4 back – slip next 2 sts onto cn and hold at back of work, k2, then k2 from cn.
cable 6 back – slip next 3 sts onto cn and hold at back of work, k3, then k3 from cn.
C4R (cross 4 right) – slip next st onto cn and hold at back of work, k3, then k1 from cn.
C4Rp – work as for C4R, but p1 from cn instead of k1.
C4L (cross 4 left) – slip next 3 sts onto cn and hold at front of work, k1, then k3 from cn.
C4Lp – work as for C4L, but k first st (st which passes behind cn).
yo (yarn over) – to work a yo between 2 k sts, take yarn to front of work between two needles, then take yarn from front to back over top of RH needle to make a new loop on RH needle; to work a yo after a k st and before a p st, take yarn to front of work between two needles, then take yarn from front to back over top of RH needle and to front again; to work a yo between 2 p sts, take yarn from front to back over top of RH needle and to front again; to work a yo after a p st and before a k st, take yarn from front to back over top of RH needle to make a new loop on RH needle.

Main cable pattern

Work main cable patt over a multiple of 12 sts as foll:
1st row (RS) *K4, p2, k4 (for the base of a cable), p2;* rep from ★ to ★.
2nd row *K2, p4, k2, p4;* rep from ★ to ★.
3rd row *K4, p2, cable 4 back, p2;* rep from ★ to ★.
4th row As 2nd row.
5th and 6th rows Rep first and 2nd rows.
These 6 rows form one patt repeat.

Diamond panel

Work diamond panel over 18 sts as foll:
1st row (RS) P6, k6, p6.
2nd row K6, p6, k6.
3rd row P6, cable 6 back, p6.
4th row As 2nd row.
5th row P5, C4R, C4L, p5.
6th row K5, p8, k5.
7th row P4, C4R, k2, C4L, p4.
8th row K4, p10, k4.
9th row P3, C4R, k4, C4L, p3.
10th row K3, p12, k3.
11th row P3, C4Lp, k4, C4Rp, p3.
12th row As 8th row.
13th row P4, C4Lp, k2, C4Rp, p4.
14th row As 6th row.
15th row P5, C4Lp, C4Rp, p5.
16th row As 2nd row.
17th–22nd rows Rep from 3rd–8th rows.
23rd–26th rows Rep from 13th–16th rows.
Rep 3rd–26th rows inclusive to form patt (first and 2nd rows are foundation rows and are not worked again).

Instructions

Back

With 2¾mm (US size 2) needles, cast on 85 [91: 95: 99: 103] sts and beg rib as foll:
1st rib row (RS) P1, *k1, p1; rep from ★ to end.
2nd rib row K1, *p1, k1; rep from ★ to end.
Rep these 2 rows once more, then rep first row again.
Inc row (WS) Keeping rib correct, rib 2 [5: 7: 5: 3], work into front and back of next st, (rib 4 [4: 3: 3: 3], work into front and back of next st) 16 [16: 20: 22: 24] times, rib rem 2 [5: 7: 5: 3] sts. 102 [108: 116: 122: 128] sts.
Change to 3mm (US size 3) needles.
First size only:
Beg main cable patt and diamond panels on next row as foll:
1st patt row (RS) Rep from ★ to ★ in first row of main cable patt once, k4, **work first row of diamond panel over next 18 sts, rep from ★ to ★ in first row of main cable patt once, k4, p2, rep from ★ to ★ in first row of main cable patt once, k4, work first row of diamond panel over next 18 sts;** now rep from ★ to ★ in first row of main cable patt once, k4.
2nd size only:
Beg main cable patt and diamond panels on next row as foll:
1st patt row (RS) K1, p2, rep from ★ to ★ in first row of main cable patt once, k4; rep from ** to ** as given for first size; now rep from ★ to ★ in first row of main cable patt once, k4, p2, k1.
3rd size only:
Beg main cable patt and diamond panels on next row as foll:
1st patt row (RS) P1, k4 (for the base of a cable), p2, rep from ★ to ★ in first row of main cable patt once, k4; rep from ** to ** as given for first size; now rep from ★ to ★ in first row of main cable patt once, k4, p2, k4 (for the base of a cable), p1.
4th size only:
Beg main cable patt and diamond panels on next row as foll:
1st patt row (RS) K2, p2, k4 (for the base of a cable), p2, rep from ★ to ★ in first row of main cable patt once, k4; rep from ** to ** as given for first size; now rep from ★ to ★ in first row of main cable patt twice, k2.
5th size only:
Beg main cable patt and diamond panels on next row as foll:
1st patt row (RS) P1, rep from ★ to ★ in first row of main cable patt twice, k4; rep from ** to ** as given for first size; now rep from ★ to ★ in first row of main cable patt twice, k4, p1.
All sizes:
2nd patt row Work first 16 [19: 23: 26: 29] sts in main cable patt as set; work 2nd row of diamond panel over next 18 sts, (k4, p2) 5 times, k4, work 2nd row of diamond panel over next 18 sts; now work last 16 [19: 23: 26: 29] sts in main cable patt.
Cont in patt as now set until back measures 15 [16: 18: 21: 23]cm/6 [6¼: 7: 8¼: 9]in from beg, ending with a WS row.
Armhole shaping
Keeping patt correct as set throughout, cast (bind) off 5 [5: 6: 6: 6] sts at beg of next 2 rows. 92 [98: 104: 110: 116] sts.

Work without shaping until back measures 25 [27: 30: 34: 37]cm/10 [10¾: 11¾: 13½: 14¾]in from beg, ending with a WS row.

Neck shaping

Next row (RS) Work first 29 [31: 33: 35: 37] sts in patt and slip these st onto a spare needle, cast (bind) off next 34 [36: 38: 40: 42] sts, work in patt to end.

Cont with rem 29 [31: 33: 35: 37] sts only, for left back.

Work one row without shaping.

**Cast (bind) off 4 sts at beg of next row (neck edge) and dec one st at neck edge on foll row.

Cast (bind) off rem 24 [26: 28: 30: 32] sts for shoulder edge.

With WS facing, rejoin yarn to neck edge of right back sts and cast (bind) off first 4 sts, then work in patt to end.

Dec one st at neck edge on next row.

Work one row without shaping.

Cast (bind) off rem 24 [26: 28: 30: 32] sts for shoulder edge.

Right front

With 2¾mm (US size 2) needles, cast on 43 [45: 49: 51: 53] sts and work 7 rows in rib as on back, so ending with a RS row.

Inc row (WS) Keeping rib correct, rib 4 [2: 4: 3: 1], work into front and back of next st, (rib 4, work into front and back of next st) 7 [8: 8: 9: 10] times, rib rem 3 [2: 4: 2: 1] sts. 51 [54: 58: 61: 64] sts.***

Change to 3mm (US size 3) needles.

Beg main cable patt and diamond panel on next row as foll:

1st patt row (RS) K1 and keep this edge st in g st, rep from * to * in first row of main cable patt once, k4, work first row of diamond panel over next 18 sts, then rep from * to * in first row of main cable patt once [once: once: twice: twice], then for first size only k4 [for 2nd size only k4, p2, k1: for 3rd size only k4, p2, k4 (for the base of a cable), p1: for 4th size only k2: for 5th size only k4, p1].

Cont in patt as now set until there is one row more than on back to beg of armhole shaping, so ending with a RS row.

Armhole shaping

Keeping patt correct as set throughout, cast (bind) off 5 [5: 6: 6: 6] sts at beg of next row. 46 [49: 52: 55: 58] sts.

Work without shaping until front measures 22 [24: 26: 30: 33]cm/8½ [9½: 10¼: 11¾: 13]in from beg, ending at centre front edge.

Neck shaping

Cast (bind) off 8 [9: 9: 10: 11] sts at beg of next row (neck edge), 4 sts at same edge on next 2 alt rows and 2 sts on next 2 alt rows, then dec one st on next 2 [2: 3: 3: 3] alt rows. 24 [26: 28: 30: 32] sts.

Work 2 [2: 4: 4: 4] rows more without shaping.

Cast (bind) off all sts for shoulder edge.

Left front

Work as for right front to ***.

Change to 3mm (US size 3) needles.

Beg main cable patt and diamond panel on next row as foll:

1st patt row (RS) Work first 16 [19: 23: 26: 29] sts given at beg of first patt row on back, work first row of diamond panel over next 18 sts, then rep from * to * in first row of main cable patt once, k4, then k one more st and keep this edge st in g st.

Cont in patt as now set and complete as for right front, but reversing shapings; work armhole shaping on same row as first casting (binding) off at back armhole and beg neck shaping one row before right front neck.

Sleeves

With 2¾mm (US size 2) needles, cast on 43 [45: 47: 49: 51] sts and work 7 rows in rib as on back, so ending with a RS row.

Inc row (WS) Keeping rib correct, rib 1 [0: 1: 0: 1], (work into front and back of next st, rib 1) 20 [22: 22: 24: 24] times, work into front and back of next st, rib 1 [0: 1: 0: 1]. 64 [68: 70: 74: 76] sts.

Change to 3mm (US size 3) needles.

First size only:

Beg main cable patt and diamond panel on next row as foll:

1st patt row (RS) P1, k4 (for the base of a cable), p2, rep from * to * in first row of main cable patt once, k4; work first row of diamond panel over next 18 sts, then rep from * to * in first row of main cable patt once, k4, p2, k4 (for the base of a cable), p1.

2nd size only:

Beg main cable patt and diamond panel on next row as foll:

1st patt row (RS) K1, p2, k4 (for the base of a cable), p2, rep from * to * in first row of main cable patt once, k4; work first row of diamond panel over next 18 sts, then rep from * to * in first row of main cable patt twice, k1.

3rd size only:

Beg main cable patt and diamond panel on next row as foll:

1st patt row (RS) Work as for 2nd size, but beg and ending k2 instead of k1.

4th size only:

Beg main cable patt and diamond panel on next row as foll:

1st patt row (RS) Rep from * to * in first row of the main cable patt twice, k4; work first row of the diamond panel pattern over next 18 sts, then rep from * to * in first row of the main cable patt twice, k4.

5th size only:
Beg main cable patt and diamond panel on next row as foll:

1st patt row (RS) P1, work all sts as given for 4th size, p1.

All sizes:
Cont in patt as now set for 2 rows more. Work in patt, inc one st at each end of next row, then on every foll 4th row 10 [10: 13: 14: 17] times and on every foll 3rd row 0 [2: 2: 3: 3] times, working all extra sts into patt. 86 [94: 102: 110: 118] sts.
Work without shaping until sleeve measures 17 [19: 22: 24: 26]cm/6¾ [7½: 8½: 9½: 10¼]in from beg.
Cast (bind) off all sts.

Finishing and borders

Do not press. Join shoulder seams, matching cable patt.

Neckband
With RS facing and 2¾mm (US size 2) needles, pick up and k23 [24: 27: 28: 29] sts evenly along right front neck edge, 39 [41: 43: 45: 47] sts across back neck and 23 [24: 27: 28: 29] sts along left front neck. 85 [89: 97: 101: 105] sts.
Beg with 2nd rib row, work 4 rows in rib as on back.
Cast (bind) off loosely in rib.

Buttonhole band
With RS facing and 2¾mm (US size 2) needles, pick up and k75 [81: 89: 101: 113] sts evenly along centre front edge (including edge of neckband) of right front for a girl or left front for a boy.
Work 2nd rib row as on back, then work first rib row.

First size only:
Make a buttonhole on next row as foll:
Buttonhole row (RS) Keeping rib correct, k1, p1, k1, (yo, k2tog, rib 15, yo, p2tog, rib 15) twice, yo, k2tog, p1, k1.

2nd size only:
Make a buttonhole on next row as foll:
Buttonhole row (RS) Keeping rib correct, (k1, p1) twice, (yo, p2tog, rib 16) 4 times, yo, p2tog, k1, p1, k1.

3rd size only:
Make a buttonhole on next row as foll:
Buttonhole row (RS) Keeping rib correct, (k1, p1) twice, (yo, p2tog, rib 18) 4 times, yo, p2tog, k1, p1, k1.

4th size only:
Make a buttonhole on next row as foll:
Buttonhole row (RS) Keeping rib correct, k1, p1, (yo, p2tog, rib 17, yo, k2tog, rib 17) twice, yo, p2tog, rib 17, yo, k2tog, p1, k1.

5th size only:
Make a buttonhole on next row as foll:

Buttonhole row (RS) Keeping rib correct, k1, p1, k1, (yo, k2tog, rib 19, yo, p2tog, rib 19) twice, yo, k2tog, rib 19, yo, p2tog, k1, p1, k1.

All sizes:
Work one row more in rib.
Cast (bind) off loosely in rib.

Button band
Work button band on other front as for buttonhole band, but omitting buttonholes.
Sew cast (bound) off edge of sleeves to sides of armholes and sew armhole cast (bind) off to last 5 [5: 6: 6: 6] rows on sides of sleeves. Join side and sleeve seams.
Sew on the buttons to correspond with the buttonholes.

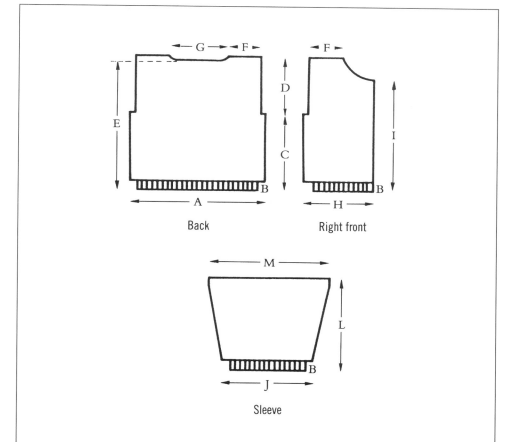

Back   Right front

Sleeve

Key

A 26 [27.5: 29.5: 31: 32.5]cm
   10¼ [10¾: 11½: 12¼: 12¾]in

B 2cm
   ¾in

C 15 [16: 18: 21: 23]cm
   6 [6¼: 7: 8¼: 9]in

D 11 [12: 13: 14: 15]cm
   4¼ [4¾: 5: 5½: 6]in

E 25 [27: 30: 34: 37]cm
   10 [10¾: 11¾: 13½: 14¾]in

F 6 [6.5: 7: 7.5: 8]cm
   2¼ [2½: 2¾: 3: 3¼]in

G 11 [11.5: 12: 12.5: 13]cm
   4¼ [4½: 4¾: 5: 5¼]in

H 13 [13.5: 14.5: 15.5: 16]cm
   5 [5¼: 5¾: 6: 6¼]in

I 22 [24: 26: 30: 33]cm
   8½ [9½: 10¼: 11¾: 13]in

J 16 [17: 18: 19: 19.5]cm
   6¼ [6¾: 7: 7½: 7¾]in

L 17 [19: 22: 24: 26]]cm
   6¾ [7½: 8½: 9½: 10¼]in

M 22 [24: 26: 28: 30]cm
   8½ [9½: 10: 11: 12]in

GIRL'S LACE YOKED BOLERO

IN SWEET'HAIR

* *

Sizes

To fit ages 2 [4: 6: 8: 10] years or 53 [58: 63: 68: 72]cm/21 [23: 25: 27: 28½]in chest
Actual width around chest (buttoned) 70 [76: 80: 86: 92]cm/28 [30½: 32: 34: 36½]in
Directions for larger sizes are in brackets [ ]; if there is only one set of figures it applies to all sizes.

Materials

PINGOUIN Sweet'Hair:
3 [4: 4: 5: 6] balls in desired pastel shade
Pair each of 3mm, 3¼mm and 3¾mm (US sizes 2, 3 and 5) needles
3 small buttons

Tension (Gauge)

Worked with 3¾mm (US size 5) needles.
Garter st: 21 sts and 42 rows to 10cm/4in over garter st; work a sample on 32 sts.

Stitches used

The main parts of the bolero are worked in garter st. The directions for the lace yoke pattern are given in the instructions.

Special abbreviations

yo (yarn over) – take yarn to front of work between two needles, then take yarn from front to back over top of RH needle to make a new loop on RH needle.
SKPO – slip one, knit one, pass slipped st over.
SK2PO – slip one, knit 2 together, pass slipped st over.

Instructions

Back

With 3¾mm (US size 5) needles, cast on 74 [80: 84: 90: 96] sts and beg g st as foll:
1st row (RS) Knit.
Mark first row as RS of work and cont in g st (k every row) until back measures 10 [12: 13: 15: 16]cm/3¾ [4½: 5: 5¾: 6¼]in from beg, ending with a WS row.
Armhole shaping
Cont in g st throughout, cast (bind) off 4 sts at beg of next 2 rows. 66 [72: 76: 82: 88] sts.
Work without shaping until back measures 20 [23: 25: 27: 29]cm/7¾ [9: 9¾: 10½: 11¼]in from beg, ending with a WS row.
Neck shaping
Divide for neck on next row as foll:
Next row (RS) K25 [27: 29: 31: 33] sts and slip these sts onto a spare needle, cast (bind) off next 16 [18: 18: 20: 22] sts, k to end.
Cont with rem 25 [27: 29: 31: 33] sts only, for left back.
K one row.
★★Cast (bind) off 3 sts at beg of next row (neck edge), then 2 sts at same edge on next 4 alt rows.
Work one row without shaping.
Dec one st at neck edge on next row and every foll alt row 5 [5: 5: 6: 6] times in all. 9 [11: 13: 14: 16] sts.
Work without shaping until back measures 26 [29: 31: 34: 36]cm/10¼ [11½: 12¼: 13½: 14¼]in from beg, ending at armhole edge in order to beg shoulder shaping.
Shoulder shaping
Cast (bind) off 4 [5: 6: 7: 8] sts at beg of next row.
Work one row without shaping.
Cast (bind) off rem 5 [6: 7: 7: 8] sts.
With WS facing, rejoin yarn to neck edge of right back sts and complete as given for left back of from ★★ to end.

Right Front

With 3¾mm (US size 5) needles, cast on 17 [18: 19: 20: 21] sts and beg g st as foll:
1st row (RS) Knit.
Mark first row as RS of work and cont in g st (k every row), inc one st at end of next row (centre front edge) and at same edge on next 12 rows. 29 [30: 31: 32: 33] sts.
K one row.
Inc one st at centre front edge on next row and every foll alt row 4 [5: 5: 7: 8] times in all, then inc one st at same edge on every foll 4th row 3 [4: 5: 5: 6] times. 37 [40: 42: 45: 48] sts.
Work in g st until front is same length as back to beg of armhole shaping, ending at armhole edge after a RS row.

Armhole shaping

Cont in g st throughout, cast (bind) off 4 sts at beg of next row. 33 [36: 38: 41: 44] sts. Work without shaping until front measures 16 [19: 21: 23: 25]cm/6¼ [7½: 8¼: 9: 9¾]in from beg, ending with at centre front edge.

Neck shaping

Cast (bind) off 5 [6: 6: 6: 7] sts at beg of next row (neck edge), 4 sts at same edge on next alt row, then 2 sts on next 3 alt rows. Work one row without shaping.
Dec one st at neck edge on next row and every foll alt row 5 [5: 5: 7: 7] times in all, then dec one st at same edge on every foll 4th row 4 times. 9 [11: 13: 14: 16] sts. Work without shaping until front is same length as back to beg of shoulder shaping, ending at armhole edge.

Shoulder shaping

Cast (bind) off 4 [5: 6: 7: 8] sts at beg of next row.
Work one row without shaping.
Cast (bind) off rem 5 [6: 7: 7: 8] sts.

Left Front

Work left front as given for right front, but reversing all shapings.

Sleeves

With 3mm (US size 2) needles, cast on 39 [41: 43: 45: 47] sts and beg rib as foll:
1st rib row (RS) P1, *k1, p1; rep from * to end.
2nd rib row K1, *p1, k1; rep from * to end.
Rep these 2 rows twice more, but inc one st at centre of last row. 40 [42: 44: 46: 48] sts. Change to 3¾mm (US size 5) needles and work 5 [7: 7: 7: 7] rows in g st.
Cont in g st throughout, inc one st at each end of next row and every foll 6th [8th: 8th: 8th: 8th] row 11 [2: 7: 12: 17] times in all, then on every foll 4th [6th: 6th: 6th: 6th] row 3 [13: 9: 5: 1] times.
68 [72: 76: 80: 84] sts.
Work without shaping until sleeve measures 25 [30: 34: 38: 42]cm/9¾ [11¾: 13¼: 15: 16½]in from beg.
Cast (bind) off all sts loosely.

Yoke

Do not press. Join shoulder seams.
With RS facing and 3¼mm (US size 3) needles, pick up and k35 [37: 37: 40: 41] sts evenly along right front neck edge, 59 [61: 61: 69: 71] sts around back neck edge and 35 [37: 37: 40: 41] sts along left front neck edge. 129 [135: 135: 149: 153] sts.
P one row.
Beg lace yoke patt on next row as foll:
1st row (RS) K4 [7: 7: 4: 6], *yo, SKPO,

k6, k2tog, yo, k1, yo, SKPO, k7;* rep from * to *, ending yo, SKPO, k3 [6: 6: 3: 5].
2nd and all WS rows (WS) Purl.
3rd row K2 [5: 5: 2: 4], *k2tog, yo, k1, yo, SKPO, k4, SK2PO, yo, k1, yo, SK2PO, k4;* rep from * to *, ending k2tog, yo, k1, yo, SKPO, k2 [5: 5: 2: 4]. 117 [123: 123: 135: 139] sts.
5th row K1 [4: 4: 1: 3], *k2tog, yo, k3, yo, SKPO, k3, k2tog, yo, k1, yo, SKPO, k3;* rep from * to *, ending k2tog, yo, k3, yo, SKPO, k1 [4: 4: 1: 3].
7th row K4 [7: 7: 4: 6], *yo, SKPO, k4, SK2PO, yo, k1, yo, SK2PO, k5;* rep from * to *, ending yo, SKPO, k3 [6: 6: 3: 5]. 105 [111: 111: 121: 125] sts.
9th row K2 [5: 5: 2: 4], *k2tog, yo, k1, yo, SKPO, k3, k2tog, yo, k1, yo, SKPO, k3;* rep from * to *, ending k2tog, yo, k1, yo, SKPO, k2 [5: 5: 2: 4].
11th row K1 [4: 4: 1: 3], *k2tog, yo, k3, yo, SKPO, k1, SK2PO, yo, k1, yo, SK2PO, k1;* rep from * to *, ending k2tog, yo, k3, yo, SKPO, k1 [4: 4: 1: 3]. 93 [99: 99: 107: 111] sts.
13th row K4 [7: 7: 4: 6], *yo, SKPO, k3, k2tog, yo, k1, yo, SKPO, k4;* rep from * to *, ending yo, SKPO, k3 [6: 6: 3: 5].
15th row K2 [5: 5: 2: 4], *k2tog, yo, k1, yo, SKPO, k1, SK2PO, yo, k1, yo, SK2PO, k1;* rep from * to *, ending k2tog, yo, k1, yo, SKPO, k2 [5: 5: 2: 4]. 81 [87: 87: 93: 97] sts.
17th row K1 [4: 4: 1: 3], *k2tog, yo, k3, yo, SKPO, k2tog, yo, k1, yo, SKPO;* rep from * to *, ending k2tog, yo, k3, yo, SKPO, k1 [4: 4: 1: 3].
19th row K7 [4: 4: 7: 3], (k2tog, k4) 11 [13: 13: 13: 15] times, k2tog, k6 [3: 3: 6: 2]. 69 [73: 73: 79: 81] sts.
Change to 3mm (US size 2) needles and beg with 2nd rib row, work 4 rows in k1, p1 rib as given on sleeve border.
Cast (bind) off loosely in rib.

Finishing and borders

Do not press g st or ribbing.
Back border
With RS facing and 3mm (US size 2) needles, pick up and k75 [81: 85: 91: 97] sts evenly along lower edge of back and beg with 2nd rib row, work 4 rows in k1, p1 rib as given on sleeve border.
Cast (bind) off loosely in rib.
Right front border
With RS facing and 3mm (US size 2) needles, pick up and k17 [18: 19: 20: 21] sts evenly along lower edge of right front, 30 [32: 36: 39: 42] sts up curved front edge and 36 [39: 42: 44: 46] sts up straight front edge including edge of yoke.
83 [89: 97: 103: 109] sts.

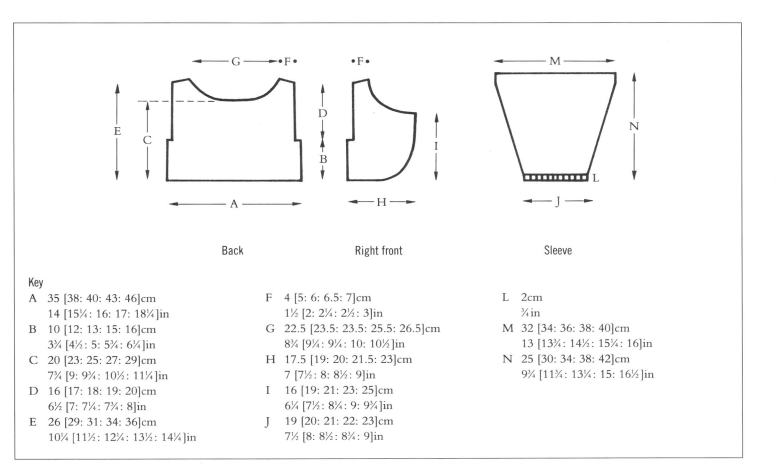

Back   Right front   Sleeve

Key

A   35 [38: 40: 43: 46]cm
    14 [15¼: 16: 17: 18¼]in
B   10 [12: 13: 15: 16]cm
    3¾ [4½: 5: 5¾: 6¼]in
C   20 [23: 25: 27: 29]cm
    7¾ [9: 9¾: 10½: 11¼]in
D   16 [17: 18: 19: 20]cm
    6½ [7: 7¼: 7¾: 8]in
E   26 [29: 31: 34: 36]cm
    10¼ [11½: 12¼: 13½: 14¼]in

F   4 [5: 6: 6.5: 7]cm
    1½ [2: 2¼: 2½: 3]in
G   22.5 [23.5: 23.5: 25.5: 26.5]cm
    8¾ [9¼: 9¼: 10: 10½]in
H   17.5 [19: 20: 21.5: 23]cm
    7 [7½: 8: 8½: 9]in
I   16 [19: 21: 23: 25]cm
    6¼ [7½: 8¼: 9: 9¾]in
J   19 [20: 21: 22: 23]cm
    7½ [8: 8½: 8¾: 9]in

L   2cm
    ¾in
M   32 [34: 36: 38: 40]cm
    13 [13¾: 14½: 15¼: 16]in
N   25 [30: 34: 38: 42]cm
    9¾ [11¾: 13¼: 15: 16½]in

Work 2nd rib row as given on sleeve border,
then work first rib row.
Keeping rib correct, work buttonholes on
next row as foll:
Buttonhole row (WS) Beg at neck edge,
k1, p1, k1, yo, k2tog, (rib 8 [10: 12: 12: 14]
sts, yo, k2tog) twice, work in rib to end.
Work one row more in rib.
Cast (bind) off loosely in rib.

Left front border
Work left front border as for right front
border, but picking up sts in reverse order
and omitting buttonholes.
Sew cast (bound) off edge of sleeves to sides
of armholes and sew armhole cast (bind) off
off to last 8 rows on sides of sleeves.
Join side seams and ends of borders, then join
sleeve seams.
Sew on the buttons to correspond with the
buttonholes.

CITY CHIC

This collection of seven chic sweaters – two for men and five for women – are perfect for city wear. The two men's designs are timeless classics and a must for any man's wardrobe. Their textured ribs have a gorgeous understated simplicity to suit even the most conventional tastes. Of the women's sweaters, the Fair Isle and cable pullover is a real test of a knitter's skill, but well worth the effort.

MAN'S RIBBED CARDIGAN

IN STAR +

*

Sizes

To fit 91 [96: 102: 107: 112]cm/36 [38: 40: 42: 44]in chest
Actual width around chest (buttoned) 106 [112: 118: 124: 128.5]cm/42½ [44½: 46¾: 49¼: 51½]in
Directions for larger sizes are in brackets [ ]; if there is only one set of figures it applies to all sizes.

Materials

PINGOUIN Star +:
16 [17: 18: 19: 20] balls Jade No. 50
Pair each of 3¾mm and 4½mm (US sizes 5 and 7) needles
5 buttons
Leather elbow patches (optional)

Tension (Gauge)

Worked with 4½mm (US size 7) needles.
Rib pattern: 21 sts and 24 rows to 10cm/4in over rib patt; work a sample on 32 sts (foll directions for rib patt on back), flattening work slightly when measuring width.

Stitches used

The cardigan is worked in a simple rib pattern with k1, p1 ribbing for lower border and cuffs. The directions for these stitches are given in the instructions.

Instructions

Back

With 3¾mm (US size 5) needles, cast on 101 [107: 113: 117: 123] sts and beg k1, p1 rib on the next row as foll:

1st rib row (RS) P1, *k1, p1; rep from * to end.
2nd rib row K1, *p1, k1; rep from * to end.
Rep these 2 rows until work measures 8cm/3in from beg, ending with a first rib row.**
Inc row (WS) Keeping rib correct, rib 6 [9: 12: 3: 6], (work into front and back of next st, rib 10) 8 [8: 8: 10: 10] times, work into front and back of next st, rib 6 [9: 12: 3: 6]. 110 [116: 122: 128: 134] sts.
Change to 4½mm (US size 7) needles.
Beg rib patt on next row as foll:
1st patt row (RS) P2, *k4, p2;* rep from * to *.
2nd patt row *K2, p4;* rep from * to *, ending k2.
Last 2 patt rows form rib patt.
Cont in rib patt until back measures 38 [39: 41: 42: 43]cm/15 [15¼: 16¼: 16½: 17]in from beg, ending with a 2nd (WS) patt row.
Armhole shaping
Keeping rib patt correct as set throughout, cast (bind) off 7 sts at beg of next 2 rows. 96 [102: 108: 114: 120] sts.
Work in patt without shaping until back measures 63 [65: 67: 69: 71]cm/24¾ [25½: 26½: 27¼: 28]in from beg, ending with a WS row.
Shoulder and neck shaping
Cast (bind) off 10 [11: 11: 12: 13] sts at beg of next 2 rows.
Next row (RS) Cast (bind) off 10 [11: 11: 12: 13] sts, work in patt until there are 17 [17: 19: 19: 19] sts on RH needle and leave these sts for right back, cast (bind) off next 22 [24: 26: 28: 30] sts, work in patt to end.
Cont with 27 [28: 30: 31: 32] sts at end of needle only, for left back.
Cast (bind) off 10 [11: 11: 12: 13] sts at beg of next row and 6 sts at neck edge on foll row.
Cast (bind) off rem 11 [11: 13: 13: 13] sts to complete shoulder shaping.
With WS facing, rejoin yarn to neck edge of right back sts and cast (bind) off first 6 sts, then work in patt to end.
Cast (bind) off rem 11 [11: 13: 13: 13] sts.

Right front

With 3¾mm (US size 5) needles, cast on 49 [53: 55: 57: 61] sts and work as for back ribbing from ** to **.
Inc row (WS) Keeping rib correct, rib 4 [11: 7: 3: 10], (work into front and back of next st, rib 9) 4 [3: 4: 5: 4] times, work into front and back of next st, rib 4 [11: 7: 3: 10]. 54 [57: 60: 63: 66] sts.***
Change to 4½mm (US size 7) needles.
Beg rib patt on next row as foll:
1st patt row (RS) K4 [1: 4: 1: 4], p2, *k4, p2;* rep from * to *.

2nd patt row *K2, p4;* rep from * to *, ending k2, p4 [1: 4: 1: 4].
Rep last 2 patt rows until front is same length as back to armhole shaping, but ending with a first (RS) patt row.
Armhole shaping
Keeping rib patt correct as set throughout, cast (bind) off 7 sts at beg of next row. 47 [50: 53: 56: 69] sts.
Work 2 rows in patt without shaping, so ending at centre front edge.
V-neck shaping
Dec one st at beg of next row (centre front edge) and every foll alt row 6 [7: 8: 10: 11] times in all, then dec one st at same edge on every foll 4th row 10 [10: 9: 9: 9] times. 31 [33: 35: 37: 39] sts.
Work in patt without shaping until front is same length as back to beg of shoulder shaping, ending at armhole edge.
Shoulder shaping
Cast (bind) off 10 [11: 11: 12: 13] sts at beg of next row and foll alt row.
Work one row without shaping.
Cast (bind) off rem 11 [11: 13: 13: 13] sts.

Left front

Work as for right front to ***.
Change to 4½mm (US size 7) needles.
Beg rib patt on next row as foll:
1st patt row (RS) P2, *k4, p2;* rep from * to *, ending k4 [1: 4: 1: 4].
2nd patt row P4 [1: 4: 1: 4], *k2, p4;* rep from * to *, ending k2.
Last 2 patt rows form rib patt.
Cont in patt as set and complete as for right front, but reversing all shapings.

Sleeves

With 3¾mm (US size 5) needles, cast on 53 [55: 55: 57: 59] sts and work as for back ribbing from ** to **.
Inc row (WS) Keeping rib correct, rib 6 [7: 7: 8: 9], (work into front and back of next st, rib 9) 4 times, work into front and back of next st, rib 6 [7: 7: 8: 9].
58 [60: 60: 62: 64] sts.
Change to 4½mm (US size 7) needles.
Beg rib patt on next row as foll:
1st patt row (RS) K1 [2: 2: 3: 4], p2, *k4, p2;* rep from * to *, ending k1 [2: 2: 3: 4].
Cont in patt as now set for 2 rows more.
Cont in patt, inc one st at each end of next row, then on every foll 4th row 17 [17: 19: 18: 18] times, then on every foll 3rd row 6 [7: 5: 7: 8] times, working extra sts into patt. 106 [110: 110: 114: 118] sts.
Work in patt without shaping until sleeve measures 52 [53: 54: 55: 56]cm/20½ [20¾: 21¼: 21½: 22]in from beg.
Cast (bind) off all sts in patt.

Finishing and front bands

Do not press. Join shoulder seams, matching rib patt.

Button band

With 3¾mm (US size 5) needles, cast on 11 sts for button band and work in rib as foll:

1st row (RS) K2, (p1, k1) 4 times, k1.

2nd row (K1, p1) 5 times, k1.

Rep these 2 rows until band, when slightly stretched, fits along front edge of right front to centre back neck.

Cast (bind) off in rib.

Sew button band to right front.

Mark positions of buttons on button band, the first to come 2cm/¾in from lower edge, the last at beg of V-neck shaping and the rem 3 evenly spaced between.

Buttonhole band

Work buttonhole band as for button band, but when positions of buttonholes are reached (ending with a RS row facing for next row) work buttonholes over 2 rows as foll:

1st buttonhole row (RS) K2, p1, k1, cast (bind) off 3, work in patt to end.

2nd buttonhole row (K1, p1) twice, cast on 3 sts onto RH needle, (p1, k1) twice.

Sew buttonhole band to left front and join front bands at centre back neck.

Sew cast-on edge of sleeves to sides of armholes and sew armhole cast (bind) off to last 8 rows on sides of sleeves.

Join side and sleeve seams.

Sew on the buttons to correspond with the buttonholes.

Sew on elbow patches if desired.

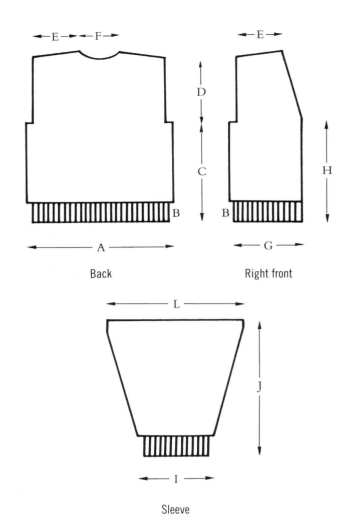

Back   Right front

Sleeve

Key

A 52 [55: 58: 61: 63.5]cm
21 [22: 23¼: 24¼: 25½]in

B 8cm
3in

C 38 [39: 41: 42: 43]cm
15 [15¼: 16¼: 16½: 17]in

D 25 [26: 26: 27: 28]cm
9¾ [10¼: 10¼: 10¾: 11]in

E 14.5 [15.5: 16.5 17.5: 18.5]cm
5¾ [6: 6½: 6¾: 7¼]in

F 16 [17: 18: 19: 20]cm
6¼ [6½: 7: 7½: 7¾]in

G 25.5 [27: 28.5: 30: 31]cm
10¼ [10¾: 11¼: 12: 12½]in

H 39 [40: 42: 43: 44]cm
15¼ [15¾: 16½: 17: 17¼]in

I 27.5 [28.5: 28.5: 29.5: 30.5]cm
11 [11½: 11½: 11¾: 12]in

J 52 [53: 54: 55: 56]cm
20½ [20¾: 21¼: 21½: 22]in

L 50.5 [52: 52: 54: 56]cm
20 [21: 21: 21¾: 22½]in

FAIR ISLE AND CABLE PULLOVER

IN FRANCE +

****

Sizes

To fit 86 to 91 [96 to 102]cm/34 to 36 [38 to 40]in bust
Actual width around bust when completed 108 [121]cm/43 [48½]in and around hips 105 [118]cm/42 [47]in
Directions for larger size are in brackets [ ]; if there is only one set of figures it applies to both sizes.

Materials

PINGOUIN France +:
12 [13] balls Opaline No. 39 (A)
1 ball Myosotis No. 76 (B)
1 ball Marron Glace No. 28 (C)
1 ball Ficelle No. 53 (D)
1 ball Ecru No. 17 (E)
Pair each of 3mm and 3¾mm (US sizes 3 and 5) needles
Cable needle (cn)

Tension (Gauge)

Worked with 3¾mm (US size 5) needles.
Fair Isle patt: 24 sts and 28 rows to 10cm/4in over Fair Isle patt; work a sample on 42 sts as foll:
Cast on with yarn A and work 2 rows in st st, then work in patt as for first size on back.
Main cable patt: 30 sts and 30 rows to 10cm/4in over main cable patt; work a sample on 42 sts. (On measurement schematic the measurements shown at lower edge are taken over Fair Isle patt and those at top over main cable patt).

Stitches used

Special abbreviations

kfb – knit into front and back of next st.
pfb – purl into front and back of next st.

T2R (twist 2 right) – pass RH needle in front of first st on LH needle and lift up 2nd st and k it leaving it on LH needle, then k first st and slip both sts off LH needle.
T2L (twist 2 left) – pass RH needle behind first st on LH needle and k into back of 2nd st leaving it on LH needle, then k into front of first st and slip both sts off LH needle.
cable 4 back – slip next 2 sts onto cn and hold at back of work, k2, then k2 from cn.
cable 4 front – slip next 2 sts onto cn and hold at front of work, k2, then k2 from cn.
C4L (cross 4 left) – slip next 2 sts onto cn and hold at front of work, p2, then k2 from cn.
C4R (cross 4 right) – slip next 2 sts onto cn and hold at back of work, k2, then p2 from cn.

Fair Isle pattern

The Fair Isle pattern is worked in st st, foll the chart as explained in the instructions. When working with 2 colours in a row, strand colour not in use loosely across WS.

Main cable pattern

Work main cable patt over a multiple of 20 sts plus 2 extra sts as foll:
1st row (RS) K1, *k2, p6, k4, p6, k2;* rep from * to *, ending k1.
2nd row K1, *p2, k6, p4, k6, p2;* rep from * to *, ending k1.
(Border st at each end of row is worked in g st to give a firm edge.)
3rd row K3, *(p6, cable 4 back) twice;* rep from * to *, ending p6, cable 4 back, p6, k3.
4th row As 2nd row.
5th row K1, *C4L, p4, k4, p4, C4R;* rep from * to *, ending k1.
6th row K1, *k2, p2, k4, p4, k4, p2, k2;* rep from * to *, ending k1.
7th row K1, *p2, C4L, p2, cable 4 back, p2, C4R, p2;* rep from * to *, ending k1.
8th row K1, *k4, p2, k2, p4, k2, p2, k4;* rep from * to *, ending k1.
9th row K1, *(k2, p2) twice, k4, (p2, k2) twice;* rep from * to *, ending k1.
10th row K1, *(p2, k2) twice, p4, (k2, p2) twice;* rep from * to *, ending k1.
11th row K1, *T2L, p2, k2, p2, cable 4 back, p2, k2, p2, T2R;* rep from * to *, ending k1.
12th row As 10th row.
13th row K1, *T2L, p2, k2, p8, k2, p2, T2R;* rep from * to *, ending k1.
14th row K1, *p2, k2, p2, k8, p2, k2, p2;* rep from * to *, ending k1.
15th row K1, *T2L, p2, C4L, p4, C4R, p2, T2R;* rep from * to *, ending k1.
16th row K1, *(p2, k4) 3 times, p2;* rep from * to *, ending k1.

17th row K1, *T2L, p4, C4L, C4R, p4, T2R;* rep from * to *, ending k1.
18th row K1, *p2, k6, p4, k6, p2;* rep from * to *, ending k1.
19th row K1, *T2L, p6, cable 4 front, p6, T2R;* rep from * to *, ending k1.
20th row As 18th row.
21st row K1, *T2L, p4, C4R, C4L, p4, T2R;* rep from * to *, ending k1.
22nd row As 16th row.
23rd row K1, *T2L, p2, C4R, p4, C4L, p2, T2R;* rep from * to *, ending k1.
24th row As 14th row.
25th row K1, *T2L, p2, k2, p2, k4, p2, k2, p2, T2R;* rep from * to *, ending k1.
26th row As 10th row.
27th row K1, *T2L, p2, k2, p2, cable 4 back, p2, k2, p2, T2R;* rep from * to *, ending k1.
28th row As 10th row.
29th row K1, *p4, k2, p2, k4, p2, k2, p4;* rep from * to *, ending k1.
30th row As 8th row.
31st row K1, *p2, C4R, p2, cable 4 back, p2, C4L, p2;* rep from * to *, ending k1.
32nd row As 6th row.
33rd row K1, *C4R, p4, k4, p4, C4L;* rep from * to *, ending k1.
34th row As 2nd row.
Rep 3rd–34th rows inclusive to form patt (first and 2nd rows are foundation rows and are not worked again).

Instructions

Back

With 3mm (US size 3) needles and yarn A, cast on 152 [172] sts and beg rib patt as foll:
1st rib row (RS) *K2, p2, k4, p2;* rep from * to *, ending k2.
2nd rib row P2, *k2, p4, k2, p2;* rep from * to *.
3rd rib row *K2, p2, T2R, T2L, p2;* rep from * to *, ending k2.
Cont to rep 2nd and 3rd rib rows until work measures 7cm/2¾in from beg, ending with a 3rd rib row.
Dec row (WS) P6 [5], (p2tog, p4, p2tog, p3) 13 [15] times, p3 [2]. 126 [142] sts.
Change to 3¾mm (US size 5) needles.
Still using yarn A, k one row.
Beg with a WS row, beg Fair Isle patt in st st from chart on next row as foll:
1st chart row (WS) P in yarn C.
2nd chart row *K1 E, 1 A;* rep from * to *.
3rd chart row *P1 E, 1 A;* rep from * to *.
4th chart row K in C.
5th chart row P in A.
6th chart row *K2D, 5 A, 4 D, 3 A;* rep from * to *, ending 0 [2] D.
7th chart row P 0 [2] A, *1 D, 1 A, 1 D,

4 A, 1 D, 3 A, 1 D, 2 A;★ rep from ★ to ★.
Cont in patt as now set until 17th chart row has been worked.

First size only:
18th chart row (RS) (K2 C, 2 E) twice, ★k2 C, 2 E, 5 C, (2 E, 1 C) twice, 2 E, 5 C, 2 E, 2 C, 2 E;★ rep from ★ to ★ 3 times more, k2 C, 2 E, 2 C.
Mark on chart the beg and end of this row.

2nd size only:
18th chart row (RS) K2 E, then rep from ★ to ★ as given for first size 5 times.

Both sizes:
Cont in patt until last row of chart has been completed, so ending with a k row.
Cont with yarn A only.
Inc row (WS) P1 [3], (pfb, p2, pfb, p3) 17 [19] times, (pfb, p2) twice. 162 [182] sts.
Now work in main cable patt (see Stitches Used) until back measures 45 [47]cm/17¾ [18½]in from beg, ending with a WS row.

Armhole shaping
Keeping main cable patt correct as set throughout, cast (bind) bind off 4 sts at beg of next 2 rows, 3 sts at beg of next 2 rows and 2 sts at beg of next 6 [8] rows, then dec one st at each end of next 2 [4] alt rows.
132 [144] sts.
Work without shaping until back measures 66 [69]cm/26 [27¼]in from beg, ending with a WS row.

Shoulder and neck shaping
Cast (bind) off 10 sts at beg of next 2 rows.
Next row (RS) Cast (bind) off 10 sts, work in patt until there are 30 [34] sts on RH needle and leave these sts for right back, cast (bind) off next 32 [36] sts, work in patt to end.
Cont with 40 [44] sts at end of needle only, for left back.
Cast (bind) off 10 sts at beg of next row and 4 sts at neck edge on foll row.
Cast (bind) off 11 [13] sts at beg of next row and 4 sts at neck edge on foll row.
Cast (bind) off rem 11 [13] sts to complete shoulder shaping.
With WS facing, rejoin yarn to neck edge of right back sts and cast (bind) off first 4 sts, then work in patt to end.
Cast (bind) off 11 [13] sts at beg of next row and 4 sts at neck edge on foll row.
Cast (bind) off rem 11 [13] sts.

Front

Work front as given for back until front measures 60 [63]cm/23½ [24¾]in from beg, ending with a WS row.

Neck shaping
Next row (RS) Work 60 [65] sts in patt and slip these sts onto a spare needle, cast (bind) off next 12 [14] sts, work in patt to end.
Cont with 60 [65] sts only, for right front.

Work one row without shaping.
★★Cast (bind) off 4 [5] sts at beg of next row (neck edge) and 4 sts at same edge on next alt row, 2 sts on next 3 alt rows.
Work one row without shaping.
Dec one st at neck edge on next row and at same edge on every foll alt row 4 times in all. 42 [46] sts.

Shoulder shaping
Keeping neck edge straight, cast (bind) off 10 sts at beg of next row and next alt row, then 11 [13] sts on next alt row.
Work one row without shaping.
Cast (bind) off rem 11 [13] sts.
With WS facing, rejoin yarn to neck edge of left front sts and complete as for right front from ★★ to end.

Sleeves

With 3mm (US size 3) needles and yarn A, cast on 62 [62] sts and work in rib patt as on back for 6cm/2¼in, ending with a 2nd rib row.
Inc row (RS) K6, (kfb, k6) 8 times. 70 sts.
Change to 3¾mm (US size 5) needles.
Still using yarn A, p one row.
Beg with 12th chart row, beg Fair Isle in st st from chart on next row as foll:
12th chart row (RS) K in C.
13th chart row ★P1 A, 1 E;★ rep from ★ to ★.
14th chart row ★K1 A, 1 E;★ rep from ★ to ★.
15th chart row P in C.
16th and 17th chart rows Work in E.
18th chart row Work as for first size on back, working sts from ★ to ★ twice.
Cont in patt as now set, but inc one st at each end of next row and again on 24th, 29th and 34th chart rows, working extra sts into patt. 78 sts.
35th chart row P in C.
Cont with yarn A only.
Inc row (RS) K4, (kfb, k2) 24 times, k2. 102 sts.
Now beg with 2nd row, work in main cable patt, inc one st at each end of every foll 8th row 4 [0] times, then every foll 6th row 8 [13] times and every foll 4th row 0 [2] times, working extra sts into patt, but always keeping border st in g st. 126 [132] sts.
Work without shaping until sleeve measures 46 [48]cm/18 [18¾]in from beg.

Top of sleeve shaping
Place a marker loop of contrasting yarn at each end of last row to indicate beg of top section.
Keeping patt correct throughout, dec one st at each end of next 2 alt rows, cast (bind) off 2 sts at beg of next 6 [8] rows, 3 sts at beg of next 2 rows and 4 [5] sts at beg of next 2 rows. Cast (bind) off rem 96 sts.

Collar

With 3mm (US size 3) needles and yarn A, cast on 142 [152] sts and work in rib patt as on back for 6cm/2¼in, ending with a 3rd rib row.
Cast (bind) off in rib patt.

Finishing and neck border

Press st st sections only, lightly on WS with a cool iron, following instructions on yarn label and avoiding ribbing and cables.

Neck border
With RS facing, 3mm (US size 3) needles and yarn A, pick up and k56 [59] sts evenly around front neck edge and 38 [41] sts across back neck. 94 [100] sts.
Beg with a p row, work 6 rows in st st.
Cast (bind) off loosely.
Join left shoulder seam, then join seam of neck border on reverse side as this border will roll over to show p side.
Sew in sleeves, placing markers level with beg of armhole cast (bind) off, then join side and sleeve seams.
Join ends of collar and sew cast-on edge to neck edges inside neck border, placing the seams level.

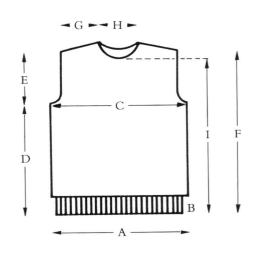
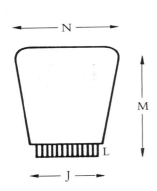

Back and front   Sleeve

Key

A 52.5 [59]cm/21 [23½]in

B 7cm/2¾in

C 54 [60.5]cm/21½ [24¼]in

D 45 [47]cm/17¾ [18½]in

E 21 [22]cm/8¼ [8¾]in

F 66 [69]cm/26 [27¼]in

G 14 [15]cm/5½ [6]in

H 16 [17]cm/6¼ [6½]in

I 60 [63]cm/23½ [24¾]in

J 29 [29]cm/11½ [11½]in

L 6cm/2¼in

M 46 [48]cm/18 [18¾]in

N 42 [44]cm/16¾ [17½]in

Fair Isle chart

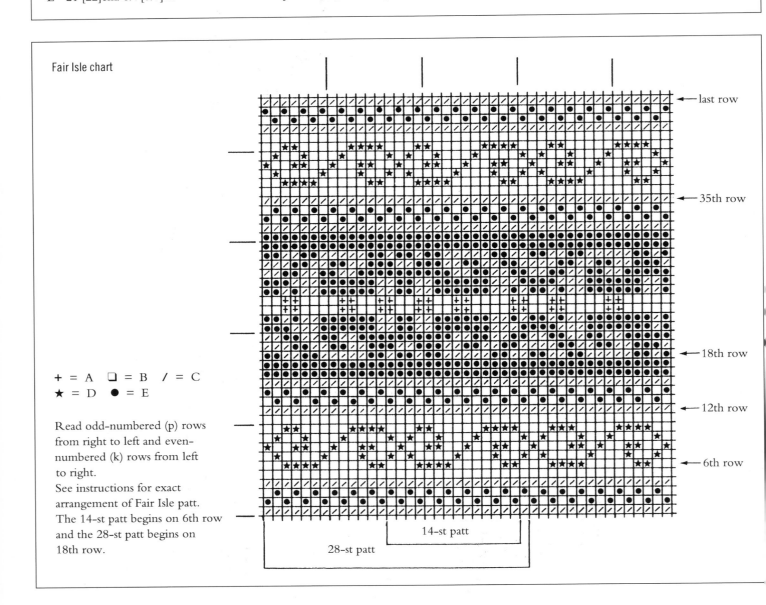

← last row

← 35th row

← 18th row

← 12th row

← 6th row

+ = A   □ = B   / = C

★ = D   ● = E

Read odd-numbered (p) rows from right to left and even-numbered (k) rows from left to right.
See instructions for exact arrangement of Fair Isle patt. The 14-st patt begins on 6th row and the 28-st patt begins on 18th row.

14-st patt

28-st patt

FAIR ISLE CARDIGAN

IN FRANCE +

** **

Sizes

To fit 86 to 91 [96: 102 to 107]cm/34 to 36 [38: 40 to 42]in bust
Actual width around bust (buttoned) 107 [115: 123]cm/42¾ [46: 49¼]in
Directions for larger sizes are in brackets [ ]; if there is only one set of figures it applies to all sizes.

Materials

PINGOUIN France +:
5 [6: 7] balls Ficelle No. 53 (A)
3 [3: 4] balls Marengo No. 66 (B)
1 ball Opaline No. 39 (C)
2 [2: 3] balls Rose No. 02 (D)
1 ball Ecru No. 17 (E)
1 ball Marengo Fonce No. 67 (F)
2 balls Tilleul No. 52 (G)
2 [2: 3] balls Vieux Rose No. 46 (H)
Pair each of 3mm and 3¾mm (US sizes 3 and 5) needles
6 buttons

Tension (Gauge)

Worked with 3¾mm (US size 5) needles.
Fair Isle patt: 24 sts and 28 rows to 10cm/4in over Fair Isle patt; work a sample on 37 sts as foll:
Cast on with D and work 2 rows, then work in patt from Chart No. 2 as given for back. When the 17 rows of this chart have been completed, begin next patt on a p row, still using Chart No. 2. Cont in this way for sample.

Stitches used

Fair Isle pattern

The Fair Isle pattern is worked in st st foll the charts. The arrangement of patt for each chart and each section of garment is explained in the instructions; mark on charts the positions where rows begin and end for size being worked.
When working with 2 colours in a row, strand colour not in use loosely across WS.

Instructions

Back

With 3mm (US size 3) needles, cast on 117 [125: 133] sts and beg rib as foll:
1st rib row (RS) P1, *k1, p1; rep from * to end.
2nd rib row K1, *p1, k1; rep from * to end.
Rep these 2 rows until work measures 6cm/2¼in from beg, ending with a first rib row.**
Inc row (WS) Keeping rib correct, rib 9 [7: 8], (work into front and back of next st, rib 10 [9: 8]) 9 [11: 13] times, work into front and back of next st, rib 8 [7: 7] sts. 127 [137: 147] sts.
Change to 3¾mm (US size 5) needles.
***Joining on colours as required, beg Fair Isle patt in st st from Chart No. 1 on next row as foll:
First size only:
1st chart row (RS) *K1 A, 3 G, 2 A, 3 G, 1 A, 3 G, 2 A, 3 G;* rep from * to * 6 times more, k1 A.
2nd chart row P1 G, *1 A, 1 G, 2 A, 1 G, (3 A, 1 G) twice, 2 A, 1 G, 1 A, 1 G;* rep from * to * 6 times more.
2nd size only:
1st chart row (RS) K2 A, 3 G, *1 A, 3 G, 2 A, 3 G, 1 A, 3 G, 2 A, 3 G;* rep from * to * 6 times more, k1 A, 3 G, 2 A.
2nd chart row P1 G, 2 A, 1 G, 1 A, 1 G, *1 A, 1 G, 2 A, 1 G, (3 A, 1 G) twice, 2 A, 1 G, 1 A, 1 G;* rep from * to * 6 times more, p1 A, 1 G, 2 A, 1 G.
3rd size only:
1st chart row (RS) K1 G, 1 A, 3 G, 2 A, 3 G, *1 A, 3 G, 2 A, 3 G, 1 A, 3 G, 2 A, 3 G;* rep from * to * 6 times more, k1 A, 3 G, 2 A, 3 G, 1 A, 1 G.
2nd chart row P1 A, 1 G, 3 A, 1 G, 2 A, 1 G, 1 A, 1 G, *1 A, 1 G, 2 A, 1 G, (3 A, 1 G) twice, 2 A, 1 G, 1 A, 1 G;* rep from * to * 6 times more, p1 A, 1 G, 2 A, 1 G, 3 A, 1 G, 1 A.
All sizes:
Cont in patt as now set and work 4 rem rows of Chart No. 1, so ending with a p row.
Now beg working from Chart No. 2 on next row as foll:
1st chart row (RS) (K1 D, 2 B) twice, *(1 D, 1 B) twice, (1 D, 2 B) twice;* rep from * to * 11 [12: 13] times more, k1 D.
Cont in patt as now set following the chart until the 17 rows of Chart No. 2 have been worked, so ending with a k row.
Now beg working from Chart No. 3 on next row as foll:
1st chart row (WS) P1 [2: 3] E, *1 B, 3 E;* rep from * to *, ending 1 B, 1 [2: 3] E.
Cont in patt as now set and work 3 rem rows of Chart No. 3, so ending with a k row.
Beg with a p row, work 3 rows in st st with yarn A only, so ending with a p row.***
These last 30 rows (from *** to ***) form one patt repeat.
Cont in patt, rep from *** to ***, until back measures 40 [42: 44]cm/15¾ [16½: 17¼]in from beg, ending with a p row.
Make a note on chart of last patt row worked.
Armhole shaping
Keeping patt correct as set throughout, cast (bind) off 4 sts at beg of next 2 rows, 3 sts at beg of next 2 rows and 2 sts at beg of next 6 rows.
Work one row without shaping.
Dec one st at each end of next row and every foll alt row 2 [3: 4] times in all. 97 [105: 113] sts.
Work in patt without shaping until back measures 61 [64: 67]cm/24 [25: 26¼]in from beg, ending with a p row.
Shoulder and neck shaping
Cast (bind) off 9 [10: 11] sts at beg of next 2 rows.
Next row (RS) Cast (bind) off 9 [10: 11] sts, work in patt until there are 13 [14: 15] sts on RH needle and leave these sts for right back, cast (bind) off next 35 [37: 39] sts, work in patt to end.
Cont with 22 [24: 26] sts at end of needle only, for left back.
Cast (bind) off 9 [10: 11] sts at beg of next row and 4 sts at neck edge on foll row.
Cast (bind) off rem 9 [10: 11] sts to complete shoulder shaping.
With WS facing, rejoin yarn to neck edge of right back sts and cast (bind) off first 4 sts, then work in patt to end.
Cast (bind) off rem 9 [10: 11] sts.

Left front

With 3mm (US size 3) needles and yarn A, cast on 57 [61: 65] sts and work as for back ribbing from ** to **.
Inc row (WS) Keeping rib correct, rib 8 [6: 4], (work into front and back of next st, rib 7) 5 [6: 7] times, work into front and back of next st, rib rem 8 [6: 4] sts. 63 [68: 73] sts.
Change to 3¾mm (US size 5) needles.
****Joining on colours as required, beg Fair Isle patt in st st from Chart No. 1 on next row as foll:
First size only:
1st chart row (RS) *K1 A, 3 G, 2 A, 3 G, 1 A, 3 G, 2 A, 3 G;* rep from * to * twice

more, k1 A, 3 G, 2 A, 3 G.

2nd size only:
1st chart row (RS) K2 A, 3 G, ★1 A, 3 G, 2 A, 3 G, 1 A, 3 G, 2 A, 3 G;★ rep from ★ to ★ twice more, k1 A, 3 G, 2 A, 3 G.

3rd size only:
1st chart row (RS) K1 G, 1 A, 3 G, 2 A, 3 G, ★1 A, 3 G, 2 A, 3 G, 1 A, 3 G, 2 A, 3 G;★ rep from ★ to ★ twice more, k1 A, 3 G, 2 A, 3 G.

All sizes:
Cont in patt as now set and work 5 rem rows of Chart No. 1, so ending with a p row.
Now beg working from Chart No. 2 on next row as foll:

First size only:
1st chart row (RS) (K1 D, 2 B) twice, ★(1 D, 1 B) twice, (1 D, 2 B) twice;★ rep from ★ to ★ 4 times more, (k1 D, 1 B) twice, 1 D, 2 B.

2nd size only:
1st chart row (RS) (K1 D, 2 B) twice, ★(1 D, 1 B) twice, (1 D, 2 B) twice;★ rep from ★ to ★ 5 times more, k1 D, 1 B.

3rd size only:
1st chart row (RS) (K1 D, 2 B) twice, ★(1 D, 1 B) twice, (1 D, 2 B) twice;★ rep from ★ to ★ 5 times more, (k1 D, 1 B) twice, 1 D, 2 B.

All sizes:
Cont in patt as now set until the 17 rows of Chart No. 2 have been worked, so ending with a k row.
Now beg working from Chart No. 3 on next row as foll:

1st chart row (WS) P1 E, ★1 B, 3 E;★ rep from ★ to ★, ending 1 B, 1 [2: 3] E.
Cont in patt as now set and work 3 rem rows of Chart No. 3, so ending with a k row.
Beg with a p row, work 3 rows in st st with yarn A only, so ending with a p row.★★★★
These last 30 rows (from ★★★★ to ★★★★) form one patt repeat for left front.
Cont in patt, rep from ★★★★ to ★★★★, until front measures 34 [36: 38]cm/13¼ [14: 15]in from beg, ending with a k row at centre front edge.

Front and armhole shaping
Keeping patt correct as set throughout, dec one st at beg of next row (centre front edge) and every foll alt row 9 [9: 10] times in all, then dec at same edge on every foll 4th row 12 [13: 13] times, **and at the same time** when front is same length as back to beg of armhole shaping and ending at armhole edge with same patt row, cast (bind) off 4 sts at beg of next row (armhole edge), 3 sts at same edge on next alt row and 2 sts on next 3 alt rows, then dec one st at armhole edge on next 2 [3: 4] alt rows and when all armhole decs are completed, keep armhole edge straight until all front decs are completed. 27 [30: 33] sts.

Work without shaping until front is same length as back to beg of shoulder shaping, ending at armhole edge, after working same patt row.

Shoulder shaping
Cast (bind) off 9 [10: 11] sts at beg of next row and foll alt row.
Work one row without shaping.
Cast (bind) off rem 9 [10: 11] sts.

Right front

Work as for left front, but reversing all patts by reading rows in reverse and also reversing all shapings.

Sleeves

With 3mm (US size 3) needles and yarn A, cast on 51 [55: 57] sts and work as for back ribbing from ★★ to ★★.
Inc row (WS) Keeping rib correct, rib 3 [5: 2], (work into front and back of next st, rib 3) 11 [11: 13] times, work into front and back of next st, rib rem 3 [5: 2] sts. 63 [67: 71] sts.
Change to 3¾mm (US size 5) needles.
Beg with a k row, work 3 rows in st st with yarn B, so ending with a k row.
Break off yarn B.
Cont in st st, work 3 rows more with yarn A, inc one st at each end of last row, so ending with a p row. 65 [69: 73] sts.
Joining on colours as required, beg Fair Isle patt in st st from Chart No. 1 on next row as foll:

First size only:
1st chart row (RS) K2 A, 3 G, ★1 A, 3 G, 2 A, 3 G, 1 A, 3 G, 2 A, 3 G;★ rep from ★ to ★ twice more, k1 A, 3 G, 2 A.

2nd size only:
1st chart row (RS) K2 G, 2 A, 3 G, ★1 A, 3 G, 2 A, 3 G, 1 A, 3 G, 2 A, 3 G;★ rep from ★ to ★ twice more, k1 A, 3 G, 2 A, 2 G.

3rd size only:
1st chart row (RS) K1 A, 3 G, 2 A, 3 G, ★1 A, 3 G, 2 A, 3 G, 1 A, 3 G, 2 A, 3 G;★ rep from ★ to ★ twice more, k1 A, 3 G, 2 A, 3 G, 1 A.

All sizes:
Cont in patt as now set, inc one st at each end of 5th chart row, then work 6th chart row of Chart No. 1 (working extra sts into patt), so ending with a p row. 67 [71: 75] sts.
Now beg working from Chart No. 2 on next row as foll:

First size only:
1st chart row (RS) (K1 D, 2 B) twice, ★(1 D, 1 B) twice, (1 D, 2 B) twice;★ rep from ★ to ★ 5 times more, k1 D.

2nd size only:
1st chart row (RS) K1 D, 1 B, (1 D, 2 B) twice, ★(1 D, 1 B) twice, (1 D, 2 B) twice;★

rep from ★ to ★ 5 times more, k1 D, 1 B, 1 D.

3rd size only:
1st chart row (RS) ★(K1 D, 1 B) twice, (1 D, 2 B) twice;★ rep from ★ to ★ 6 times more, (k1 D, 1 B) twice, 1 D.

All sizes:
Cont in patt as now set, inc one st at each end of 5th, 11th and 17th chart row of Chart No. 2, so ending with a k row.
Now beg working from Chart No. 3 on next row as foll:

1st chart row (WS) ★P1 B, 3 E;★ rep from ★ to ★, ending 1 B.
Cont in patt as now set and work 3 rem rows of Chart No. 3, so ending with a k row.
Beg with a p row, work 3 rows in st st with yarn A only, inc one st at each end of last row, so ending with a p row. 75 [79: 83] sts.
This completes first 30-row patt repeat.
Taking care to keep all patt panels in line with previous ones, cont in patt, working incs on same patt rows 2 [3: 3] times more, then inc at each end of every foll 4th row [11: 12: 12] times. 101 [107: 113] sts.
Work in patt without shaping until sleeve measures 42 [44: 46]cm/16½ [17¼: 18]in from beg or desired length to underarm, ending with same patt row as back armhole.

Top of sleeve shaping
Keeping patt correct throughout, cast (bind) off 4 sts at beg of next 2 rows and 2 sts at beg of next 6 rows.
Work one row without shaping.
Dec one st at each end of next row and every foll alt row 10 times in all.
Cast (bind) off 2 sts at beg of next 10 [12: 14] rows and 4 sts at beg of next 4 rows.
Cast (bind) off rem 19 [21: 23] sts.

Finishing and front bands

Press lightly on WS with a cool iron, following instructions on yarn label and avoiding ribbing. Join shoulder seams.
Button band
With 3mm (US size 3) needles and yarn A, cast on 11 sts for button band and work in rib as foll:
1st row (RS) K2, (p1, k1) 4 times, k1.
2nd row (K1, p1) 5 times, k1.
Rep these 2 rows until band, when slightly stretched, fits along front edge of left front to centre back neck.
Cast (bind) off in rib.
Sew button band to left front.
Mark positions of buttons on button band, the first to come 2cm/¾in from lower edge, the last at beg of V-neck shaping and the rem 4 evenly spaced between.
Buttonhole band
Work buttonhole band as for button band,

but when positions of buttonholes are reached (ending with a RS row facing for next row) work buttonholes over 2 rows as foll:

1st buttonhole row (RS) K2, p1, k1, cast (bind) off 3, work in patt to end.

2nd buttonhole row (K1, p1) twice, cast on 3 sts onto RH needle, (p1, k1) twice.

Sew buttonhole band to right front and join front bands at centre back neck.

Sew in sleeves, then join side and sleeve seams, matching patt.

Sew on the buttons to correspond with the buttonholes.

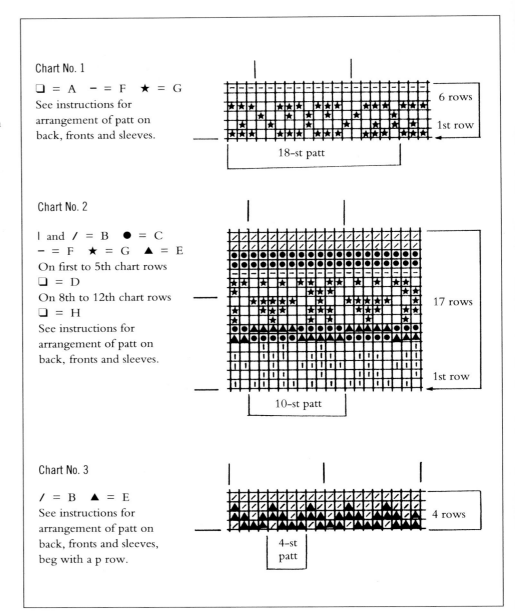

Chart No. 1

☐ = A – = F ★ = G

See instructions for arrangement of patt on back, fronts and sleeves.

18-st patt

6 rows
1st row

Chart No. 2

I and / = B ● = C
– = F ★ = G ▲ = E

On first to 5th chart rows
☐ = D

On 8th to 12th chart rows
☐ = H

See instructions for arrangement of patt on back, fronts and sleeves.

17 rows
1st row

10-st patt

Chart No. 3

/ = B ▲ = E

See instructions for arrangement of patt on back, fronts and sleeves, beg with a p row.

4 rows

4-st patt

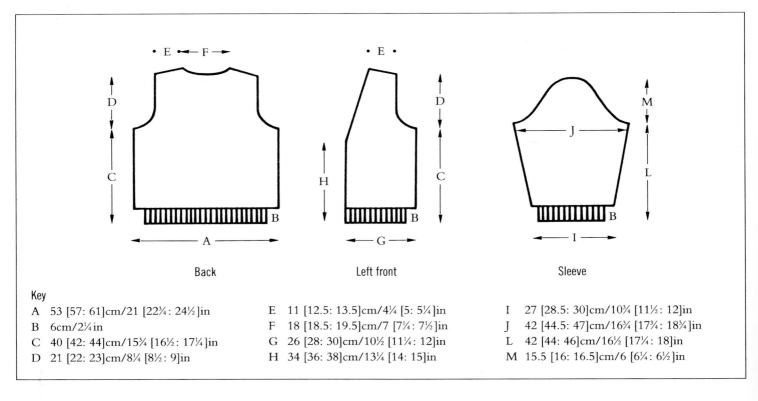

Back

Left front

Sleeve

Key

A 53 [57: 61]cm/21 [22¾: 24½]in
B 6cm/2¼in
C 40 [42: 44]cm/15¾ [16½: 17¼]in
D 21 [22: 23]cm/8¼ [8½: 9]in

E 11 [12.5: 13.5]cm/4¼ [5: 5¼]in
F 18 [18.5: 19.5]cm/7 [7¼: 7½]in
G 26 [28: 30]cm/10½ [11¼: 12]in
H 34 [36: 38]cm/13¼ [14: 15]in

I 27 [28.5: 30]cm/10¾ [11½: 12]in
J 42 [44.5: 47]cm/16¾ [17¾: 18¾]in
L 42 [44: 46]cm/16½ [17¼: 18]in
M 15.5 [16: 16.5]cm/6 [6¼: 6½]in

MAN'S SLEEVELESS PULLOVER

IN FRANCE +

*

Sizes

To fit 91 [96: 102: 107: 112 to 117]cm/36 [38: 40: 42: 44 to 46]in chest
Actual width around chest when completed 105 [110: 116: 122: 128]cm/42 [44: 46½: 49: 51]in
Directions for larger sizes are in brackets [ ]; if there is only one set of figures it applies to all sizes.

Materials

PINGOUIN France +:
8 [8: 9: 9: 10] balls in desired shade
Pair each of 3mm and 3¾mm (US sizes 3 and 5) needles
3mm (US size 3) circular needle

Tension (Gauge)

Worked with 3¾mm (US size 5) needles.
Patt st: 28 sts and 30 rows to 10cm/4in over patt st; work a sample on 37 sts as foll:
1st row (RS) P11, k5, p5, k5, p11.
2nd row K11, p5, k5, p5, k11.
Rep these 2 rows for sample and flatten work slightly when measuring tension (gauge).

Stitches used

The sweater is worked in a simple knit and purl pattern stitch and has k1, p1 ribbing for lower border, armbands and neckband. The directions for these stitches are given in the instructions.

Instructions

Back

With 3mm (US size 3) needles, cast on 129 [137: 143: 151: 157] sts and beg k1, p1 rib.

1st rib row (RS) P1, *k1, p1; rep from * to end.
2nd rib row K1, *p1, k1; rep from * to end.
Rep these 2 rows until work measures 7cm/2¾in from beg, ending with a first rib row.
Inc row (WS) Keeping rib correct, rib 5 [9: 5: 9: 5], (work into front and back of next st, rib 6) 17 [17: 19: 19: 21] times, work into front and back of next st, rib 4 [8: 4: 8: 4].
147 [155: 163: 171: 179] sts.
Change to 3¾mm (US size 5) needles.
Beg patt st on next row as foll:

First size only:
1st patt row (RS) K1, p5, k5, *p13, k5, p5, k5:* rep from * to * 3 times more, p13, k5, p5, k1.
2nd patt row P1, k5, p5, k13, *p5, k5, p5, k13:* rep from * to * 3 times more, p5, k5, p1.

2nd size only:
1st patt row (RS) K5, p5, k5, *p13, k5, p5, k5:* rep from * to * 4 times more.
2nd patt row *P5, k5, p5, k13:* rep from * to * 4 times more, p5, k5, p5.

3rd size only:
1st patt row (RS) P4, k5, p5, k5, *p13, k5, p5, k5:* rep from * to * 4 times more, p4.
2nd patt row K4, *p5, k5, p5, k13:* rep from * to * 4 times more, p5, k5, p5, k4.

4th size only:
1st patt row (RS) P8, k5, p5, k5, *p13, k5, p5, k5:* rep from * to * 4 times more, p8.
2nd patt row K8, *p5, k5, p5, k13:* rep from * to * 4 times more, p5, k5, p5, k8.

5th size only:
1st patt row (RS) P12, k5, p5, k5, *p13, k5, p5, k5:* rep from * to * 4 times more, p12.
2nd patt row K12, *p5, k5, p5, k13:* rep from * to * 4 times more, p5, k5, p5, k12.

All sizes:
Last 2 patt rows form patt st.
Cont in patt st until back measures 36 [37: 38: 39: 40]cm/14 [14½: 15: 15½: 15¾]in from beg, ending with a 2nd (WS) patt row.**

Armhole shaping

Keeping patt st correct as set throughout, cast (bind) off 4 sts at beg of next 2 rows, 3 sts at beg of next 2 rows and 2 sts at beg of next 8 rows, then dec one st at each end of next 4 [5: 6: 7: 8] alt rows.
109 [115: 121: 127: 133] sts.
Work in patt without shaping until back measures 61 [63: 65: 66: 68]cm/24 [24¾: 25½: 26: 26¾]in from beg, ending with a WS row.

Shoulder and neck shaping

Cast (bind) off 9 [10: 10: 11: 11] sts at beg of next 2 rows.
Next row (RS) Cast (bind) off 9 [10: 10: 11: 11] sts, work in patt until there are 14 [14: 16: 16: 18] sts on RH needle and leave these

sts for right back, cast (bind) off next 45 [47: 49: 51: 53] sts, work in patt to end.
Cont with 23 [24: 26: 27: 29] sts at end of needle only, for left back.
Cast (bind) off 9 [10: 10: 11: 11] sts at beg of next row and 5 sts at neck edge on foll row.
Cast (bind) off rem 9 [9: 11: 11: 13] sts to complete shoulder shaping.
With WS facing, rejoin yarn to neck edge of right back sts and cast (bind) off first 5 sts, then work in patt to end.
Cast (bind) off rem 9 [9: 11: 11: 13] sts.

Front

Work front as given for back to **.
Armhole and neck shaping
Keeping patt st correct as set throughout, cast (bind) off 4 sts at beg of next 2 rows and 3 sts at beg of foll row, so ending with a RS row.
Next row (WS) Cast (bind) off 3 sts, work in patt until there are 66 [70: 74: 78: 82] sts on RH needle and slip these sts onto a spare needle, cast (bind) off one st, work in patt to end.
Cont with rem 66 [70: 74: 78: 82] sts only, for left front.
***Cast (bind) off 2 sts at beg of next row (armhole edge) and at same edge on next 3 alt rows, then dec one st at armhole edge on next 4 [5: 6: 7: 8] alt rows, **and at the same time** dec one st at neck edge on every alt row 22 [23: 23: 25: 26] times, then dec at neck edge on every foll 4th row 5 [5: 6: 5: 5] times.
When all decs have been completed, work rem 27 [29: 31: 33: 35] sts without shaping until front is same length as back to beg of shoulder shaping, ending at armhole edge.
Shoulder shaping
Cast (bind) off 9 [10: 10: 11: 11] sts at beg of next row and next alt row.
Work one row without shaping.
Cast (bind) off rem 9 [9: 11: 11: 13] sts.
With RS facing, rejoin yarn to right front sts and work in patt to end.
Complete as for left front from *** to end, reversing all shapings and working first dec at neck edge on next row.

Finishing and borders

Do not press. Join shoulder seams, matching patt stitch.
Neckband
With RS facing and 3mm (US size 3) circular needle, beg at centre front neck and pick up and k73 [76: 78: 78: 81] sts evenly up right front neck edge, 53 [55: 57: 59: 61] sts across back neck and 73 [76: 78: 78: 81] sts down left front neck edge.
199 [207: 213: 215: 223] sts.
Do not work in rounds, but work back and forth in rows on circular needle (centre front seam will be joined when neckband is complete).
Beg with 2nd rib row as on back, work one row in k1, p1 rib.
Keeping rib correct at set, dec one st at each end of next 8 rows.
Cast (bind) off loosely in rib.
Armbands
With RS facing and 3mm (US size 3) needles, pick up and k145 [151: 157: 157: 163] sts evenly around one armhole edge.
Beg with 2nd rib row as on back, work 9 rows in k1, p1 rib.
Cast (bind) off loosely in rib.
Work other armband in same way.
Join side seams and armband seams.
Join shaped ends of neckband, making a neat mitred point at centre front.

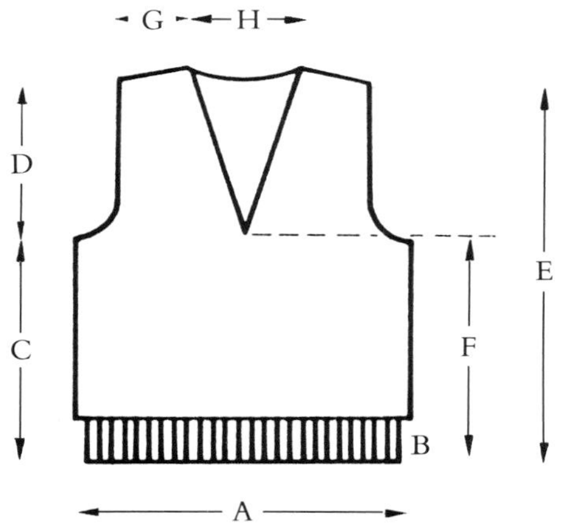

Back and front

Key

A 52.5 [55: 58: 61: 64]cm
21[22: 23¼: 24½: 25½]in
B 7cm
2¾in
C 36 [37: 38: 39: 40]cm
14 [14½: 15: 15½: 15¾]in
D 25 [26: 27: 27: 28]cm
10 [10¼: 10½: 10½: 11]in
E 61 [63: 65: 66: 68]cm
24 [24¾: 25½: 26: 26¾]in
F 37 [38: 39: 40: 41]cm
14¼ [14¾: 15¼: 15¾: 16]in
G 9.5 [10: 11: 11.5: 12.5]cm
3¾ [4: 4¼: 4½: 5]in
H 19.5 [20: 21: 21.5: 22.5]cm
7½ [7¾: 8¼: 8½: 8¾]in

Irish Moss Stitch Pullover

in Tempo

✳

Sizes

To fit 81 [86: 91: 96: 102]cm/32 [34: 36: 38: 40]in bust
Actual width around bust when completed 96 [101: 108: 114: 120]cm/38½ [40½: 43½: 45½: 48]in
Directions for larger sizes are in brackets [ ]; if there is only one set of figures it applies to all sizes.

Materials

PINGOUIN Tempo:
9 [10: 11: 12: 13] balls Ecru No. 17
Pair each of 3¼mm and 4mm (US sizes 3 and 6) needles
Shoulder pads (optional)

Tension (Gauge)

Rib patt: 27 sts and 32 rows to 10cm/4in measured over unstretched rib patt and worked using 3¼mm (US size 3) needles; work a sample on 37 sts.
Irish moss st: 23 sts and 30 rows to 10cm/4in measured over Irish moss st and worked using 4mm (US size 6) needles; work a sample on 33 sts.

Stitches used

Special abbreviations

yo (yarn over) – to work a yo after a p st and before a k st, take yarn from front to back over top of RH needle to make a new loop on RH needle; to work a yo after a k st and before a p st, take yarn to front of work between two needles, then take yarn from front to back over top of RH needle and to front again.

Rib pattern

Work rib patt over a multiple of 6 sts plus one st extra as foll:
1st rib row (RS) *K1, p1, k3, p1;* rep from * to *, ending k1.
2nd rib row P1, *k1, p3, k1, p1:* rep from * to *.
3rd rib row *K1, p1, yo, k3tog, yo, p1;* rep from * to *, ending k1.
4th rib row As 2nd row.
These 4 rows form one patt repeat.

Irish moss stitch

Work Irish moss st over an odd number of sts as foll:
1st row (RS) *K1, p1;* rep from * to *, ending k1.
2nd row P1, *k1, p1:* rep from * to *.
3rd row As 2nd row.
4th row As first row.
These 4 rows form one patt repeat.

Instructions

Back

With 3¼mm (US size 3) needles, cast on 97 [103: 109: 115: 121] sts.
Work rows 1–4 of rib patt 4 times, then work rows 1–3 once more (a total of 19 rows), so ending with a RS row.
Inc row (WS) Keeping rib patt correct, work first 9 [12: 9: 12: 9] sts in patt, (work into front and back of next st, work next 5 sts in patt) 13 [13: 15: 15: 17] times, work into front and back of next st, work rem 9 [12: 9: 12: 9] sts in patt. 111 [117: 125: 131: 139] sts.
Change to 4mm (US size 6) needles.
Work in Irish moss st (see Stitches Used) until back measures 32 [33: 34: 35: 36]cm/ 12½ [13: 13¼: 13¾: 14]in from beg, ending with a WS row.
Armhole shaping
Keeping patt correct as set throughout, cast (bind) off 4 sts at beg of next 2 rows and 2 sts at beg of next 6 rows.
Work one row without shaping.
Dec one st at each end of next row and every foll alt row 3 [3: 4: 5: 5] times in all. 85 [91: 97: 101: 109] sts.
Work without shaping until back measures 54 [56: 57: 59: 61]cm/21¼ [22: 22¼: 23¼: 24]in from beg, ending with a WS row.
Shoulder and neck shaping
Next row (RS) Cast (bind) off 7 [8: 9: 9: 10] sts, work in patt until there are 22 [23: 24: 26: 27] sts on RH needle and leave these sts for right back, cast (bind) off next 27 [29: 31: 31: 35] sts, work in patt to end.
Cont with 29 [31: 33: 35: 37] sts at end of needle only, for left back.

Cast (bind) off 7 [8: 9: 9: 10] sts at beg of next row and 3 sts at neck edge on foll row; rep last 2 rows again.

Cast (bind) off rem 9 [9: 9: 11: 11] sts to complete shoulder shaping.

With WS facing, rejoin yarn to neck edge of right back sts and cast (bind) off first 3 sts, then work in patt to end.

Cast (bind) off 7 [8: 9: 9: 10] sts at beg of next row and 3 sts at neck edge on foll row.

Cast (bind) off rem 9 [9: 9: 11: 11] sts.

Front

Work front as given for back until front measures 48 [50: 50: 52: 54]cm/18¾ [19½: 19½: 20½: 21¼]in from beg, ending with a WS row.

Neck shaping

Next row (RS) Work 36 [38: 41: 43: 46] sts in patt and slip these sts onto a spare needle, cast (bind) off next 13 [15: 15: 15: 17] sts, work in patt to end.

Cont with 36 [38: 41: 43: 46] sts only, for right front.

Work one row without shaping.

★★★Cast (bind) off 3 sts at beg of next row (neck edge) and 2 sts at same edge on next 3 [3: 3: 3: 4] alt rows, then dec one st at neck edge on next 4 [4: 5: 5: 4] alt rows. 23 [25: 27: 29: 31] sts.

Work 2 rows without shaping, so ending at armhole edge.

Shoulder shaping

Cast (bind) off 7 [8: 9: 9: 10] sts at beg of next row and next alt row.

Work one row without shaping.

Cast (bind) off rem 9 [9: 9: 11: 11] sts.

With WS facing, rejoin yarn to neck edge of left front sts and complete as for right front from ★★★ to end.

Sleeves

With 3¼mm (US size 3) needles, cast on 43 [49: 49: 55: 55] sts and work in rib patt for 19 rows as for back, so ending with a RS row.

Inc row (WS) Keeping rib patt correct, work first 5 [2: 2: 6: 6] sts in patt, (work into front and back of next st, work next 2 [4: 4: 5: 5] sts in patt) 11 [9: 9: 7: 7] times, work into front and back of next st, work rem 4 [1: 1: 6: 6] sts in patt. 55 [59: 59: 63: 63] sts.

Change to 4mm (US size 6) needles.

Work in Irish moss st, inc one st at each end of every foll 6th row 8 [9: 9: 10: 8] times, then on every foll 4th row 13 [12: 13: 12: 16] times, working extra sts into patt. 97 [101: 103: 107: 111] sts.

Work without shaping until sleeve measures 42 [43: 44: 45: 46]cm/16½ [17: 17¼: 17¾: 18]in from beg, ending with a WS row.

Top of sleeve shaping

Keeping patt correct throughout, cast (bind) off 2 sts at beg of next 8 rows.

Dec one st at each end of every foll alt row 12 [13: 12: 13: 13] times.

Cast (bind) off 2 sts at beg of next 12 [12: 14: 14: 16] rows and 4 sts at beg of next 4 rows.

Cast (bind) off rem 17 [19: 19: 21: 21] sts.

Finishing and neckband

Do not press. Join right shoulder seam.

Neckband

With RS facing and 3¼mm (US size 3) needles, pick up and k56 [59: 63: 63: 66] sts evenly around front neck edge and 41 [44: 46: 46: 49] sts across back neck. 97 [103: 109: 109: 115] sts.

Beg with a 2nd rib row, work 20 rows in rib patt.

Cast (bind) off loosely in patt.

Join left shoulder seam and neckband seam. Sew in sleeves, then join side and sleeve seams. (Sew on shoulder pads if desired.)

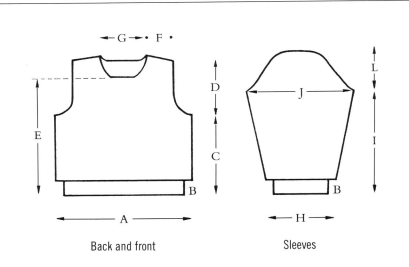

Back and front   Sleeves

Key

A 48 [50.5: 54: 57: 60]cm
   19¼ [20¼: 21¾: 22¾: 24]in

B 6cm
   2¼in

C 32 [33: 34: 35: 36]cm
   12½ [13: 13¼: 13¾: 14]in

D 22 [23: 23: 24: 25]cm
   8¾ [9: 9: 9½: 10]in

E 48 [50: 50: 52: 54]cm
   18¾ [19½: 19½: 20½: 21¼]in

F 10 [10.5: 11.5: 12.5: 13.5]cm
   4 [4¼: 4½: 5: 5¼]in

G 17 [17.5: 18.5: 18.5: 20]cm
   6½ [6¾: 7¼: 7¼: 7¾]in

H 24 [25.5: 25.5: 27: 27]cm
   9½ [10¼: 10¼: 11: 11]in

I 42 [43: 44: 45: 46]cm
   16½ [17: 17¼: 17¾: 18]in

J 42 [44: 44.5: 46.5: 48]cm
   16¾ [17½: 18: 18½: 19¼]in

L 16 [16.5: 16.5: 17: 18]cm
   6¼ [6½: 6½: 6¾: 7]in

TEXTURED SLEEVELESS TOP

IN FIL D'ECOSSE NO.4

*

Sizes

To fit 81 [86: 91: 96: 102]cm/32 [34: 36: 38: 40]in bust

Actual width around bust (buttoned) 93.5 [99: 105: 110: 116.5]cm/37½ [39¼: 42: 44: 46¼]in

Directions for larger sizes are in brackets [ ]; if there is only one set of figures it applies to all sizes.

Materials

PINGOUIN Fil d'Ecosse No. 4:
7 [8: 9: 10: 11] balls Naturel No. 407
Pair each of 3mm and 3¾mm (US sizes 3 and 5) needles
6 buttons

Tension (Gauge)

Worked with 3¾mm (US size 5) needles.
Patt st: 26 sts and 32 rows to 10cm/4in over patt st; work a sample on 40 sts.

Stitches used

Special abbreviations

pk2 – purl next 2 sts tog without slipping them off LH needle, then k the same 2 sts tog and slip them off LH needle.

Pattern stitch

Work pattern st over an even number of sts as foll:
1st row (RS) Knit.
2nd row K1, *pk2;* rep from * to *, ending k1.
3rd row Knit.
4th row K1, p1, *pk2;* rep from * to *, ending p1, k1.
These 4 rows form one patt repeat.

Note: When shaping, take care to work pk2 over correct sts always keeping one or 2 border sts at side edges.

Instructions

Back

With 3mm (US size 3) needles, cast on 101 [107: 113: 119: 127] sts and beg k1, p1 rib as foll:
★★1st rib row (RS) P1, *k1, p1; rep from * to end.
2nd rib row K1, *p1, k1; rep from * to end.
Rep these 2 rows until work measures 10cm/4in from beg, ending with a first rib row.★★
Inc row (WS) Keeping rib correct, rib 5 [8: 2: 5: 9], (work into front and back of next st, rib 8) 10 [10: 12: 12: 12] times, work into front and back of next st, rib rem 5 [8: 2: 5: 9] sts. 112 [118: 126: 132: 140] sts.
Change to 3¾mm (US size 5) needles.
Work 13 [13: 13: 15: 15] rows in patt st (see Stitches Used), so ending with a RS row.
Working extra sts into patt, cont in patt st, inc one st at each end of next row and every foll 14th [14th: 14th: 16th: 16th] row 4 times in all. 120 [126: 134: 140: 148] sts.
Work in patt st without shaping until back measures 32 [33: 34: 35: 36]cm/12½ [13: 13¼: 13¾: 14]in from beg, ending with a WS row.
Armhole shaping
Keeping patt st correct as set throughout, cast (bind) off 2 sts at beg of next 6 rows.
Work one row without shaping.
Dec one st at each end of next row and every foll alt row 4 [4: 5: 5: 6] times in all. 100 [106: 112: 118: 124] sts.
Work without shaping until back measures 54 [56: 58: 60: 62]cm/21¼ [22: 22¾: 23½: 24½]in from beg, ending with a WS row.
Shoulder and neck shaping
Next row (RS) Cast (bind) off 10 [10: 11: 12: 12] sts, k until there are 29 [31: 32: 33: 35] sts on RH needle and leave these sts for right back, cast (bind) off next 22 [24: 26: 28: 30] sts, k to end.
Cont with 39 [41: 43: 45: 47] sts at end of needle only, for left back.
Cast (bind) off 10 [10: 11: 12: 12] sts at beg of next row and 5 sts at neck edge on foll row; rep last 2 rows again.
Cast (bind) off rem 9 [11: 11: 11: 13] sts to complete shoulder shaping.
With WS facing, rejoin yarn to neck edge of right back sts and cast (bind) off first 5 sts, then work in patt to end.
Cast (bind) off 10 [10: 11: 12: 12] sts at beg of next row and 5 sts at neck edge on foll row.
Cast (bind) off rem 9 [11: 11: 11: 13] sts.

Right front

With 3mm (US size 3) needles, cast on 49 [53: 57: 61: 65] sts and work as for back ribbing from ★★ to ★★.

Inc row (WS) Keeping rib correct, rib 3 [5: 7: 9: 11], (work into front and back of next st, rib 6) 6 times, work into front and back of next st, rib rem 3 [5: 7: 9: 11] sts. 56 [60: 64: 68: 72] sts.

Change to 3¾mm (US size 5) needles.

Work 13 [13: 13: 15: 15] rows in patt st, so ending with a RS row.

Working extra sts into patt, cont in patt st, inc one st at beg of next row (armhole edge) and at same edge on every foll 14th [14th: 14th: 16th: 16th] row 4 times in all. 60 [64: 68: 72: 76] sts.

Work in patt st without shaping until front is same length as back to beg of armhole shaping, ending at centre front edge after a WS row.

V-neck and armhole shaping

Keeping patt st correct as set throughout, dec one st at beg of next row (centre front edge), then cast (bind) off 2 sts at beg of foll row (armhole edge).

Cont to dec one st at centre front edge on next row and on every foll alt row 9 [12: 12: 14: 15] times in all, then at same edge on every foll 4th row 11 [10: 11: 11: 11] times, **and at the same time** cast (bind) off 2 sts at armhole edge on next 2 alt rows, then dec one st at armhole edge on next 4 [4: 5: 5: 6] alt rows.

When all decs have been completed, cont on rem 29 [31: 33: 35: 37] sts until front is same length as back to beg of shoulder shaping, ending at armhole edge.

Shoulder shaping

Cast (bind) off 10 [10: 11: 12: 12] sts at beg of next row and foll alt row.

Work one row without shaping.

Cast (bind) off rem 9 [11: 11: 11: 13] sts.

Left front

Work left front as for right front, but reversing all shapings.

Finishing and borders

Do not press k1, p1 ribbing or patt st.

Buttonhole band

With RS facing and 3mm (US size 3) needles, pick up and k26 sts evenly up centre front edge of right front ribbing, 57 [60: 62: 65: 68] sts up remainder of right front edge to beg of V-neck shaping and 58 [61: 63: 66: 69] sts along sloping edge to shoulder. 141 [147: 151: 157: 163] sts.

Work 2nd rib row as on back.

Keeping rib correct, work buttonholes over next 2 rows as foll:

1st buttonhole row (RS) Beg at lower edge, rib 3, cast (bind) off 2, ★rib until there are 8 sts on RH needle after buttonhole, cast (bind) off 2,★ rep from ★ to ★ once more, ★★rib until there are 16 [17: 18: 19: 20] sts on RH needle after buttonhole, cast (bind) off 2,★★ rep from ★★ to ★★ twice more, rib to end.

2nd buttonhole row Work in rib, casting on 2 sts over each buttonhole.

Work one row more in rib.

Cast (bind) off loosely in rib.

Button band

Work button band on left front as for buttonhole band, but picking up sts in reverse order and omitting buttonholes.

Back neckband

With RS facing and 3mm (US size 3) needles, pick up and k45 [47: 49: 51: 53] sts evenly across back neck edge.

Beg with a 2nd rib row as on back, work 4 rows in rib.

Cast (bind) off loosely in rib.

Armbands

Join shoulder seams and ends of bands.

With RS facing and 3mm (US size 3) needles, pick up and k123 [129: 135: 141: 147] sts evenly around one armhole edge.

Work ribbing as for back neckband.

Work other armband in same way.

Join side seams and armband seams.

Sew on the buttons to correspond with the buttonholes.

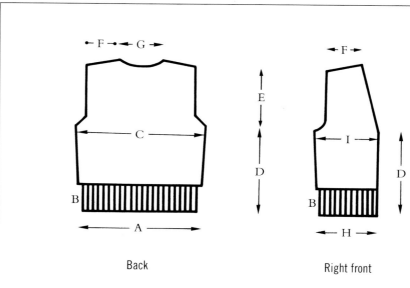

Back

Right front

Key

A 43 [45: 48.5: 50.5: 53.5]cm
17¼ [18: 19¼: 20¼: 21½]in

B 10cm
4in

C 46 [48.5: 51.5: 53.5: 57]cm
18½ [19¼: 20½: 21½: 22¾]in

D 32 [33: 34: 35: 36]cm
12½ [13: 13¼: 13¾: 14]in

E 22 [23: 24: 25: 26]cm
8¾ [9: 9½: 9¾: 10½]in

F 11 [12: 12.5: 13.5: 14]cm
4¼ [4¾: 5: 5¼: 5½]in

G 16 [17: 17.5: 18.5: 19]cm
6¼ [6½: 6¾: 7¼: 7½]in

H 21.5 [23: 24.5: 26: 27.5]cm
8½ [9¼: 9¾: 10½: 11]in

I 23 [24.5: 26: 27.5: 29]cm
9¼ [9¾: 10½: 11: 11½]in

PLAID AND CABLE PULLOVER

IN FRANCE + AND SOFT'HAIR

✳✳✳

Sizes

To fit 86 [91: 96 to 102]cm/34 [36: 38 to 40]in bust
Actual width around bust when completed
106 [113: 120]cm/42½ [45: 48]in
Directions for larger sizes are in brackets [ ]; if there is only one set of figures it applies to all sizes.

Materials

PINGOUIN France +:
12 [13: 14] balls Marengo Fonce No. 67 (A)
PINGOUIN Soft'Hair:
2 balls Outremer No. 41 (B)
Small amount Menthe No. 36 (C)
Pair each of 3mm and 3 3/4 mm (US sizes 3 and 5) needles
3mm (US size 3) circular needle for neckband
Cable needle (cn)

Tension (Gauge)

Worked with 3¾mm (US size 5) needles.
St st or rev st st: 23 sts and 30 rows to 10cm/4in over st st or rev st st, using yarn A; work a sample on 34 sts.
Plaid patt: 23 sts and 27 rows to 10cm/4in over plaid patt; work a sample on 34 sts as foll:
Cast on with yarn B and p one row, then using Chart No. 1, miss the first 11 sts from RH edge and work next 34 sts in patt; cont working on these sts for sample.
Cable: measures 5cm/2in in width; work a sample on 30 sts, working 3 sts in rev st st at each end of row.

Stitches used

Special abbreviations

pfb – purl into front and back of next st.
kfb – knit into front and back of next st.
cable 12 back – slip next 6 sts onto cn and hold at back of work, k6, then k6 from cn.
cable 12 front – slip next 6 sts onto cn and hold at front of work, k6, then k6 from cn.

Plaid pattern

The plaid pattern is worked from Chart No. 1, 2 or 3 according to size, as explained in the instructions. When working the patt, take care to twist yarns when changing from the plain st st sections to the plaid section.
Note: The vertical lines in yarn C are embroidered on afterwards, so the sts shown in this colour on the chart should be worked in patt.

Cable pattern

Work the cable pattern over 24 sts as foll:
1st row (RS) K24.
2nd and all WS rows Purl.
3rd row As first row.
5th row Cable 12 back, cable 12 front.
7th and 9th rows As first row.
10th row As 2nd row.
These 10 rows form one patt repeat.

Instructions

Back

With 3mm (US size 3) needles and yarn A, cast on 113 [119: 125] sts and beg rib as foll:
1st rib row (RS) P1, *k1, p1; rep from * to end.
2nd rib row K1, *p1, k1; rep from * to end.
Rep these 2 rows until work measures 4cm/1½in from beg, ending with a first rib row.
Inc row (WS) Keeping rib correct, rib 8 [4: 2], work into front and back of next st, (rib 11 [10: 9], work into front and back of next st) 8 [10: 12] times, rib rem 8 [4: 2] sts. 122 [130: 138] sts.
Change to 3¾mm (US size 5) needles.
Beg with a k row, work in st st until back measures 42 [44: 46]cm/16½ [17¼: 18]in from beg, ending with a p row.
Armhole shaping
Cont in st st throughout, cast (bind) off 5 sts at beg of next 2 rows. 112 [120: 128] sts.
Work without shaping until back measures 65 [68: 71]cm/25½ [26¾: 28]in from beg, ending with a p row.
Shoulder and neck shaping
To begin the shoulder shaping, cast (bind) off 9 [10: 11] sts at beg of next 2 rows.
Next row (RS) Cast (bind) off 9 [10: 11] sts, k until there are 27 [28: 29] sts on RH needle and leave these sts for right back, cast (bind) off next 22 [24: 26] sts, k to end.
Cont with 36 [38: 40] sts at end of needle only, for left back.
Cast (bind) off 9 [10: 11] sts at beg of next row and 4 sts at neck edge on foll row; rep last 2 rows again.
Cast (bind) off rem 10 sts to complete shoulder shaping.
With WS facing, rejoin yarn to neck edge of right back sts and cast (bind) off first 4 sts, then p to end.
Cast (bind) off 9 [10: 11] sts at beg of next row and 4 sts at neck edge on foll row.
Cast (bind) off rem 10 sts.

Right front section

With 3¾mm (US size 5) needles and yarn A, cast on 52 [56: 60] sts for right front section (lower ribbing is worked later).
P one row.
Break off yarn A and join in yarn B.
Using Chart No. 1, 2 or 3 according to size, beg plaid patt on next row as foll:
1st chart row (RS) K border st in B, k28 [30: 32] B, join on A, (k3 A, 3 B) 3 [4: 4] times, k3 [0: 2] A, 1 [0: 0] B, then k border st in B [A: A].
Cont in st st, working plaid patt as now set and working border sts in either colour and always twisting yarns when changing from plain st st section to plaid section, until front measures 30 [33: 36]cm/11¾ [13: 14]in from beg, ending with a WS row.
Front and armhole shaping
Keeping plaid patt correct throughout, dec one st at beg of next row (centre front edge) and at same edge on next 0 [2: 4] alt rows, then dec one st at same edge on every foll 4th row 18 [17: 16] times, **and at the same time** keep side edge straight until front measures 38 [40: 42]cm/15 [15¾: 16½]in from beg (ending at straight armhole edge), cast (bind) off 5 sts at beg of next row and then keep armhole edge straight until all front decs have been completed. 28 [31: 34] sts.
Work without shaping until front measures 61 [64: 67]cm/24 [25¼: 26½]in from beg, ending at armhole edge.
Shoulder shaping
Cast (bind) off 9 [10: 11] sts at beg of next row and next alt row.
Work one row without shaping.
Cast (bind) off rem 10 [11: 12] sts.

Left front section

Work left front section as for right front section, but reversing all shapings.

Front cable panel

With 3¾mm needles and yarn A, cast on 18 sts and beg front cable panel as foll:
1st row (RS) P3, k12, p3.
2nd row K3, pfb 12 times, k3. 30 sts.
These first 2 rows count as first and 2nd rows of cable patt.
3rd row P3, k24, p3.
4th row K3, p24, k3.
5th row P3, work 5th row of cable over next 24 sts (see Stitches Used), p3.
Cont in patt as now set until 9 [10: 11] cable patt repeats have been completed, then work 3 rows more in patt, so ending with a 3rd cable patt row.
4th row K3, p12, turn, cast on 3 sts onto RH needle, p12, k3. 33 sts.
5th row P3, cable 12 back, pfb 3 times, cable 12 front, p3. 36 sts.
6th row K3, p12, k6, p12, k3.
7th row P3, kfb 12 times, p6, kfb 12 times, p3. 60 sts.
8th row K3, p24, k6, p24, k3.
9th row P3, k24, p6, k24, p3.
Work 5 rows more in patt as set, so ending with 4th row of 11th [12th: 13th] patt repeat.
5th row (RS) P3, cable 12 back, cable 12 front, p3, then turn leaving rem 30 sts on a st holder for right front panel.
Cont in patt on these 30 sts only, for left front panel.
Work in patt as set until side edge of panel fits along front edge of left front section from lower edge to top of shoulder edge, ending with a RS row.
Cast (bind) off, working p2tog 12 times over cable during cast (bind) off.

With RS facing, rejoin yarn A to 30 sts on st holder and p3, cable 12 back, cable 12 front, p3. Complete as for left front panel.

Sleeves

With 3mm (US size 3) needles and yarn A, cast on 53 [55: 57] sts and work in rib as on back for 4cm/1½in, ending with a first rib row.
Inc row (WS) Keeping rib correct, rib 2 [3: 4], (work into front and back of next st, rib 2) 16 times, work into front and back of next st, rib rem 2 [3: 4] sts. 70 [72: 74] sts.
Change to 3¾mm (US size 5) needles.
Beg patt on next row as foll:
1st row (RS) P23 [24: 25], work first row of cable over next 24 sts (see Stitches Used), p23 [24: 25].
Cont in patt as set (working cable at centre with sts at sides in rev st st), work 4 rows more in patt.
Cont in patt, inc one st at each end of next row, then on every foll 6th row 9 [8: 9] times, then on every foll 4th row 14 [17: 17] times, working all extra sts in rev st st. 118 [124: 128] sts.
Work without shaping until sleeve measures 48 [50: 52]cm/18¾ [19¾: 20½]in from beg, ending with a RS row.
Cast off all sts, working p2tog 12 times over cable during cast (bind) off.

Finishing and borders

Press lightly on WS with a cool iron, following instructions on yarn label and omitting ribbing and cables.
Sew sides of cable panel to front sections.
Lower front ribbing
With RS facing, 3mm (US size 3) needles and yarn A, pick up and k113 [119: 125] sts evenly across entire lower edge of front.
Beg with a 2nd rib row, work in rib as on back for 4cm/1½in.
Cast (bind) off loosely in rib.
Embroidery
Using yarn C and a tapestry needle, work vertical lines in Swiss darning (duplicate st) on plaid patt as shown on chart.
Neckband
Join shoulder seams, easing in front shoulders to fit back.
With RS facing, 3mm (US size 3) circular needle and yarn A, beg at centre front neck and pick up and k80 sts evenly up right front neck edge of cable panel, 41 [43: 45] sts across back neck and 80 sts down left front neck edge.
201 [203: 205] sts.
Do not work in rounds, but work back and forth in rows on circular needle (centre front seam will be joined when neckband is complete).
Beg with 2nd rib row as on back, work one row in rib.
Keeping rib correct at set, dec one st at each end of next 19 rows.
Cast (bind) off loosely in rib.
Join shaped ends of neckband, making a neat mitred point at centre front.
Sew cast (bound) off edge of sleeves to sides of armholes and sew armhole cast (bind) off to last 7 rows on sides of sleeves.
Join side and sleeve seams.

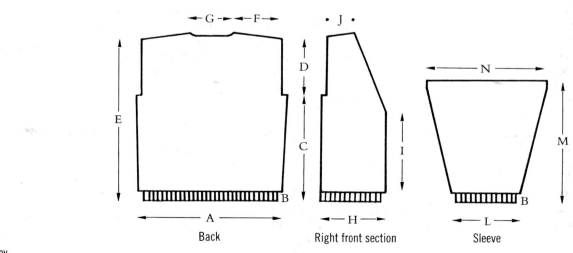

Back Right front section Sleeve

Key
A 53 [56.5: 60]cm/21¼ [22½: 24]in
B 4cm/1½in
C 42 [44: 46]cm/16½ [17¼: 18]in
D 23 [24: 25]cm/9 [9½: 10]in
E 65 [68: 71]cm/25½ [26¾: 26¾: 28]in

F 16 [17: 18.5]cm/6¼ [6¾: 7¼]in
G 16.5 [17: 18]cm/6½ [6¾: 7]in
H 22.5 [24: 26]cm/9 [9¾: 10½]in
I 30 [33: 36]cm/11¾ [13: 14]in
J 12 [13.5: 14.5]cm/4¾ [5¼: 5¾]in

L 25 [25.5: 26.5]cm/9¾ [10: 10½]in
M 48 [50: 52]cm/18¾ [19¾: 20½]in
N 46 [48.5: 50]cm/18 [19: 20]in

Chart No. 1
First size

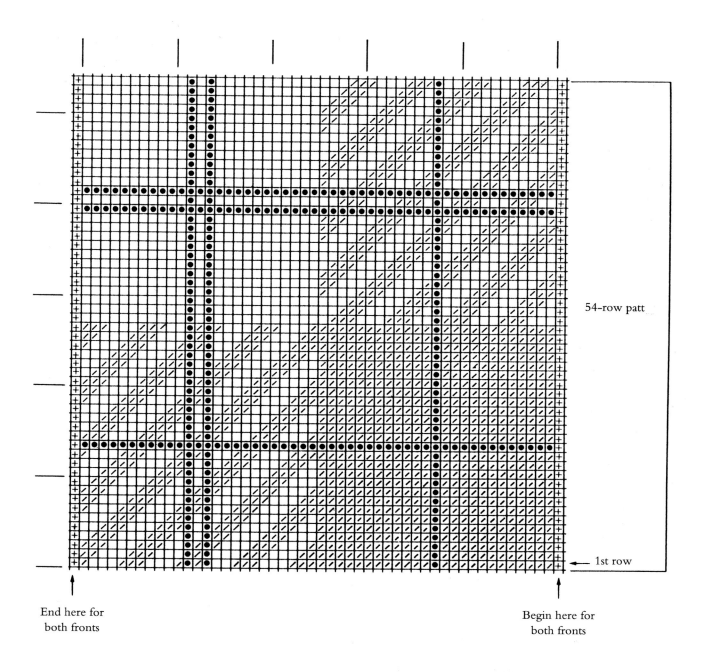

54-row patt

1st row

End here for
both fronts

Begin here for
both fronts

☐ = A / = B ● = C + = border st worked in any colour

Sts forming the vertical lines in C should be worked in patt and embroidered
afterwards in Swiss darning (duplicate st) using C.

Chart No. 2
2nd size

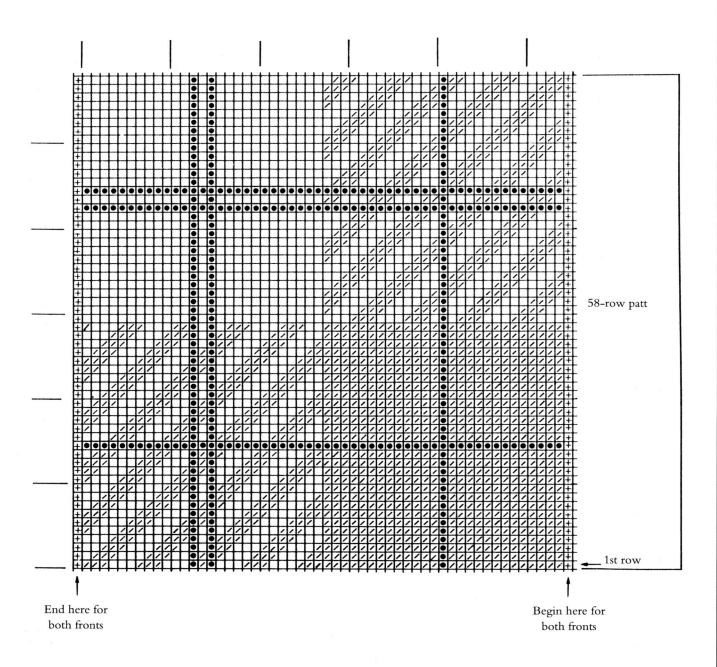

58-row patt

1st row

End here for
both fronts

Begin here for
both fronts

☐ = A   / = B   ● = C   + = border st worked in any colour

Sts forming the vertical lines in C should be worked in patt and embroidered
afterwards in Swiss darning (duplicate st) using C.

Chart No. 3
3rd size

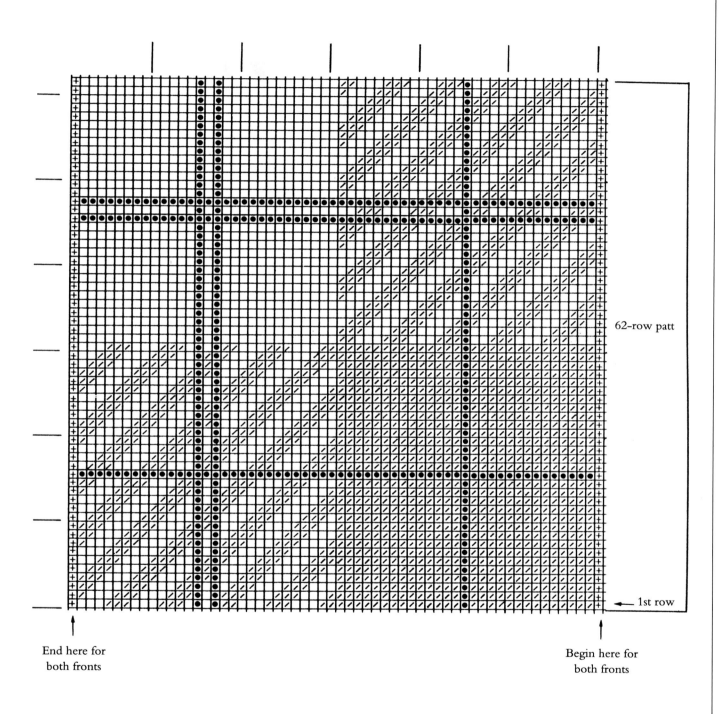

62-row patt

1st row

End here for
both fronts

Begin here for
both fronts

□ = A   / = B   ● = C   + = border st worked in any colour

Sts forming the vertical lines in C should be worked in patt and embroidered
afterwards in Swiss darning (duplicate st) using C.

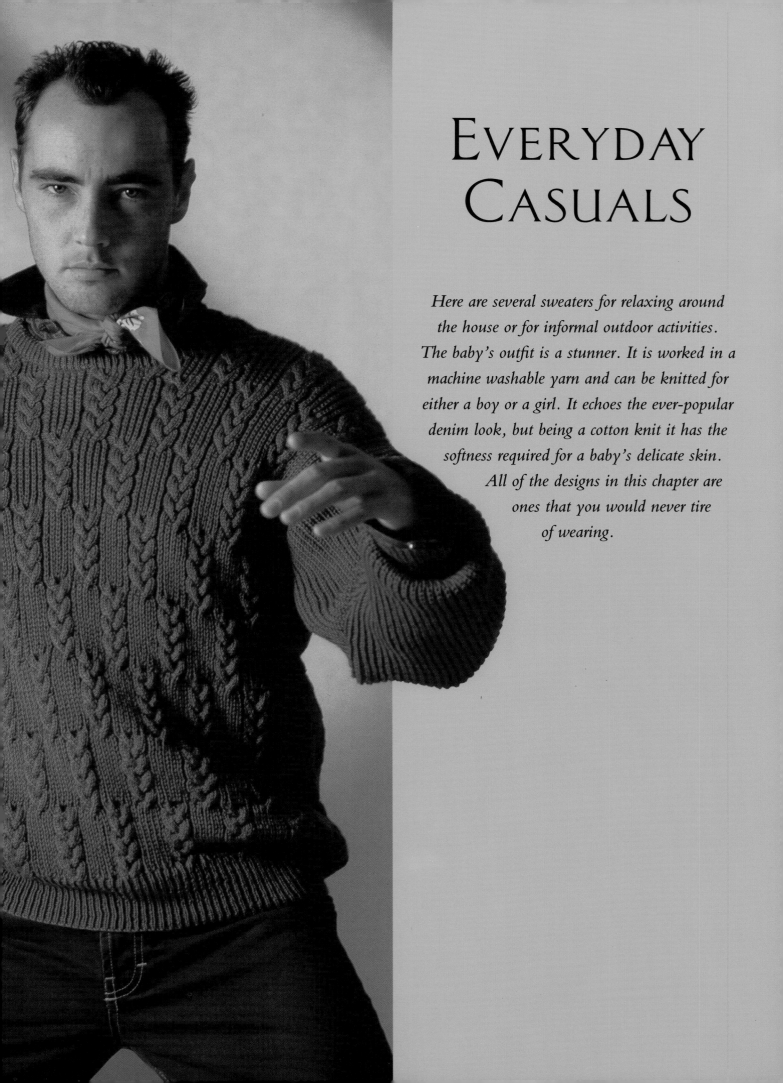

EVERYDAY CASUALS

Here are several sweaters for relaxing around
the house or for informal outdoor activities.
The baby's outfit is a stunner. It is worked in a
machine washable yarn and can be knitted for
either a boy or a girl. It echoes the ever-popular
denim look, but being a cotton knit it has the
softness required for a baby's delicate skin.
All of the designs in this chapter are
ones that you would never tire
of wearing.

CHILD'S HOODED JACKET IN SWEET'HAIR

*

Sizes

To fit ages 2 [4: 6: 8: 10] years or 53 [58: 63: 68: 72]cm/21 [23: 25: 27: 28½]in chest
Actual width around chest (buttoned) 72 [76.5: 83.5: 86: 91]cm/28¾ [30¾: 32¾: 34¾: 36¾]in
Directions for larger sizes are in brackets [ ]; if there is only one set of figures it applies to all sizes.

Materials

PINGOUIN Sweet'Hair:
5 [6: 6: 7: 7] balls Myosotis No. 37
Pair each of 3mm and 3¾mm (US sizes 3 and 5) needles
7 small buttons

Tension (Gauge)

Worked with 3¾mm (US size 5) needles.
Patt st: 22 sts and 46 rows to 10cm/4in over patt st; work a sample on 31 sts.

Stitches used

Special abbreviations

d inc (double increase) – into next st p into front, then k into back, then p again into front of same st.
k1 below – insert RH needle from front to back through st below next st on LH needle and knit this st, allowing st above to drop off LH needle as st is completed.

Pattern stitch

Work patt st over a multiple of 2 sts plus one extra st.
1st row (RS) K all sts.
2nd row K1, *k1 below, p1;* rep from * to * to last 2 sts, k1 below, k1.

These 2 rows form one patt repeat.
Note: When casting (binding) off over this patt, cast (bind) off loosely in normal k1, p1 rib as sts appear.

Instructions

Back

With 3mm (US size 3) needles, cast on 69 [75: 81: 85: 91] sts and beg k1, p1 rib as foll:
★★1st rib row (RS) K1, *p1, k1; rep from * to end.
2nd rib row P1, *k1, p1; rep from * to end.
Rep these 2 rows until work measures 4cm/1½in from beg, ending with a first rib row.**★★**
Inc row (WS) Keeping rib correct, rib 8 [10: 14: 16: 18], (d inc, rib 17) 3 times, d inc, rib rem 6 [10: 12: 14: 18] sts.
77 [83: 89: 93: 99] sts.
Change to 3¾mm (US size 5) needles.
Work in patt st (see Stitches Used) until back measures 20 [23: 25: 27: 29]cm/7¾ [8¾: 9¾: 10½: 11]in from beg, ending with a 2nd (WS) patt row.
Armhole shaping
Keeping patt st correct throughout, cast (bind) off 6 sts at beg of next 2 rows. 65 [71: 77: 81: 87] sts.
Work without shaping until back measures 35 [39: 42: 45: 48]cm/13¾ [15¼: 16½: 17¾: 18¾]in from beg, ending with a 2nd (WS) patt row.
Shoulder and neck shaping
Cast (bind) off 6 [6: 7: 8: 8] sts at beg of next 2 rows.
Next row (RS) Cast (bind) off 6 [6: 7: 8: 8] sts, k until there are 10 [12: 12: 12: 14] sts on RH needle and leave these sts for right back, cast (bind) off next 21 [23: 25: 25: 27] sts, k to end.
Cont with these 16 [18: 19: 20: 22] sts at end of needle only, for left back.
Cast (bind) off 6 [6: 7: 8: 8] sts at beg of next row and 4 sts at neck edge on foll row.
Cast (bind) off rem 6 [8: 8: 8: 10] sts to complete shoulder shaping.
With WS facing, rejoin yarn to neck edge of right back sts and cast (bind) off first 4 sts, then work in patt to end.
Cast (bind) off rem 6 [8: 8: 8: 10] sts.

Right front

With 3mm (US size 3) needles, cast on 35 [37: 41: 43: 45] sts and work in rib as for back from ★★ to ★★.
Inc row (WS) Keeping rib correct, rib 8 [10: 12: 12: 14], d inc, rib 17, d inc, rib rem 8 [8: 10: 12: 12] sts. 39 [41: 45: 47: 49] sts.
Change to 3¾mm (US size 5) needles.
Work in patt st until front is same length as

back to beg of armhole shaping, but ending with a first (RS) patt row.
Armhole shaping
Keeping patt st correct throughout, cast (bind) off 6 sts at beg of row (armhole edge). 33 [35: 39: 41: 43] sts.
Work without shaping until front measures 31 [35: 37: 40: 43]cm/12¼ [13¾: 14½: 15¾: 17]in from beg, ending at straight centre front edge.
Neck shaping
Cast (bind) off 6 sts at beg of next row (neck edge) and 2 sts at same edge on next 3 alt rows, then dec one st at neck edge on next 3 [3: 5: 5: 5] alt rows. 18 [20: 22: 24: 26] sts.
Work without shaping until front is same length as back to beg of shoulder shaping, ending at armhole edge.
Shoulder shaping
Cast (bind) off 6 [6: 7: 8: 8] sts at beg of next row and next alt row.
Work one row without shaping.
Cast (bind) off rem 6 [8: 8: 8: 10] sts.

Left front

Work left front as given for right front, but reversing all shapings.

Sleeves

With 3mm (US size 3) needles, cast on 37 [37: 41: 43: 43] sts and work in rib as for back from ★★ to ★★.
Inc row (WS) Keeping rib correct, rib 2 [2: 4: 6: 6], (d inc, rib 7) 4 times, d inc, rib rem 2 [2: 4: 4: 4] sts. 47 [47: 51: 53: 53] sts.
Change to 3¾mm (US size 5) needles.
Work in patt st, inc one st at each end of every foll 10th row 0 [0: 8: 10: 11] times, then every foll 8th row 10 [12: 4: 4: 5] times, working extra sts into patt. 67 [71: 75: 81: 85] sts.
Work in patt st without shaping until sleeve measures 26 [30: 34: 38: 42]cm/10¼ [11¾: 13¾: 15: 16½]in from beg, ending with a 2nd (WS) patt row.
Cast (bind) off loosely in rib.

Hood

The hood is worked in one piece, beg at neck edge of right half of hood and worked to centre top of head, then left half of hood is cont from top of head to neck edge.
Right half of hood
With 3¾mm (US size 5) needles, cast on 37 [39: 43: 43: 45] sts.
Work 9 [11: 11: 9: 11] rows in patt st, so ending with a first (RS) patt row.
Back edge shaping
Working extra sts into patt, inc one st at beg of next row, then at same edge on every foll

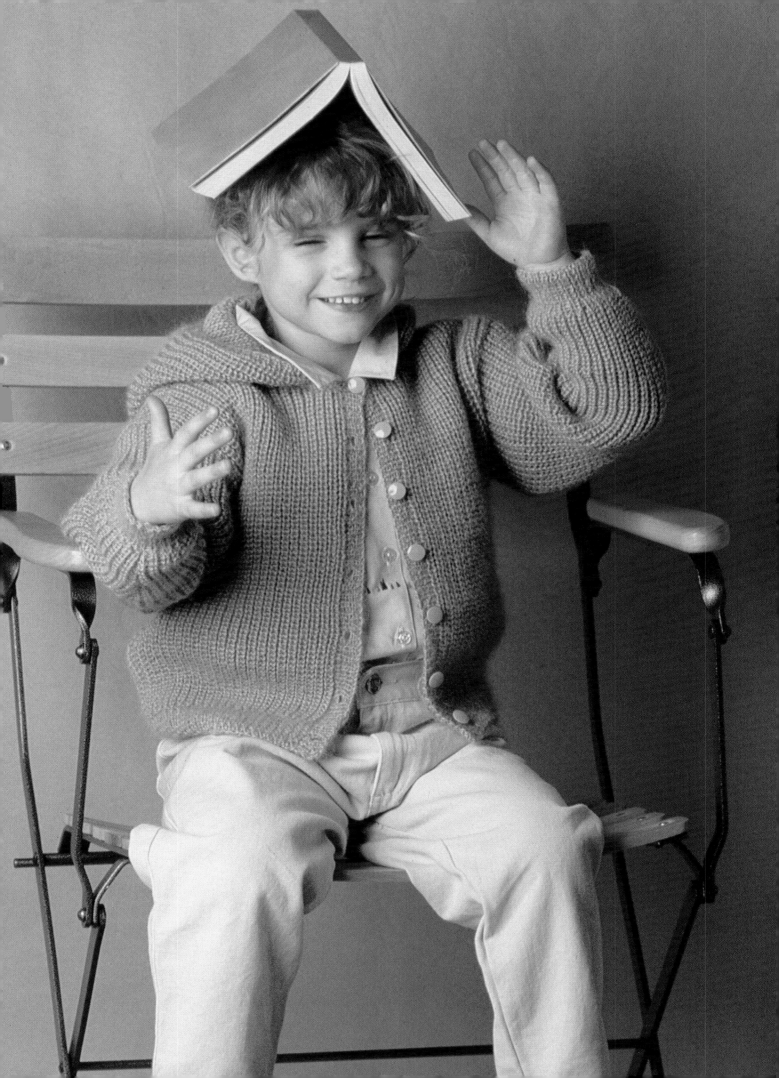

12th row 0 [1: 5: 0: 4] times, then on every foll 10th row 7 [6: 2: 9: 5] times. 45 [47: 51: 53: 55] sts.
Cont in patt st throughout, work without shaping until hood measures 20 [21: 23: 24: 26]cm/7¾ [8¼: 9: 9½: 10¼]in from beg, ending at shaped edge.
Make a note of the number of rows worked since last inc row.

Top edge shaping
Keeping patt st correct throughout, dec one st at beg of next row.
Work 5 rows without shaping.
Dec one st at beg of next row, then on every foll 4th row 3 times more, then on every alt row 4 times, then dec one st at same edge on next 5 rows. 31 [33: 37: 39: 41] sts.
Work one row without shaping.

Left half of hood
Inc one st at shaped edge on next 6 rows, then at same edge on every alt row 4 times, then on every foll 4th row 3 times.
Work 5 rows without shaping.
Inc one st at shaped edge on next row. 45 [47: 51: 53: 55] sts.
Work same number of rows as were worked after last inc on right side of hood.
Dec one st at shaped edge on next row, then on every foll 10th row 7 [6: 2: 9: 5] times, then on every foll 12th row 0 [1: 5: 0: 4] times. 37 [39: 43: 43: 45] sts.
Work 9 [11: 11: 9: 11] rows without shaping.
Cast (bind) off loosely in rib.

Finishing and front borders

Do not press. Join shoulder seams.

Neckband
With RS facing and 3mm (US size 3) needles, pick up and k22 [22: 25: 26: 26] sts evenly up right front neck edge, 35 [37: 39: 39: 41] sts across back neck and 22 [22: 25: 26: 26] sts down left front neck. 79 [81: 89: 91: 93] sts.
Beg with 2nd rib row, work 4 rows in k1, p1 rib as on back.
Cast (bind) off loosely in rib.

Buttonhole band
With RS facing and 3mm (US size 3) needles, pick up and k83 [93: 101: 107: 115] sts evenly along front edge of right front for girl or left front for boy, including edge of neckband.
Beg with 2nd rib row, work 2 rows in k1, p1 rib, so ending with a RS row.
1st buttonhole row (WS) Keeping rib correct, rib 4 [3: 4: 4: 5], cast (bind) off 2, *rib until there are 10 [12: 13: 14: 15] sts on RH needle after previous buttonhole, cast off 2;* rep from * to * 5 times more, rib to end.
2nd buttonhole row Work in rib, casting on 2 sts over each buttonhole.
Work 3 rows more in rib.
Cast (bind) off loosely in rib.

Button band
Work button band on other front as for buttonhole band (working 7 rows of k1, p1 rib), but omitting buttonholes.

Hood border
With RS facing and 3mm (US size 3) needles, pick up and k135 [141: 151: 157: 167] sts evenly along entire straight front edge of hood.
Beg with 2nd rib row, work 7 rows in k1, p1 rib. Cast (bind) off loosely in rib.
Sew cast (bound) off edge of sleeves to sides of armholes and sew armhole cast (bind) off to last 12 rows on sides of sleeves.
Join side and sleeve seams.
Join back seam of hood; sew lower edges to neckline inside neckband, easing hood to fit so that front edges come to within 4cm/1½in of cast (bound) off edge of front bands.
Sew on the buttons to correspond with the buttonholes.

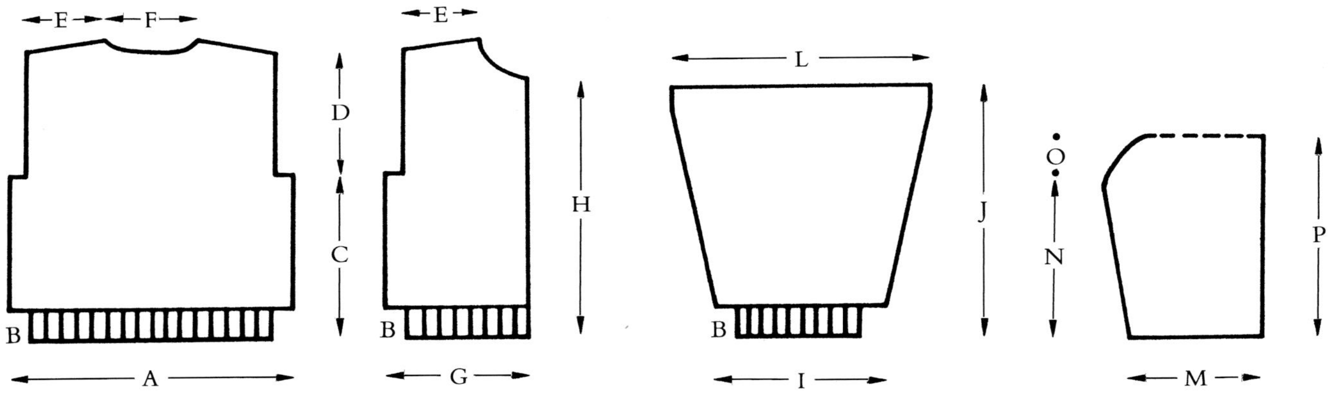

Back | Right front | Sleeve | Right half of hood

Key

A 35 [37.5: 40.5: 42: 45]cm
14 [15: 16: 17: 18]in

B 4cm
1½in

C 20 [23: 25: 27: 29]cm
7¾ [8¾: 9¾: 10½: 11]in

D 15 [16: 17: 18: 19]cm
6 [6½: 6¾: 7¼: 7¾]in

E 8 [9: 10: 11: 11.5]cm
3 [3½: 4: 4¼: 4½]in

F 13 [14: 15: 15: 16]cm
5 [5½: 6: 6: 6¼]in

G 17.5 [18.5: 20.5: 21: 22]cm
7 [7½: 8: 8½: 9]in

H 31 [35: 37: 40: 43]cm
12¼ [13¾: 14½: 15¾: 17]in

I 21 [21: 23: 24: 24]cm
8½ [8½: 9¼: 9½: 9½]in

J 26 [30: 34: 38: 42]cm
10¼ [11¾: 13¼: 15: 16½]in

L 30.5 [32: 34: 36.5: 38.5]cm
12 [13: 13½: 14¾: 15½]in

M 16.5 [17.5: 19.5: 19.5: 20.5]cm
6¾ [7: 7¾: 7¾: 8]in

N 20 [21: 23: 24: 26]cm
7¾ [8¼: 9: 9½: 10¼]in

O 7cm
2¾in

P 27 [28: 30: 31: 33]cm
10½ [11: 11¾: 12¼: 13]in

BABY'S EVERYDAY OUTFIT

IN CORRIDA 3

✳✳

BABY'S JACKET

The baby's jacket can be worked for a baby to go with the long trousers, the plain shorts or the shorts with the bib. It can also be worked to go with either of the shorts for a young child up to 2 years old.

Sizes

To fit 6 months [9 to 12 months: 18 months: 2 years]
Actual width around chest when completed 57 [60.5: 63: 66.5]cm/23 [24: 25½: 26½]in
Directions for larger sizes are in brackets [ ]; if there is only one set of figures it applies to all sizes.

Materials

PINGOUIN Corrida 3:
2 [2: 3: 3] balls Bleu Givre No. 410 (A)
Small amount of Ecru No. 312 (B)
Pair each of 2¾mm and 3mm (US sizes 2 and 3) needles
6 small buttons

Tension (Gauge)

Worked with 3mm (US size 3) needles.
St st: 27 sts and 38 rows to 10cm/4in over st st; work a sample on 40 sts.

Stitches used

Special abbreviations

yo (yarn over) – to work a yo between 2 p sts, take yarn from front of work to back over top of RH needle and to front again to make a new loop on RH needle.

Embroidery

The jacket is worked in plain st st with k1, p1 ribbing. The top stitching is worked after the knitting has been completed and consists of simple running st using yarn B doubled.
To work the vertical lines of running stitch, pass over 2 rows and under 2 rows while stitching.
To work the horizontal lines, pass over 2 sts and under one st while stitching. See the instructions for positions of lines.

Instructions

Back

With 2¾mm (US size 2) needles and yarn A, cast on 71 [75: 79: 83] sts and beg rib as foll:
✳✳1st rib row (RS) P1, *k1, p1; rep from * to end.
2nd rib row K1, *p1, k1; rep from * to end.
Rep these 2 rows 3 times more, then rep first row again.✳✳
Inc row (WS) Keeping rib correct, rib 5 [7: 9: 11], (work into front and back of next st, rib 11) 5 times, work into front and back of next st, rib rem 5 [7: 9: 11] sts. 77 [81: 85: 89] sts.
Change to 3mm (US size 3) needles.
Beg with a k row, work in st st until back measures 17 [19: 21: 23]cm/6½ [7½: 8¼: 9]in from beg.
Cast (bind) off all sts.
Note: Yoke is worked separately.

Fronts

With 2¾mm (US size 2) needles and yarn A, cast on 33 [35: 37: 39] sts for right front and work ribbing as for back from ✳✳ to ✳✳.
Inc row (WS) Keeping rib correct, (rib 7 [8: 9: 9], work into front and back of next st) 3 times, rib rem 9 [8: 7: 9] sts.
36 [38: 30: 42] sts.
Change to 3mm (US size 3) needles.
Beg with a k row, work in st st until front measures 17 [19: 21: 23]cm/6½ [7½: 8¼: 9]in from beg.
Cast (bind) off all sts.
Work left front in exactly the same way.

Yoke

The two front sections of the yoke are worked first, then joined across back neck.
Right front yoke
With 3mm (US size 3) needles and yarn A, cast on 35 [37: 39: 41] sts.
Beg with a k row, work 12 [14: 18: 20] rows in st st, so ending with a p row.
Neck shaping
✳✳✳Cont in st st throughout, cast (bind) off 4

sts at beg of next row (neck edge) and 2 sts at same edge on next alt row, then dec one st at neck edge on next 5 [6: 6: 7] alt rows. 24 [25: 27: 28] sts.✳✳✳
Work 5 rows without shaping, so ending at shaped edge after a p row.
Place a marker loop of contrasting yarn at each end of last row to indicate shoulder line, then cont for right back section.
Right back yoke
Cast on for back neck 2 sts at beg of next row and 4 sts at same edge on next alt row. 30 [31: 33: 34] sts.
P one row.
Break off yarn and leave these sts on a spare needle.
Left front yoke
With 3mm (US size 3) needles and yarn A, cast on 35 [37: 39: 41] sts.
Beg with a k row, work 13 [15: 19: 21] rows in st st, so ending with a k row.
Neck shaping
Work neck shaping as given for right front yoke from ✳✳✳ to ✳✳✳.
Work 4 rows without shaping, so ending at shaped edge after a p row.
Place a marker loop of contrasting yarn at each end of last row to indicate shoulder line, then cont for left back section.
Left back yoke
K one row.
Cast on for back neck 2 sts at beg of next row and 4 sts at same edge on next alt row. 30 [31: 33: 34] sts.
Join right and left yokes
Next row (RS) K30 [31: 33: 34] sts of left back yoke, then onto RH needle cast on 17 [19: 21] sts, then k sts of right back yoke. 77 [81: 85: 89] sts.
Work without shaping until back yoke measures 8 [9: 10: 11]cm/3¼ [3½: 3¾: 4¼]in from shoulder-line markers.
Cast (bind) off.

Sleeves

With 2¾mm (US size 2) needles and yarn A, cast on 41 [43: 45: 47] sts and work ribbing as for back from ✳✳ to ✳✳.
Inc row (WS) Keeping rib correct, rib 3 [3: 4: 2], work into front and back of next st, (rib 4 [5: 5: 5], work into front and back of next st) 7 [6: 6: 7] times, rib rem 2 [3: 4: 2] sts. 49 [50: 52: 55] sts.
Change to 3mm (US size 3) needles.
Beg with a k row, work in st st, inc one st at each end of every foll 6th row 8 [9: 9: 10] times, then on every foll 4th row 0 [1: 3: 3] times. 65 [70: 76: 81] sts.
Work in st st without shaping until sleeve measures 17 [20: 22: 24]cm/6½ [7¾: 8½: 9½]in from beg.
Cast (bind) off all sts.

Finishing and borders

Press lightly on WS with a cool iron, following instructions on yarn label and avoiding ribbing.

Lap yoke slightly over fronts (with WS of yoke to RS of fronts) and with RS facing and yarn A, backstitch cast-on edges of yoke to upper edge of fronts, stitching just above edge. Then sew cast-off edge of back yoke to upper edge of back in same way.

Button band

With 2¾mm (US size 2) needles and yarn A, cast on 15 sts and beg with a first rib row, work in rib as on back until band, when slightly stretched, fits from lower edge of ribbing to neck edge on yoke, ending with a 2nd (WS) rib row.

Break off yarn and leave sts on a st holder to be worked later into neckband.

Sew button band to left front for girl or right front for boy, taking care that RS of band is on RS of jacket (yarn end will be at RH edge of band and, with RS facing, next row of band begins with a p st).

Mark positions of buttons on button band, the first to come 1.5cm/½in from lower edge, the last to come one row above top edge (in 2nd row of neckband) and the rem 4 evenly spaced between.

Buttonhole band

Work buttonhole band as for button band, but working buttonholes on a RS row when reached as foll:

Buttonhole row (RS) (P1, k1) 3 times, p1, yo, p2tog, rib 6.

After ending on a 2nd (WS) rib row, leave sts on a st holder.

Sew buttonhole band to other front, again taking care that RS of band is on RS of jacket.

Neckband

With RS facing, 2¾mm (US size 2) needles and yarn A, rejoin yarn to right front band and rib these 15 sts, then onto same needle pick up and k18 [20: 20: 22] sts evenly along right front neck edge to shoulder-line marker, 33 [35: 35: 37] sts around back neck edge between markers and 18 [20: 20: 22] sts along left front neck edge, then rib 15 sts of left front band. 99 [105: 105: 111] sts.

Work one row in rib.

Rib next row, making another buttonhole above previous ones.

Work 3 rows more in rib.

Cast (bind) off loosely in rib.

Embroidery

Using a tapestry needle and yarn B doubled, work the lines of top stitching (see Stitches Used) as foll:

On each front yoke, work a horizontal line 2 rows above the seam joining yokes to fronts

and another in same position on back yoke. On main part of right front, work a vertical line 2 sts from seam joining on front band, beg on first row of st st and ending just below yoke; miss next 9 sts, then work another line. Work 2 lines in same positions on left front. On sleeves, work a vertical line at centre placing it on a st for first and 4th sizes and between 2 sts for 2nd and 4th sizes, then work a horizontal line 3 rows below cast (bound) off edge, thus leaving one row for seam.

On each side edge of back and fronts mark a point 12 [13: 14: 15]cm/4¾ [5: 5½: 6]in below shoulder-line markers for armholes and sew cast (bound) off edges of sleeves between outer markers. Remove all markers. Join side and sleeve seams.

Sew on the buttons to correspond with the buttonholes.

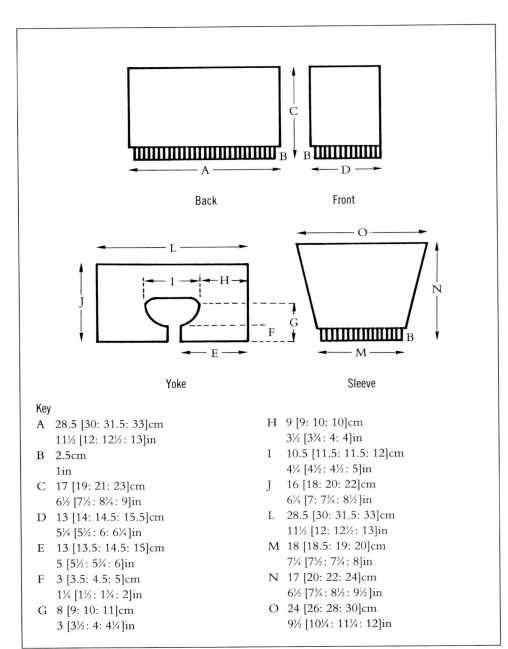

Back Front

Yoke Sleeve

Key

A 28.5 [30: 31.5: 33]cm
11½ [12: 12½: 13]in

B 2.5cm
1in

C 17 [19: 21: 23]cm
6½ [7½: 8¼: 9]in

D 13 [14: 14.5: 15.5]cm
5¼ [5½: 6: 6¼]in

E 13 [13.5: 14.5: 15]cm
5 [5½: 5¾: 6]in

F 3 [3.5: 4.5: 5]cm
1¼ [1½: 1¾: 2]in

G 8 [9: 10: 11]cm
3 [3½: 4: 4¼]in

H 9 [9: 10: 10]cm
3½ [3¾: 4: 4]in

I 10.5 [11.5: 11.5: 12]cm
4¼ [4½: 4½: 5]in

J 16 [18: 20: 22]cm
6¼ [7: 7¾: 8½]in

L 28.5 [30: 31.5: 33]cm
11½ [12: 12½: 13]in

M 18 [18.5: 19: 20]cm
7¼ [7½: 7¾: 8]in

N 17 [20: 22: 24]cm
6½ [7¾: 8½: 9½]in

O 24 [26: 28: 30]cm
9½ [10¼: 11¼: 12]in

BABY'S STRIPED TROUSERS

The baby's striped trousers are worked in two pieces – back and front. Each piece is worked from side to side and the borders are worked later.

Sizes

To fit 3 months [6 months: 9 to 12 months]
Actual width around hips when completed
54 [56: 60]cm/22 [23: 24]in
Directions for larger sizes are in brackets [ ]; if there is only one set of figures it applies to all sizes.

Materials

PINGOUIN Corrida 3:
1 [1: 2] balls Ecru No. 312 (A)
1 ball Bleu Givre No. 410 (B)
Pair each of 2¾mm and 3mm (US sizes 2 and 3) needles
2 small buttons
Elastic thread for waistband

Tension (Gauge)

Worked with 3mm (US size 3) needles.
St st or main patt: 27 sts and 38 rows to 10cm/4in over st st or main patt; work a sample on 42 sts, working in st st.
Note: When working patt from Chart No. 2, the tension (gauge) will be different, but this chart is only used for the straps and does not affect the size of the garment.

Stitches used

Main pattern

Working in st st, work the main patt (which is shown on Chart No. 1) as foll:
1st row (RS) Using A, k to end.
2nd row Using A, p to end.
3rd row Using A or B as indicated, k1 A, *2 B, 2 A;* rep from * to *, ending k2 B, 1 A.
4th–17th rows Cont in st st and work 14 rows in stripes, working 2 rows A, 4 rows B, 4 rows A, one row B, 2 rows A, one row B. These 17 rows form one patt repeat.
Note: For 2nd and every alt patt repeat, beg with a p row, reading p for k and vice versa.
Patt sequence for first size only:
Work 6 complete 17-row patt repeats as given above, then work 2 rows A. Total of 104 rows.
Patt sequence for 2nd size only:
Working in st st, beg with a k row and work

one row A, one row B, then work 6 complete 17-row patt repeats as given above, then work from first-4th rows of patt. Total of 108 rows.
Patt sequence for 3rd size only:
Working in st st, beg with a k row and work (2 rows A, one row B) twice, then work 6 complete 17-row patt repeats as given above, then work from first-8th rows of patt. Total of 116 rows.

Instructions

Back

The back is worked from side to side.
Right half back
With 3mm (US size 3) needles and yarn A, cast on 84 [96: 108] sts.
Work in main patt in sequence for correct size (see Stitches Used) until 52 [54: 58] rows have been worked, so ending after a p row (first row of 4th patt repeat).
Crutch (crotch) shaping
Break off yarn and with RS facing, slip first 36 [40: 44] sts onto a spare needle, then rejoin yarn to rem 48 [56: 64] sts and k to end.
Cont in patt throughout, work one row without shaping.
Cast (bind) off 4 sts at beg of next row, then dec one st at same edge on next 3 rows, then again on foll alt row.
Cast (bind) off rem 40 [48: 56] sts.
This completes right half of back.
Left half of back
With 3mm (US size 3) needles and yarn A, cast on 40 [48: 56] sts for second leg and beg as foll:
1st row (WS) Using A, k to end.
2nd row Using A, p to last st, work into front and back of last st.
3rd row Using A, k to end.
4th row Using B, as 2nd row.
5th row Using A, work into front and back of first st, k to end.
6th row Using A, as 2nd row.
7th row Using B, cast on 4 sts, k to end.
8th row Using A, p to end.
Break off yarn and leave these 48 [56: 64] sts on a spare needle.
Next row (RS) Return to sts of right half of back and with RS facing, k all 36 [40: 44] sts, then k48 [56: 64] sts of 2nd leg.
84 [96: 108] sts.
Work rem 51 [53: 57] rows of patt sequence as set (see Stitches Used).
Cast (bind) off all sts.

Front

Work front of trousers exactly as given for back of trousers.

Shoulder straps

With 3mm (US size 3) needles and yarn A, cast on 14 sts and beg working in patt from Chart No. 2 as foll:
1st chart row (RS) Using A, k to end.
2nd chart row Using A, p to end.
3rd chart row Using A or B as indicated, *k2 A, 2 B, 1 A, 1 B;* rep from * to * again, k2 A.
4th chart row P4 A, 1 B, 1 A, 1 B, 3 A, (1 B, 1 A) twice.
Cont in patt from chart as now set until·strap measures 32 [36: 40]cm/12½ [14: 15½]in from beg.
Cast (bind) off all sts.
Make a second strap in the same way.

Finishing and borders

Press lightly on WS with a cool iron, following instructions on yarn label.
Back waistband
With RS facing, 2¾mm (US size 2) needles and yarn A, pick up and k67 [71: 77] sts evenly along upper edge of back.
Beg k1, p1 rib as foll:
1st rib row (WS) K1, *p1, k1; rep from * to end.
2nd rib row P1, *k1, p1; rep from * to end.
Rep first rib row once more.
Make buttonholes on next row as foll:
1st buttonhole row (RS) Keeping rib correct, rib 22 [24: 26], cast (bind) off 2, rib until there are 19 [19: 21] sts on RH needle after buttonhole, cast (bind) off 2, rib to end.
2nd buttonhole row Work in rib, casting on 2 sts over each buttonhole.
Work 3 rows more in rib.
Cast (bind) off loosely in rib.
Front waistband
Work as for back waistband along upper edge of front, but omitting buttonholes.
Join side seams and waistband seams.
Leg border
With RS facing, 2¾mm (US size 2) needles and yarn A, pick up and k71 [75: 79] sts evenly all around lower edge of one leg.
Rep first and 2nd rib rows 4 times.
Cast (bind) off loosely in rib.
Work other leg border in same way.
Join short centre back and front seams along shaped edges, then join inner leg seams.
Strap borders
With RS facing, 2¾mm (US size 2) needles and yarn A, pick up and k92 [104: 116] sts evenly along one side edge of one of the shoulder straps.
K one row.
Cast (bind) off knitwise.
Work another border in the same way along the other side edge of this strap and then on

both edges of the other strap.

Sew cast-on edge of shoulder straps inside front waistband, placing them so that centres are about 10cm/4in apart.

Pass a row of elastic thread through WS of waistband on 2nd and 7th rib rows, securing ends in a seam.

Sew a button to other end of each strap and cross them at back to fasten.

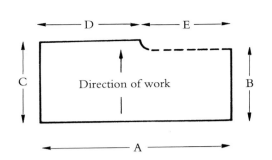

Right half back or Left half front

Key

A 31 [35.5: 40]cm/12½ [14¼ : 16]in

B 13.5 [14: 15]cm/5½ [5¾ : 6]in

C 15.5 [16: 17]cm/6¼ [6½ : 6¾]in

D 14.5 [17.5: 20.5]cm/6 [7: 8¼]in

E 16.5 [18: 19.5]cm/6½ [7¼ : 7¾]in

Chart No. 1
Back and front

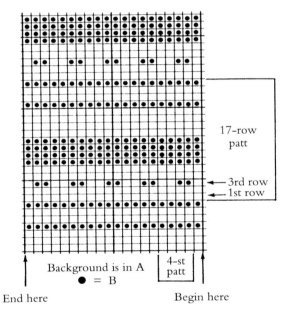

17-row patt

←— 3rd row
←— 1st row

4-st patt

Background is in A
● = B

End here

Begin here

Chart No. 2
Shoulder straps

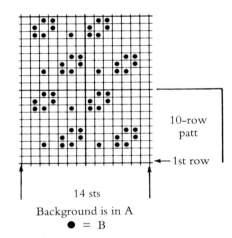

10-row patt

←— 1st row

14 sts

Background is in A
● = B

Work this patt on both shoulder straps.

Note: The 4-st patt repeat only applies to 3rd patt row. The patt sequence begins on a different row according to size; see instructions.

BABY'S SHORTS

The baby's shorts can be worked as part of a set to go with the jacket or on their own to be worn with a T-shirt.

Sizes

To fit 3 months [6 months: 9 to 12 months: 18 months: 2 years], fitting loosely
Actual width around hips when completed 60 [64: 66: 70: 72]cm/24 [26: 27: 28: 29]in
Directions for larger sizes are in brackets [ ]; if there is only one set of figures it applies to all sizes.

Materials

PINGOUIN Corrida 3:
1 [1: 2: 2: 2] balls Bleu Givre No. 410 (A)
Small amount of Ecru No. 312 (B)
Pair each of 2¾mm and 3mm (US sizes 2 and 3) needles
Tape or flat seam binding for facing leg edges
Elastic thread for waistband

Tension (Gauge)

Worked with 3mm (US size 3) needles.
St st: 27 sts and 38 rows to 10cm/4in over st st; work a sample on 40 sts.

Stitches used

Embroidery

The shorts are worked in plain st st with k1, p1 ribbing. The top stitching is worked after the knitting has been completed and consists of simple running st using yarn B doubled. Work the running st as directed in the instructions.

Instructions

Back

Back of shorts is begun at lower edge of legs. The two legs are worked separately to the crutch (crotch), then joined.
First leg
With 3mm (US size 3) needles and yarn A, cast on 49 [51: 53: 55: 57] sts.
Beg with a k row, work 12 [12: 12: 16: 16] rows in st st, so ending with a p row.★★
Crotch (crutch) shaping
Cont in st st, cast (bind) off 2 sts at beg of next row and next alt row, so ending with a k row. 45 [47: 49: 51: 53] sts.
P one row.

Break off yarn and leave sts on a spare needle.
Second leg
Work second leg in same way as first to ★★.
K one row.
Crutch (crotch) shaping
Cont in st st, cast (bind) off 2 sts at beg of next row and next alt row, so ending with a p row. 45 [47: 49: 51: 53] sts.
(Do not break off yarn.)
Join legs
Next row (RS) K45 [47: 49: 51: 53] sts of second leg, then k sts of first leg. 90 [94: 98: 102: 106] sts.
P one row.
Next row (RS) K42 [44: 46: 48: 50], k2tog, k2 (2 centre sts), sl 1-k1-psso, k42 [44: 46: 48: 50].
Cont in st st, cont to dec at each side of centre 2 sts in this way on next 3 alt rows. 82 [86: 90: 94: 98] sts.
Work in st st without shaping until shorts measure 19 [21: 22: 24: 25]cm/7½ [8¼: 8½: 9½: 9¾]in from beg, ending with a k row.
Dec row (WS) P4 [6: 8: 2: 4], (p2tog, p6) 9 [9: 9: 11: 11] times, p2tog, p rem 4 [6: 8: 2: 4] sts. 72 [76: 80: 82: 86] sts.
Change to 2¾mm (US size 2) needles.
Work 8 rows in k1, p1 rib.
Cast (bind) off loosely in rib.

Front

Work front of shorts exactly as given for back of shorts.

Finishing and trimming

Press lightly on WS with a cool iron, following instructions on yarn label and avoiding ribbing.
Join short centre back and front seams along the cast (bound) off edges. Then join inner leg seams.
Join side seams leaving the first 18 rows open at lower edge. Pass a row of elastic thread through WS of waistband, on 2nd and 7th rib rows, securing ends in a seam.
Embroidery
Using a tapestry needle and yarn B doubled, work a line of running stitches along side slits and around lower edge as foll:
Beg at top of one slit and 2 sts from edge, pass the yarn over 2 rows and under 2 rows; cont until 2 rows above cast-on edge, then work a horizontal line of stitches all around lower edge, passing under one st and over 2 sts. Finally work along other side edge of slit in same way as before, then work trimming in same way on other leg.
Face lower edge of legs and sides of slits with the tape or seam binding to strengthen edges and prevent curling.

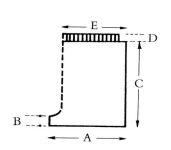

Right half back or Left half front

Key
A 18 [19: 19.5: 20: 21]cm
    7¼ [7½: 7¾: 8: 8½]in
B 3 [3: 3: 4: 4]cm
    1¼ [1¼: 1¼: 1½: 1½]in
C 19 [21: 22: 24: 25]cm
    7½ [8¼: 8½: 9½: 9¾]in
D 3cm
    1¼in
E 15 [16: 16.5: 17.5: 18]cm
    6 [6½: 6¾: 7: 7¼]in

BABY'S SHORTS WITH BIBS

The baby's shorts with bibs can be worked as part of a set to go with the jacket or on their own to be worn with a T-shirt.

Sizes

To fit 6 months [9 to 12 months: 18 months: 2 years]
Actual width around hips when completed 56 [60: 62: 66]cm/23 [24: 25: 26]in
Directions for larger sizes are in brackets [ ]; if there is only one set of figures it applies to all sizes.

Materials

PINGOUIN Corrida 3:
2 [2: 3: 3] balls Bleu Givre No. 410 (A)
Small amount of Ecru No. 312 (B)
Pair each of 2¾mm and 3mm (US sizes 2 and 3) needles
4 small buttons
Tape or flat seam binding for facing leg edges

Tension (Gauge)

Worked with 3mm (US size 3) needles.
St st: 27 sts and 38 rows to 10cm/4in over st st; work a sample on 40 sts.

Stitches used

Special abbreviations

yo (yarn over) – to work a yo between 2 k sts, take yarn to front of work between two needles, then take yarn from front to back over top of RH needle to make a new loop on RH needle.

Embroidery

The shorts are worked in plain st st with k1, p1 ribbing. The top stitching is worked after the knitting has been completed and consists of simple running st using yarn B doubled. To work the vertical lines of running stitch, pass over 2 rows and under 2 rows while stitching. To work the horizontal lines, pass over 2 sts and under one st while stitching. See the instructions for positions of lines.

Instructions

Front

Front of shorts is begun at lower edge of legs. The two legs are worked separately to the crutch (crotch), then joined.

First leg
With 3mm (US size 3) needles and yarn A, cast on 34 [36: 36: 38] sts.
Beg with a k row, work 3 [3: 3: 5] rows in st st, so ending with a k row.

Leg shaping
Cont in st st throughout, inc one st at each end of next row, then on every foll 4th row 1 [3: 4: 5] times, then on every alt row 3 [1: 1: 0] times. 44 [46: 48: 50] sts.
Work 2 [2: 2: 4] rows without shaping, so ending with a p row.★★

Crotch (crutch) shaping
Cast (bind) off 2 sts at beg of next row. 42 [44: 46: 48] sts.
P one row.
Break off yarn and leave sts on a spare needle.

Second leg
Work second leg in same way as first to ★★.
K one row.

Crutch (crotch) shaping
Cast (bind) off 2 sts at beg of next row, so ending with a p row. 42 [44: 46: 48] sts. (Do not break off yarn.)

Join legs
Join legs tog on next row as foll:
Next row (RS) K42 [44: 46: 48] sts of second leg, then k sts of first leg. 84 [88: 92: 96] sts.
P one row.
Dec on next row as foll:
Next row (RS) K39 [41: 43: 45], k2tog, k2 (2 centre sts), sl 1-k1-psso, k39 [41: 43: 45].
Cont to dec at each side of centre 2 sts in this way on next 3 alt rows. 76 [80: 84: 88] sts.★★★
Work without shaping until shorts measure 11 [13: 14: 16]cm/4¼ [5: 5½: 6¼]in from beg, ending with a p row.

Pocket shaping
Next row (RS) K3, sl 1-k1-psso, k to last 5 sts, k2tog, k3.
Next row P to end.
Rep last 2 rows 16 [18: 20: 22] times more.
Cast (bind) off rem 42 sts.

Front pockets

With 3mm (US size 3) needles and yarn A, cast on 20 [22: 24: 26] sts.
Beg with a k row, work in st st for 10 [11: 12: 13]cm/4 [4½: 4¾: 5¼]in.
Cast (bind) off all sts.
Make a second pocket in same way.

Back

Work back as given for front to ★★★.
Work without shaping until shorts are same length as front to upper edge (thus omitting pocket shaping).
Cast (bind) off all sts.

Back bib

With 3mm (US size 3) needles and yarn A, cast on 76 [80: 84: 88] sts.
Beg with a k row, work 4 rows in st st, so ending with a p row.

Armhole shaping
Next row (RS) K3, sl 1-k1-psso, k to last 5 sts, k2tog, k3.
Work 3 rows in st st without shaping.
First size only:
There are now 74 sts.
2nd size only:
Rep last 4 rows once more. 76 sts.
3rd size only:
Rep last 4 rows 3 times more. 76 sts.
4th size only:
Rep last 4 rows 4 times more. 78 sts.
All sizes:
Cont in st st throughout, dec in same positions at each end of next row (RS) and next 18 alt rows, so ending with a k row. 36 [38: 38: 40] sts.
K next row (WS) to make a firm edge.
Cast (bind) off all sts knitwise.

Front bib

Before beg front bib, work lining for the mock pocket.
Mock pocket lining
With 3mm (US size 3) needles and yarn A, cast on 22 [22: 24: 24] sts.
P one row, then k one row.
Leave these sts on a spare needle.
Bib
Work main part of bib as given for back bib until 30 [34: 38: 42] rows have been worked from beg, so ending with a p row. 52 [54: 58: 60] sts.
Next row K3, sl 1-k1-psso, k10 [11: 12: 13], cast (bind) off next 22 [22: 24: 24] sts purlwise to make a ridge on RS, k to last 5 sts, k2tog, k3.
On foll row p the sts of the mock pocket lining in place of those cast (bound) off.
Cont as for back bib for 10 [10: 14: 14] rows more, so ending with a p row. 40 [42: 42: 44] sts.
Make buttonholes on next row as foll:
Buttonhole row (RS) K3, sl 1-k1-psso, k1, yo, k2tog, k to last 8 sts, k2tog, yo, k1, k2tog, k3.
P one row.
Work decs on next row as usual. 36 [38: 38: 40] sts.
K one row (WS) to make a firm edge.
Cast (bind) off all sts knitwise.

Shoulder straps

With 3mm (US size 3) needles and yarn A, cast on 9 sts.

Beg with a k row, work in st st for 13 [15: 17: 19]cm/5 [6: 6½: 7½]in.
Cast (bind) off all sts.
Make a second strap in same way.

Mock front border

With 3mm (US size 3) needles and yarn A, cast on 7 sts.
Beg with a k row, work in st st for 8 [9: 10: 11]cm/3 [3½: 4: 4¼]in, ending with with a p row.
Next row (RS) K1, sl 1-k1-psso, k to end.
Cont in st st throughout, dec in this same position on next 3 alt rows.
P one row on rem 3 sts.
Now cast (bind) off 2 sts, leaving one st on RH needle; slip this st onto a 2¾mm (US size 2) needle and along left side edge pick up and k30 [33: 36: 39] sts.
K one row.
Cast (bind) off all sts.

Mock belt loops

With 3mm (US size 3) needles and yarn A, cast on 10 sts.
Beg with a k row, work 14 rows in st st.
Cast (bind) off all sts.
Make a second belt loop in same way.

Finishing and trimming

Press pieces lightly on WS with a cool iron, following instructions on yarn label.
Pocket edging
With RS facing, 2¾mm (US size 2) needles and yarn A, pick up and k31 [34: 38: 41] sts evenly along sloping edge of one pocket on lower part of front.
Cast (bind) off knitwise.
Work similar edging on other pocket.
Armhole edging
With RS facing, 2¾mm (US size 2) needles and yarn A, pick up and k39 [42: 48: 51] sts evenly along right back armhole edge.
Cast (bind) off knitwise.
Work similar edging on left back armhole and both front armholes.
Strap edging
With RS facing, 2¾mm (US size 2) needles and yarn A, pick up and k37 [43: 49: 55] sts evenly along one side edge of one of the shoulder straps.
Cast (bind) off knitwise.
Work similar edging on other side of this strap and on both side edges of other strap.
Embroidery
Using a tapestry needle and yarn B doubled, work the lines of top stitching (see Stitches Used) as foll:
On pocket shapings work a vertical line on the 3rd st from each edge, that is the st next to the decs, then embroider vertical lines in same positions on armhole edges of back and front bibs. Work a horizontal line 2 rows below mock pocket opening on front bib, then on WS slip stitch pocket lining in place. Work a horizontal line 2 rows below cast (bound) off edge of back and front bib. On each shoulder strap, work a vertical line at centre of 2nd st from each side edge. Work a vertical line in same positions on belt loops and also a horizontal line 2 rows above cast-on edge and 2 rows below cast (bound) off edge. On mock front border, work a vertical line at centre of 2nd st from RH edge and cont along shaped edge. Slip stitch border at centre of trouser section of front placing cast-on edge level with upper edge of front (see photo).
With RS of pockets to WS of front, pin pockets in place having upper edges level and lower edge of pockets extending 1cm/½in below beg of pocket shaping. Slip stitch side and lower edges of pockets to WS of front. Join side seams catching in the lower 1cm/½in of pockets.
Embroider a horizontal line all around each leg 2 rows above cast-on edge; join inner leg seams.
Face lower edge of legs with tape or seam binding to strengthen edges and prevent them from curling.

Lap bib sections slightly over shorts (with WS of bib to RS of shorts) and with RS facing and yarn A, backstitch cast-on edges of bibs to shorts, stitching just above edge and catching in mock front border. Sew mock belt loops to front so that they overlap upper edge of pocket shapings and waist seams (see photo).
Sew a button to one end of each shoulder strap and sew other end of straps to upper edge of back bib. Sew rem 2 buttons to front at sides of waist seam.

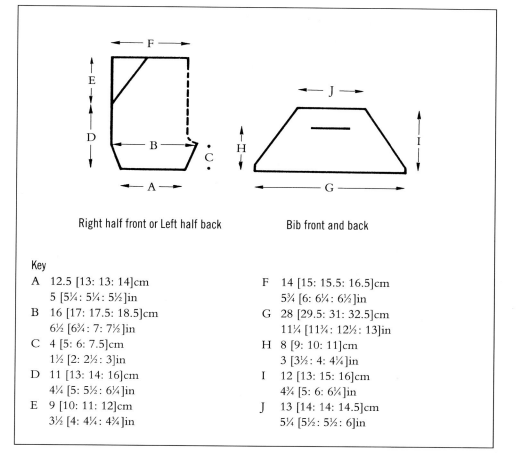

Right half front or Left half back   Bib front and back

Key

A   12.5 [13: 13: 14]cm   F   14 [15: 15.5: 16.5]cm
    5 [5¼: 5¼: 5½]in   5¾ [6: 6¼: 6½]in
B   16 [17: 17.5: 18.5]cm   G   28 [29.5: 31: 32.5]cm
    6½ [6¾: 7: 7½]in   11¼ [11¾: 12½: 13]in
C   4 [5: 6: 7.5]cm   H   8 [9: 10: 11]cm
    1½ [2: 2½: 3]in   3 [3½: 4: 4¼]in
D   11 [13: 14: 16]cm   I   12 [13: 15: 16]cm
    4¼ [5: 5½: 6¼]in   4¾ [5: 6: 6¼]in
E   9 [10: 11: 12]cm   J   13 [14: 14: 14.5]cm
    3½ [4: 4¼: 4¾]in   5¼ [5½: 5½: 6]in

Hooded Cabled Pullover

in Andes

✳✳✳

Sizes

To fit 86 [91 to 96: 102: 107 to 112]cm/34 [36 to 38: 40: 42 to 44]in bust
Actual width around bust when completed 108 [117: 126: 135]cm/42½ [46: 49½: 53]in
Directions for larger sizes are in brackets [ ]; if there is only one set of figures it applies to all sizes.

Materials

Pingouin Andes:
19 [21: 23: 25] balls Mandarine No. 03
Pair each of 3mm and 3¾mm (US sizes 3 and 5) needles
3mm (US size 3) circular needle for hood border
Cable needle (cn)

Tension (Gauge)

Worked with 3¾mm (US size 5) needles.
Patt panels between cables: 32 sts and 30 rows to 10cm/4in over patt panels between cables; work a sample on 47 sts as foll:
1st row (WS) (K5, p2) 6 times, k5.
2nd row (P5, T2L) 6 times, p5.
Rep these 2 rows for sample.
Plaited (braided) cable: measures 5cm/2in in width.
Rib patt on hood: 23 sts and 32 rows to 10cm/4in over rib patt on hood; work a sample on 37 sts, working rows as for first size on right side section of the hood but without shaping.

Stitches used

Special abbreviations

T2L (twist 2 left) – pass RH needle behind first st on LH needle and k into back of 2nd st leaving it on LH needle, then k into front of first st and slip both sts off LH needle.
k1 below – insert RH needle from front to back through st below next st on LH needle and knit this st, allowing st above to drop off LH needle as st is completed.
cable 12 back – slip next 6 sts onto cn and hold at back of work, k6, then k6 from cn.
cable 12 front – slip next 6 sts onto cn and hold at front of work, k6, then k6 from cn.

Plaited (braided) cable

Work the plaited (braided) cable over 18 sts as foll:
1st row (RS) K18.
2nd and all WS rows P18.
3rd row As first row.
5th row Cable 12 back, k6.
7th, 9th and 11th rows As first row.
13th row K6, cable 12 front.
15th row As first row.
16th row P18.
These 16 rows form one patt repeat.
Note: When casting (binding) off over this cable, work (k2tog, k1) 6 times during cast (bind) off.

Instructions

Back

With 3mm (US size 3) needles, cast on 133 [143: 153: 163] sts and beg k1, p1 rib as foll:
1st rib row (RS) P1, *k1, p1; rep from * to end.
2nd rib row K1, *p1, k1; rep from * to end.
Rep these 2 rows until work measures 7cm/2¾in from beg, ending with a 2nd rib row.
Inc row (RS) Keeping rib correct, p1, (work into front and back of next st, rib 2, work into front and back of next st, rib 1) 26 [28: 30: 34] times, work into front and back of next st, p1. 186 [200: 214: 228] sts.
Change to 3¾mm (US size 5) needles.
Work foundation row for patt as foll:
Foundation row (WS) K2, (p2, k5) 1 [2: 3: 4] times, p18, *k5, p2, k5, p18;* rep from * to * 4 times more, (k5, p2) 1 [2: 3: 4] times, k2.
Beg patt on next row as foll:
1st patt row (RS) P2, (T2L, p5) 1 [2: 3: 4] times, *work first row of plaited (braided) cable over next 18 sts, p5, T2L, p5;* rep from * to * 4 times more, work first row of plaited (braided) cable over next 18 sts, (p5, T2L) 1 [2: 3: 4] times, p2.
2nd patt row As foundation row.
Cont in patt as now set (working the T2L on every RS row) until back measures 70 [73: 75: 78]cm/27½ [28¾: 29½: 30¾]in from beg, ending with a WS row.
Cast (bind) off all sts.

Front

Work as given for back until front measures 67 [70: 72: 75]cm/26¼ [27½: 28¼: 29½]in from beg, ending with a WS row.
Neck shaping
Keeping patt correct throughout, divide for neck on next row as foll:
Next row (RS) Work 67 [72: 79: 84] sts in patt, then turn leaving rem sts on spare needle.
Cont on these sts only, for left front.
Cast (bind) off 6 sts at beg of next row (neck edge), 4 sts at same edge on next alt row and 2 sts on next 3 alt rows.
Cast (bind) off rem 51 [56: 63: 68] sts for shoulder edge.
With RS facing, rejoin yarn to sts left unworked and work centre 52 [56: 56: 60] sts in patt, then turn leaving rem sts on a spare needle.
Cont on these centre sts only.
Work without shaping for 7cm/2¾in.
Cast (bind) off all sts.
With RS facing, rejoin yarn to rem 67 [72: 79: 84] sts of right front and cont as for left front from ★★ to ★★.
Work one row without shaping.
Cast (bind) off rem 51 [56: 63: 68] sts for shoulder edge.

Sleeves

With 3mm (US size 3) needles, cast on 55 [57: 57: 59] sts and work in rib as on back for 6cm/2½in, ending with a 2nd rib row.
Inc row (RS) Keeping rib correct, rib 1 [2: 1: 2], work into front and back of each of next 53 [53: 55: 55] sts, rib 1 [2: 1: 2]. 108 [110: 112: 114] sts.
Change to 3¾mm (US size 5) needles.
Work foundation row for patt as foll:
Foundation row (WS) K0 [1: 2: 3], p18, *k5, p2, k5, p18;* rep from * to * twice more, k0 [1: 2: 3].
Beg patt on next row as foll:
1st patt row (RS) P0 [1: 2: 3], *work first row of plaited (braided) cable over next 18 sts, p5, T2L, p5;* rep from * to * twice more, work first row of plaited (braided) cable over next 18 sts, p0 [1: 2: 3].
2nd patt row As foundation row.
Cont in patt as now set, inc one st at each end of next row, on every foll 6th row twice [once: once: once], on every foll 4th row 21 [23: 23: 22] times, then on every alt row 0 [1: 4: 7] times, working all extra sts at sides in patt of p5, T2L, in same way as at sides of back. 156 [162: 170: 176] sts.
Work in patt without shaping until sleeve measures 43 [44: 46: 47]cm/17 [17¼: 18: 18½]in from beg.
Cast (bind) off all sts.

Hood

The hood is worked in two sections.

Right side section

With 3¾ mm (US size 5) needles, cast on 48 [50: 50: 52] sts and beg rib patt as foll:

1st row (RS) K all sts.

2nd row P4 [6: 6: 8], *k1 below, p10;* rep from * to *.

These last 2 rows form patt repeat.

Cont in patt for 3 rows more, so ending with a RS row.

Hood shaping

Cont in patt, inc one st at beg on next row, then at same edge on every foll 6th row 7 times more, working extra sts into patt. 56 [58: 58: 60] sts.

Work in patt without shaping until hood measures 28cm/11in from beg, ending at shaped edge.

Keeping patt correct throughout, dec one st at beg of next row and at same edge on next 9 alt rows, then cast (bind) off 2 sts at same edge on next 10 alt rows.

Cast (bind) off rem 26 [28: 28: 30] sts.

Left side section

With 3¾ mm (US size 5) needles, cast on 48 [50: 50: 52] sts and beg rib patt as foll:

1st row (RS) K all sts.

2nd row *P10, k1 below;* rep from * to *, ending p4 [6: 6: 8].

These last 2 rows form patt repeat.

Cont in patt and complete as for right side section, but reversing all shapings.

Finishing and hood border

Do not press. Join shoulder edges of front to corresponding width on cast (bound) off edge of back, matching patt and leaving centre section of back open.

Join shaped back edges of hood sections, but leaving cast (bound) off edges open. Sew lower edges of hood to the shaped neck edges of front and across back neck. Sew the sides of the extension section at centre front to the first 7cm/2¾ in on front edges of hood.

Hood border

With RS facing and using 3mm (US size 3) circular needle, pick up and k83 sts evenly along remainder of left front edge of hood, 41 [45: 45: 49] sts across cast (bound) off edge of front neck extension and 83 sts along remainder of right front edge of hood. 207 [211: 211: 215] sts.

Working back and forth in rows on circular needle and beg with 2nd rib row, work 8 rows in k1, p1 rib as on back.

Cast (bind) off loosely in rib.

Join upper edge of hood and ends of border with a neat backstitch seam.

On each side edge of back and front mark a point 23 [24: 25: 26]cm/9 [9¼: 9¾: 10¼]in below shoulder seam for armholes, ensuring that these markers are placed on same patt row. Sew cast (bound) off edge of sleeves between markers.

Join side and sleeve seams.

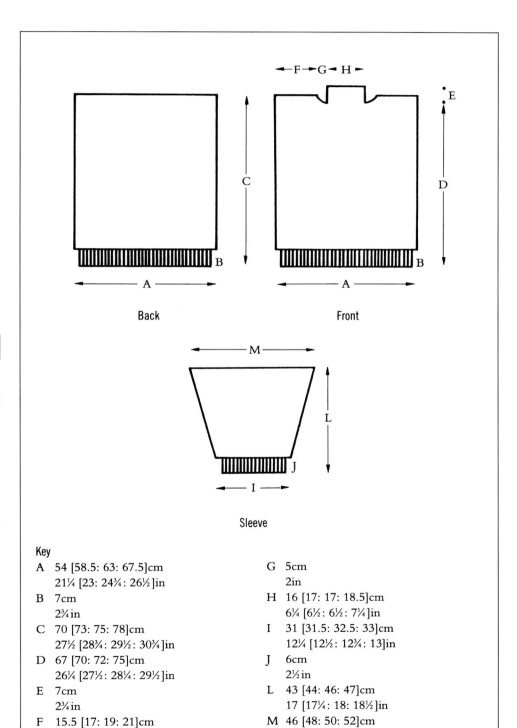

Back

Front

Sleeve

Key

A 54 [58.5: 63: 67.5]cm
   21¼ [23: 24¾: 26½]in

B 7cm
   2¾ in

C 70 [73: 75: 78]cm
   27½ [28¾: 29½: 30¾]in

D 67 [70: 72: 75]cm
   26¼ [27½: 28¼: 29½]in

E 7cm
   2¾ in

F 15.5 [17: 19: 21]cm
   6 [6½: 7½: 8¼]in

G 5cm
   2in

H 16 [17: 17: 18.5]cm
   6¼ [6½: 6½: 7¼]in

I 31 [31.5: 32.5: 33]cm
   12¼ [12½: 12¾: 13]in

J 6cm
   2½ in

L 43 [44: 46: 47]cm
   17 [17¼: 18: 18½]in

M 46 [48: 50: 52]cm
   18 [18¾: 19½: 20½]in

CHILD'S DIAMOND PULLOVER

IN PURE LAINE NO.5

✳✳

Sizes

To fit ages 6 [8: 10: 12: 14] years or 63 [68: 72: 76: 81]cm/25 [27: 28½: 30: 32]in chest
Actual width around chest when completed 80 [86: 90: 96: 100]cm/32 [34: 36: 38: 40]in
Directions for larger sizes are in brackets [ ]; if there is only one set of figures it applies to all sizes.

Materials

PINGOUIN Pure Laine No. 5:
7 [8: 9: 10: 11] balls Bouteille No. 10
Pair each of 4½mm and 5mm (US sizes 7 and 8) needles

Tension (Gauge)

Worked with 5mm (US size 8) needles.
Rib patt: 24 sts and 24 rows to 10cm/4in over rib patt; work a sample on 37 sts.

Stitches used

The pullover is worked in rev st st with a textured yoke and textured diamond shapes worked in rib pattern. The diamond shapes are worked from the chart.

Instructions

Back

With 4½mm (US size 7) needles, cast on 97 [103: 109: 115: 121] sts and beg rib patt as foll:
1st patt row (RS) K1 tbl, *p2, k1 tbl;* rep from * to *.
2nd patt row *P1 tbl, k2;* rep from * to *, ending row with p1 tbl.
These 2 rows form the rib patt.
Cont in rib patt until back measures 5 [5: 6: 6: 7]cm/2 [2: 2¼: 2¼: 2¾]in from beg, ending with a 2nd patt row.
Change to 5mm (US size 8) needles.
Cont in rib patt for 2 [4: 6: 6: 6] rows more, so ending with a WS row.
Beg with row marked '1st row' on chart, beg working diamond patt from chart on next row as foll:
1st chart row (RS) P0 [3: 6: 9: 12], *over next 24 sts which form 24-st patt repeat work p3, (k1 tbl, p2) 7 times;* rep from * to * 3 times more, p1 [4: 7: 10: 13].
2nd chart row K1 [4: 7: 10: 13], *over 24-st patt repeat work (k2, p1 tbl) 7 times, k3;* rep from * to * 3 times more, k10 [3: 6: 9: 12].
3rd–6th chart rows Rep first and 2nd rows twice.
7th chart row P0 [3: 6: 9: 12], *over 24-st patt repeat work p6, (k1 tbl, p2) 4 times, k1 tbl, p5;* rep from * to * 3 times more, p1 [4: 7: 10: 13].
This sets the position of 24-st patt repeats across back.
Cont in patt from chart as now set until back measures 26 [27: 29: 30: 32]cm/10¼ [10½: 11¼: 11¾: 12¼]in from beg, ending with a WS row.
Armhole shaping
Keeping patt correct as set, cast (bind) off 6 sts at beg of next 2 rows. 85 [91: 97: 103: 109] sts.
Cont working from chart until last chart row has been completed.
Work 8 rows in rev st st.✳✳
Work in rib patt as at beg of back until back measures 45 [47: 50: 52: 55]cm/17¾ [18½: 19½: 20½: 21½]in from beg, ending with a WS row.
Shoulder and neck shaping
During foll rows always cast (bind) off in rib patt.
Cont in rib patt and keeping rib patt correct throughout, cast (bind) off 8 [8: 9: 10: 10] sts at beg of next 2 rows.
Next row (RS) Cast (bind) off 8 [8: 9: 10: 10] sts, work in patt until there are 14 [16: 16: 16: 18] sts on RH needle and leave these sts for right back, cast (bind) off next 25 [27: 29: 31: 33] sts, work in patt to end.
Cont with these 22 [24: 25: 26: 28] sts at end of needle only, for left back.
Cast (bind) off 8 [8: 9: 10: 10] sts at beg of next row and 6 sts at neck edge on foll row.
Cast (bind) off rem 8 [10: 10: 10: 12] sts to complete shoulder shaping.
With WS facing, rejoin yarn to neck edge of right back sts and cast (bind) off first 6 sts, then work in patt to end.
Cast (bind) off rem 8 [10: 10: 10: 12] sts.

Front

Work front exactly as given for back to ★★.
Then work in rib patt as at beg of back
until front measures 38 [40: 43: 45: 48]cm/15
[15¾: 16¾: 17¾: 18¾]in from beg, ending
with a WS row.

Neck shaping
During rem rows always cast (bind) off in
rib patt. Cont in rib patt and keeping rib patt
correct throughout, divide for neck on next
row as foll:
Next row (RS) Work 35 [37: 39: 41: 43] sts
in patt and slip these sts onto a spare needle,
cast (bind) off next 15 [17: 19: 21: 23] sts,
work in patt to end.
Cont with these 35 [37: 39: 41: 43] sts only,
for right front.
Work one row without shaping.
★★★Cast (bind) off 4 sts at beg of next row
(neck edge) and 2 sts at same edge on next 2
alt rows, then dec one st at neck edge on
next 3 alt rows. 24 [26: 28: 30: 32] sts.
Work without shaping until front is same
length as back to beg of shoulder shaping,
ending at armhole edge.

Shoulder shaping
Cast (bind) off 8 [8: 9: 10: 10] sts at beg of
next row and next alt row.
Work one row without shaping.
Cast (bind) off rem 8 [10: 10: 10: 12] sts.
With WS facing, rejoin yarn to neck edge of
left front sts and complete as for right front
from ★★★ to end.

Sleeves

With 4½mm (US size 7) needles, cast on 51
[53: 55: 57: 59] sts and beg rib patt as foll:
1st patt row (RS) P1 [2: 0: 1: 2], *k1 tbl,
p2;* rep from * to *, ending k1 tbl, p1 [2: 0:
1: 2].
2nd patt row K1 [2: 0: 1: 2], p1 tbl, *k2, p1
tbl;* rep from * to *, ending k1 [2: 0: 1: 2].
Rep these 2 rows until sleeve measures 5 [5:
6: 6: 7]cm/2 [2: 2¼: 2¼: 2¾]in from beg,
ending with a 2nd patt row.
Change to 5mm (US size 8) needles.
Beg with row marked '1st row' on chart, beg
working diamond patt from chart on next
row as foll:

First size only:
1st chart row (RS) P1, *over next 24 sts
which form 24-st patt repeat work p3,
(k1 tbl, p2) 7 times;* rep from * to * once
more, p2.
2nd size only:
1st chart row (RS) P2, *over next 24 sts
which form 24-st patt repeat work p3,
(k1 tbl, p2) 7 times;* rep from * to * once
more, p3.
3rd size only:
1st chart row (RS) K1 tbl, p2, *over next

24 sts which form 24-st patt repeat work p3,
(k1 tbl, p2) 7 times;* rep from * to * once
more, p3, k1 tbl.
4th size only:
1st chart row (RS) P1, k1 tbl, p2, *over
next 24 sts which form 24-st patt repeat work
p3, (k1 tbl, p2) 7 times;* rep from * to *
once more, p3, k1 tbl, p1.
5th size only:
1st chart row (RS) P2, k1 tbl, p2, *over
next 24 sts which form 24-st patt repeat work
p3, (k1 tbl, p2) 7 times;* rep from * to *
once more, p3, k1 tbl, p2.
All sizes:
This sets the position of 24-st patt repeats
across sleeve.
Cont in patt from chart as now set for 2
rows more.
Working extra sts into patt, cont in patt, inc
one st at each end of next row, then on every
foll 4th row 1 [1: 2: 3: 4] times, then on
every foll 3rd row 10 [12: 15: 19: 21] times,
then on every alt row 8 [8: 5: 2: 0] times,
and at the same time when last row of
chart has been completed, cont in rev st st for
2 [4: 4: 6: 8] rows, then work in rib patt
taking care to keep the k1 tbl ribs in line
with those of patt.
When incs have been completed, cont on 91

[97: 101: 107: 111] sts without shaping until
sleeve measures 33 [36: 40: 44: 47]cm/13
[14: 15¾: 17¼: 18½]in from beg.
Cast (bind) off in patt.

Finishing and neckband

Do not press. Join right shoulder seam,
matching patt.
Neckband
With RS facing and 4½mm (US size 7)
needles, pick up and k51 [53: 55: 57: 59] sts
evenly around front neck edge and 37 [39:
41: 43: 45] sts across back neck. 88 [92: 96:
100: 104] sts.
Work in k1, p1 rib for 5 rows.
Cast (bind) off loosely in rib.
Join left shoulder seam and neckband seam.
Sew cast (bound) off edge of sleeves to sides
of armholes and sew armhole cast (bind) off
to last 6 rows on sides of sleeves.
Join side and sleeve seams.

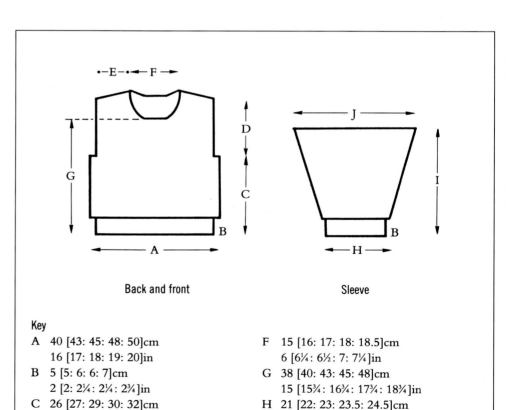

Back and front

Sleeve

Key

A 40 [43: 45: 48: 50]cm
   16 [17: 18: 19: 20]in
B 5 [5: 6: 6: 7]cm
   2 [2: 2¼: 2¼: 2¾]in
C 26 [27: 29: 30: 32]cm
   10¼ [10½: 11¼: 11¾: 12¼]in
D 19 [20: 21: 22: 23]cm
   7½ [8: 8¼: 8¾: 9¼]in
E 10 [10.5: 11.5: 12.5: 13]cm
   4 [4¼: 4½: 4¾: 5]in

F 15 [16: 17: 18: 18.5]cm
   6 [6¼: 6½: 7: 7¼]in
G 38 [40: 43: 45: 48]cm
   15 [15¾: 16¾: 17¾: 18¾]in
H 21 [22: 23: 23.5: 24.5]cm
   8½ [8¾: 9: 9½: 9¾]in
I 33 [36: 40: 44: 47]cm
   13 [14: 15¾: 17¼: 18½]in
J 38 [40: 42: 44.5: 46]cm
   15 [16: 16¾: 17¾: 18½]in

Diamond chart

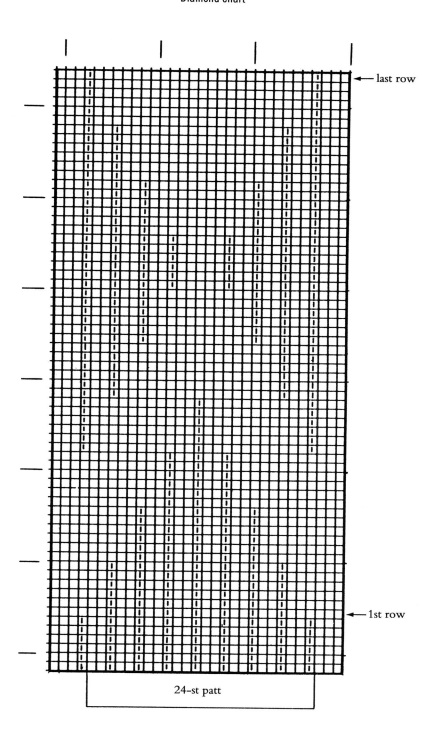

← last row

← 1st row

24-st patt

See instructions for arrangement of patt on back, front and sleeves. On back and front the rib patt continues for some rows before the patt begins then the patt is worked over 97 sts with sts at sides in rev st st for 2nd, 3rd, 4th and 5th sizes. On sleeves the patt begins directly after the cuff and is worked across all sts.

☐ = p on RS, k on WS

| = k1 tbl on RS, p1 tbl on WS

MAN'S CABLED PULLOVER

IN FRANCE +

✳✳✳

Sizes

To fit 86 to 91 [96 to 107]cm/34 to 36 [38 to 42]in chest
Actual width around chest when completed 103 [119]cm/41½ [47½]in
Directions for larger size are in brackets [ ]; if there is only one set of figures it applies to both sizes.

Materials

PINGOUIN France +:
14 [16] balls in desired shade
Pair each of 3mm, 3¼mm and 3¾mm (US sizes 2, 3 and 5) needles
Cable needle (cn)

Tension (Gauge)

Main patt: 28 sts and 38 rows to 10cm/4in measured over main patt and worked using 3¾mm (US size 5) needles; work a sample on 35 sts, working from first row to 25th row, then 34th row to 57th row.
Fisherman's rib patt: 23 sts and 46 rows to 10cm/4in measured over fisherman's rib patt and worked using 3¼mm (US size 3) needles; work a sample on 29 sts, beg with 2nd patt row.

Stitches used

Special abbreviations

k1 B (k1 below) – insert RH needle from front to back through st below next st on LH needle and knit this st, allowing st above to drop off LH needle as st is completed.
cable 6 back – slip next 3 sts onto cn and hold at back of work, k3, then k3 from cn.
cable 6 front – slip next 3 sts onto cn and hold at front of work, k3, then k3 from cn.

Fisherman's rib pattern

Work fisherman's rib patt over an odd number of sts as foll:
1st row (RS) K1, p1, *k1 B, p1;* rep from * to *, ending k1.
2nd row K all sts.
These 2 rows form one patt repeat.
Note: When casting (binding) off over this patt, cast (bind) off loosely in normal k1, p1 rib as sts appear.

Main pattern

Work main patt over a multiple of 22 sts plus 13 sts extra as foll:
1st row (RS) *(P2, k9);* rep from * to * to last 13 sts, ending p2, k9, p2.
2nd row K13, *p9, k13;* rep from * to *.
3rd row *P2, (k1 B, p1) 4 times, k1 B, p2, cable 6 back, k3;* rep from * to * to last 13 sts, ending p2, (k1 B, p1) 4 times, k1 B, p2.
4th row As 2nd row.
5th row *P2, (k1 B, p1) 4 times, k1 B, p2, k9;* rep from * to * to last 13 sts, ending p2, (k1 B, p1) 4 times, k1 B, p2.
6th row As 2nd row.
7th row *P2, (k1 B, p1) 4 times, k1 B, p2, k3, cable 6 front;* rep from * to * to last 13 sts, ending p2, (k1 B, p1) 4 times, k1 B, p2.
8th row As 2nd row.
9th row As 5th row.
10th-33rd rows Rep 2nd-9th rows 3 times.
34th row K2, p9, *k13, p9;* rep from * to * to last 2 sts, ending k2.
35th row *P2, cable 6 back, k3, p2, (k1 B, p1) 4 times, k1 B;* rep from * to * to last 13 sts, ending p2, cable 6 back, k3, p2.
36th row As 34th row.
37th row *P2, k9, p2, (k1 B, p1) 4 times, k1 B;* rep from * to * to last 13 sts, ending p2, k9, p2.
38th row As 34th row.
39th row *P2, k3, cable 6 front, p2, (k1 B, p1) 4 times, k1 B;* rep from * to * to last 13 sts, ending p2, k3, cable 6 front, p2.
41st row As 37th row.
42nd-65th rows Rep 34th-41st rows 3 times.
Rep 2nd-65th rows inclusive to form patt (first row is foundation row and is not worked again).

Instructions

Back

With 3mm (US size 2) needles, cast on 117 [135] sts and beg k1, p1 rib as foll:
1st rib row (RS) K1, *p1, k1; rep from * to end.
2nd rib row P1, *k1, p1; rep from * to end.
Rep these 2 rows until work measures 7cm/

2¾in from beg, ending with a first rib row.
Inc row (WS) Keeping rib correct, rib 4 [5], (work into front and back of next st, rib 3) 27 [31] times, work into front and back of next st, rib rem 4 [5] sts. 145 [167] sts.**
Change to 3¾mm (US size 5) needles.
Beg with first row, work in main patt (see Stitches Used) until 65th row has been completed.
Cont in patt, rep 2nd-65th rows until back measures 37 [41]cm/14½ [16]in from beg, ending with a WS row.
Armhole shaping
Keeping patt correct throughout, cast (bind) off 11 sts at beg of next 2 rows. 123 [145] sts.
Work without shaping until back measures 62 [68]cm/24½ [26¾]in from beg, ending with a WS row.
Shoulder and neck shaping
Cast (bind) off 9 [11] sts at beg of next 2 rows.
Next row (RS) Cast (bind) off 9 [11] sts, work in patt until there are 28 [32] sts on RH needle and leave these sts for right back, cast (bind) off next 31 [37] sts, work in patt to end.
Cont with these 37 [43] sts at end of needle only, for left back.
Cast (bind) off 9 [11] sts at beg of next row and 5 sts at neck edge on foll row; rep last 2 rows again.
Cast (bind) off rem 9 [11] sts to complete shoulder shaping.
With WS facing, rejoin yarn to neck edge of right back sts and cast (bind) off first 5 sts, then work in patt to end.
Cast (bind) off 9 [11] sts at beg of next row and 5 sts at neck edge on foll row.
Cast (bind) off rem 9 [11] sts.

Front

Work front exactly as given for back to **.
Change to 3¾mm (US size 5) needles.
Work first row of main patt (see Stitches Used).
Then work 34th-65th rows of main patt.
Now work 2nd-33rd rows of main patt.
This reverses position of panels for front.
Cont in patt as set (rep 34th-65th patt rows, then 2nd-33rd rows) until front is same length as back to armhole.
Armhole shaping
Keeping patt correct throughout, cast (bind) off 11 sts at beg of next 2 rows. 123 [145] sts.
Work without shaping until front measures 55 [61]cm/21¾ [24]in from beg, ending with a WS row.
Neck shaping
Next row (RS) Work 51 [59] sts in patt and slip these sts onto a spare needle, cast (bind) off next 21 [27] sts, work in patt to end.
Cont with these rem 51 [59] sts only, for

right front (leaving rem sts for later).
Work one row without shaping.
★★★Cast (bind) off 3 sts at beg of next row (neck edge) and 2 sts at same edge on next 3 alt rows, then dec one st at neck edge on next 6 alt rows. 36 [44] sts.
Work without shaping until front is same length as back to beg of shoulder shaping, ending at armhole edge.

Shoulder shaping
Cast (bind) off 9 [11] sts at beg of next row and next 2 alt rows.
Work one row without shaping.
Cast (bind) off rem 9[11] sts.
With WS facing, rejoin yarn to neck edge of left front sts and complete as for right front from ★★★ to end.

Sleeves

With 3mm (US size 2) needles, cast on 53 [59] sts and work in k1, p1 rib as on back for 7cm/2¾in, ending with a 2nd rib row.
Inc row (RS) Keeping rib correct, rib 7 [9], (into next st p into front, k into back and p again into front of same st, rib 9) 4 times, into next st p into front, k into back and p again into front of same st, rib rem 5 [9] sts. 63 [69] sts.
Change to 3¼mm (US size 3) needles.
K one row (WS).
Work fisherman's rib patt, inc one st at each

end of every foll 6th row 21 [23] times, then on every foll 4th row 5 times, working extra sts into patt (but do not k1 below on the border st at sides). 115 [125] sts.
Work in patt as now set without shaping until sleeve measures 53 [56]cm/20¾ [22]in from beg, ending with a RS row.
Cast (bind) off loosely in normal k1, p1 rib.

Finishing and neckband

Do not press. Join right shoulder seam.
Neckband
With RS facing and 3mm (US size 2) needles, pick up and k62 [67] sts evenly around front neck edge and 47 [52] sts across back neck. 109 [119] sts.
Beg with 2nd rib row, work in k1, p1 rib as on back for 4cm/1½in.
Cast (bind) off loosely in rib.
Join left shoulder seam and neckband seam.
Sew cast (bound) off edge of sleeves to sides of armholes and sew armhole cast (bind) off to last 15 rows on sides of sleeves.
Join side and sleeve seams.

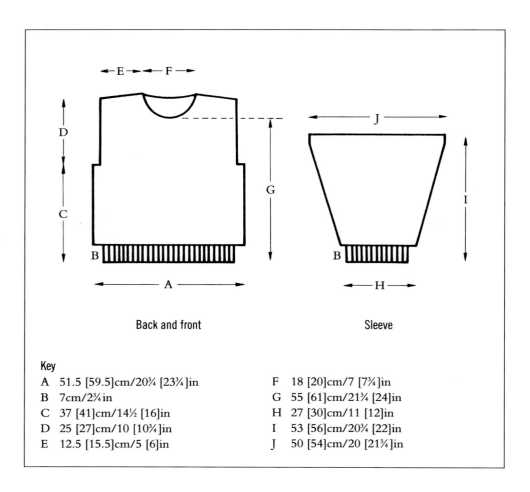

Back and front

Sleeve

Key

A	51.5 [59.5]cm/20¾ [23¾]in		F	18 [20]cm/7 [7¾]in
B	7cm/2¾in		G	55 [61]cm/21¾ [24]in
C	37 [41]cm/14½ [16]in		H	27 [30]cm/11 [12]in
D	25 [27]cm/10 [10¾]in		I	53 [56]cm/20¾ [22]in
E	12.5 [15.5]cm/5 [6]in		J	50 [54]cm/20 [21¾]in

BROAD CABLE CARDIGAN
IN CORRIDA 4
✳✳✳

Sizes

To fit 86 [91: 96: 102: 107]cm/34 [36: 38: 40: 42]in bust
Actual width around bust (buttoned) 106.5 [111: 116.5: 122.5: 127]cm/42¾ [44¼: 46¾: 49: 51]in
Directions for larger sizes are in brackets [ ]; if there is only one set of figures it applies to all sizes.

Materials

PINGOUIN Corrida 4:
17 [18: 19: 20: 21] balls Ficelle No. 550
Pair each of 3¼mm and 4mm (US sizes 3 and 6) needles
Cable needle (cn)
5 buttons

Tension (Gauge)

Worked with 4mm (US size 6) needles.
Patt: 29 sts and 28 rows to 10cm/4in over patt; work a sample on 42 sts as foll:
1st row (RS) P5, work first row of plaited (braided) cable over next 12 sts, p8, work first row of plaited (braided) cable over next 12 sts, p5.
Cont as now set, working 2 plaited (braided) cables, and working sts between them and at sides in rev st st.

Stitches used

Special abbreviations

cable 8 front – slip next 4 sts onto cn and hold at front of work, k4, then k4 from cn.
cable 8 back – slip next 4 sts onto cn and hold at back of work, k4, then k4 from cn.

Plaited (braided) cable

Work the plaited (braided) cable over 12 sts as foll:
1st row (RS) K12.
2nd row P12.
3rd row K12.
4th and all WS rows P12.
5th row Cable 8 front, k4.
7th row As 3rd row.
9th row K4, cable 8 back.
10th row P12.
Rep 3rd–10th rows inclusive to form patt.

Instructions

Back

With 3¼mm (US size 3) needles, cast on 109 [115: 121: 127: 133] sts and beg rib as foll:
1st rib row (RS) P1, ✶k1, p1; rep from ✶ to end.
2nd rib row K1, ✶p1, k1; rep from ✶ to end.
Rep these 2 rows 6 times more, then rep first row once, so ending with a RS row.
Inc row (WS) Keeping rib correct, rib 3 [5: 6: 5: 6], (work into front and back of next st, rib 2) 34 [35: 36: 39: 40] times, work into front and back of next st, rib rem 3 [4: 6: 4: 6] sts. 144 [151: 158: 167: 174] sts.
Change to 4mm (US size 6) needles.
Beg patt on next row as foll:
1st patt row (RS) P3 [3: 3: 4: 4], ✶work first row of plaited (braided) cable over next 12 sts, p6 [7: 8: 9: 10];✶ rep from ✶ to ✶ 6 times more, work first row of plaited (braided) cable over next 12 sts, p3 [3: 3: 4: 4].
2nd patt row K3 [3: 3: 4: 4], work 2nd row of plaited (braided)·cable over next 12 sts, ✶k6 [7: 8: 9: 10], work 2nd row of plaited (braided) cable over next 12 sts;✶ rep from ✶ to ✶ 6 times more, k3 [3: 3: 4: 4].
Cont in patt as now set (working 8 cables with sts at sides and between them worked in rev st st), inc one st at each end of every foll 28th rows 3 times, working these extra sts in rev st st. 150 [157: 164: 173: 180] sts.
Work in patt without shaping until back measures 43 [44: 46: 47: 48]cm/16¼ [17¼: 18: 18½: 19]in from beg, ending with a WS row.

Armhole shaping

Keeping patt correct as set throughout, cast (bind) off 4 sts at beg of next 2 rows, 3 sts at beg of next 2 rows and 2 sts at beg of next 8 rows, then dec one st at each end of next 3 [3: 3: 4: 4] alt rows.
114 [121: 128: 135: 142] sts.
There are now 6 cables with 6 [7: 8: 9: 10] sts in rev st st at each side.
Work without shaping until back measures 67 [69: 72: 74: 76]cm/26¼ [27: 28¼: 29: 30]in from beg, ending with a WS row.

Shoulder and neck shaping

Next row (RS) Cast (bind) off 11 [12: 13: 13: 14] sts, work in patt until there are 32 [33: 35: 37: 38] sts on RH needle and leave these sts for right back, cast (bind) off next 28 [31: 32: 35: 38] sts, work in patt to end.
Cont with these 43 [45: 48: 50: 52] sts at end of needle only, for left back.
Cast (bind) off 11 [12: 13: 13: 14] sts at beg of next row and 5 sts at neck edge on foll row; rep last 2 rows again.
Cast (bind) off rem 11 [11: 12: 14: 14] sts to complete shoulder shaping.
With WS facing, rejoin yarn to neck edge of right back sts and cast (bind) off first 5 sts, then work in patt to end.
Cast (bind) off 11 [12: 13: 13: 14] sts at beg of next row and 5 sts at neck edge on foll row.
Cast (bind) off rem 11 [11: 12: 14: 14] sts.

Right front

With 3¼mm (US size 3) needles, cast on 55 [57: 61: 65: 67] sts and work 15 rows in rib as on back, so ending with a RS row.
Inc row (WS) Keeping rib correct, rib 2 [1: 3: 5: 3], (work into front and back of next st, rib 2) 17 [18: 18: 18: 20] times, work into front and back of next st, rib rem 1 [1: 3: 5: 3] sts. 73 [76: 80: 84: 88] sts.✶✶
Change to 4mm (US size 6) needles.
Beg patt on next row as foll:
1st patt row (RS) P4 [4: 5: 5: 6], ✶work first row of plaited (braided) cable over next 12 sts, p6 [7: 8: 9: 10];✶ rep from ✶ to ✶ twice more, work first row of plaited (braided) cable over next 12 sts, p3 [3: 3: 4: 4].
Work 28 rows in patt as now set (working 4 cables with sts at sides and between them worked in rev st st), so ending at side edge after a RS row.
Cont in patt, inc one st at beg of next row, then at same edge on every foll 28th row twice more, working these extra sts in rev st st. 76 [79: 83: 87: 91] sts.
Work in patt without shaping until front measures 41 [42: 44: 45: 46]cm/16 [16½: 17¼: 17¾: 18]in from beg, ending at straight centre front edge.

Front and armhole shaping

Keeping patt correct as set throughout, dec one st at beg of next row (centre front edge) and at same edge on next 8 [8: 8: 8: 11] alt rows, then dec one st at same edge on every foll 3rd row 16 [17: 18: 19: 18] times, **and at the same time** keep armhole edge straight until front is same length as back to beg of armhole shaping (ending at armhole edge), then cast (bind) off 4 sts at beg of next row (armhole edge), 3 sts at same edge on next alt row, 2 sts on next 4 alt rows, dec one st at armhole edge on next 3 [3: 3: 4: 4] alt rows, then keep armhole edge straight until all front decs have been completed. 33 [35: 38: 40: 42] sts.

Work without shaping until front is same length as back to beg of shoulder shaping, ending at armhole edge.

Shoulder shaping

Cast (bind) off 11 [12: 13: 13: 14] sts at beg of next row and next alt row.

Work one row without shaping.

Cast (bind) off rem 11 [11: 12: 14: 14] sts.

Left front

Work as given for right front to **.

Change to 4mm (US size 6) needles.

Beg patt on next row as foll:

1st patt row (RS) P3 [3: 3: 4: 4], *work first row of plaited (braided) cable over next 12 sts, p6 [7: 8: 9: 10];* rep from * to * twice more, work first row of plaited (braided) cable over next 12 sts, p4 [4: 5: 5: 6].

Cont in patt as now set and complete as for right front, but reversing all shapings.

Sleeves

With 3¼mm (US size 3) needles, cast on 51 [53: 55: 57: 59] sts and work 15 rows in rib as on back, so ending with a RS row.

Inc row (WS) Keeping rib correct, rib 3 [3: 1: 1: 1], (work into front and back of next st, rib 1) 22 [23: 26: 27: 28] times, work into front and back of next st, rib rem 3 [3: 1: 1: 1] sts. 74 [77: 82: 85: 88] sts.

Change to 4mm (US size 6) needles.

Beg patt on next row as foll:

1st patt row (RS) P4 [4: 5: 5: 5], *work first row of plaited (braided) cable over next 12 sts, p6 [7: 8: 9: 10];* rep from * to * twice more, work first row of plaited (braided) cable over next 12 sts, p4 [4: 5: 5: 5].

Work 2 rows in patt as now set.

Cont in patt, inc one st at each end of next row, then on every foll 4th row 17 times, then on every foll 3rd row 9 [10: 11: 12: 13] times, **and at the same time** work extra sts into patt as foll: keep next 2 [3: 3: 4: 5] sts added at each side in rev st sts, then on next 12 sts form another plaited (braided) cable at each side, then work the rem 13 [13: 14: 14: 14] sts added at each side in rev st st. 128 [133: 140: 145: 150] sts.

Work in patt without shaping until sleeve measures 43 [44: 45: 46: 47]cm/17 [17¼: 17¾: 18: 18½]in from beg.

Top of sleeve shaping

Keeping patt correct as set throughout, cast (bind) off one st at beg of next 4 rows, 2 sts at beg of next 6 rows and 3 sts at beg of next 4 rows.

Cast (bind) off rem 100 [105: 112: 117: 122] sts.

Finishing and borders

Do not press. The ribbed front bands and the back neckband are worked before shoulder seams are joined.

Buttonhole band

With RS facing and 3¼mm (US size 3) needles, pick up and k90 [92: 97: 99: 101] sts evenly up straight centre front edge of right front to beg of neck shaping and 57 [59: 62: 64: 66] sts up sloping edge to shoulder. 147 [151: 159: 163: 167] sts.

Beg with 2nd rib row, work 3 rows in rib as on back, so ending with a WS row.

1st buttonhole row (RS) Beg at lower edge and keeping rib correct, rib 4 [3: 4: 5: 3] sts, cast (bind) off 2, *rib until there are 18 [19: 20: 20: 21] sts on RH needle after buttonhole, cast off 2;* rep from * to * 3 times more, rib to end.

2nd buttonhole row Work in rib, casting on 2 sts over each buttonhole.

Work 3 rows more in rib.

Cast (bind) off loosely in rib.

Button band

Work button band on left front as for buttonhole band (working 8 rows in rib), but picking up groups of sts in reverse order and omitting buttonholes.

Back neckband

With RS facing and 3¼mm (US size 3) needles, pick up and k41 [43: 45: 47: 49] sts across back neck.

Beg with 2nd rib row, work 8 rows in rib as on back. Cast (bind) off loosely in rib.

Join shoulder seams, matching patt and join ends of front bands to ends of back neckband. Sew in sleeves. Join side and sleeve seams. Sew on the buttons to correspond with the buttonholes.

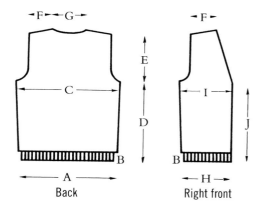

Back

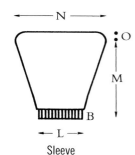

Right front

Sleeve

Key

A 49.5 [52: 54.5: 57.5: 60]cm
19¾ [20¾: 21¾: 23: 24]in

B 5cm
2in

C 51.5 [54: 56.5: 59.5: 62]cm
20½ [21½: 22½: 23¾: 24¾]in

D 43 [44: 46: 47: 48]cm
16¾ [17¼: 18: 18½: 19]in

E 24 [25: 26: 27: 28]cm
9½ [9¾: 10¼: 10½: 11]in

F 11 [12: 13: 13.5: 14.5]cm
4¼ [4¾: 5: 5¼: 5¾]in

G 16.5 [17.5: 18: 19: 20]cm
6½ [6¾: 7: 7½: 7¾]in

H 25 [26: 27.5: 29: 30]cm
10 [10½: 11: 11½: 12]in

I 26 [27: 28.5: 30: 31]cm
10½ [10¾: 11½: 12: 12½]in

J 41 [42: 44: 45: 46]cm
16 [16½: 17¼: 17¾: 18]in

L 25.5 [26.5: 28: 29: 30]cm
10¼ [10½: 11¼: 11¾: 12]in

M 43 [44: 45: 46: 47]cm
17 [17¼: 17¾: 18: 18½]in

N 48 [50: 52.5: 54: 56]cm
19 [19½: 20½: 21: 22]in

O 5cm
2in

BRIGHT MODERNS

Bold colours and simple geometric shapes are the theme of these six particularly stylish sweaters. Although the emphasis here is on strong colour, you could achieve a completely different look by substituting white for the black in several of the designs, or by choosing a whole set of softer tones. If you want to try intarsia knitting for the first time, the baby's circle and stripe top or the diamond and zigzag pullover would be a good introduction.

COLOUR BLOCK CARDIGAN

IN STAR +

*

Sizes

To fit 81 to 86 [91: 96 to 102: 107]cm/32 to 34 [36: 38 to 40: 42]in bust
Actual width around bust (buttoned) 99.5 [108.5: 115: 124.5]cm/40 [43¾: 46 : 49¾]in
Directions for larger sizes are in brackets [ ]; if there is only one set of figures it applies to all sizes.

Materials

PINGOUIN Star +:
4 balls Bouteille No. 24 (A)
3 balls Bleu Franc No. 16 (B)
2 balls Blanc No. 01 (C)
2 balls Rose Indien No. 12 (D)
2 balls Noir No. 20 (E)
Pair each of 3¾mm and 4½mm (US sizes 5 and 7) needles
7 buttons

Tension (Gauge)

Worked with 4½mm (US size 7) needles.
St st: 18 sts and 24 rows to 10cm/4in over st st; work a sample on 26 sts.

Stitches used

Striped pattern

The striped patt on the cardigan is worked in st st as explained in the instructions.

Instructions

Back

With 3¾mm (US size 5) needles and yarn E, cast on 81 [87: 93: 101] sts and beg rib as foll:
★★1st rib row (RS) P1, *k1, p1; rep from * to end.

2nd rib row K1, *p1, k1; rep from * to end.
Rep these 2 rows until work measures 6cm/2¼in from beg, ending with a first rib row.★★
Inc row (WS) Keeping rib correct, rib 9 [3: 6: 10], (work into front and back of next st, rib 8) 7 [9: 9: 9] times, work into front and back of next st, rib rem 8 [2: 5: 9] sts. 89 [97: 103: 111] sts.
Change to 4½mm (US size 7) needles.
Break off yarn E and change to yarn B.
Beg with a k row and using yarn B, work in st st until back measures 28 [29: 29: 30]cm/ 10¾ [11½: 11½: 11¾]in from beg, ending with a p row.
Break off yarn B and change to yarn E.
Beg with a k row and using yarn E, work 10 rows in st st. Break off yarn E.
Armhole shaping
Cont in st st throughout and using yarn A, cast (bind) off 6 sts at beg of next 2 rows. 77 [85: 91: 99] sts.
Still using yarn A, work without shaping until back measures 52 [54: 55: 57]cm/20¼ [21¼: 21½: 22¼]in from beg, ending with a p row.
Break off yarn A and change to yarn E.
Using yarn E, work 3 rows more without shaping, so ending with a k row.
Neck shaping
Using yarn E for remainder of back, beg neck shaping on next row as foll:
Next row (WS) P28 [31: 33: 36] sts and slip these sts onto a spare needle, cast (bind) off next 21 [23: 25: 27] sts, p to end.
Cont with rem 28 [31: 33: 36] sts only, for right back.
Work one row without shaping.
Cast (bind) off 4 sts at beg of next row (neck edge), then dec one st at same edge on foll row. 23 [26: 28: 31] sts.
Work one row without shaping.
Cast (bind) off all sts for shoulder edge.
With RS facing, rejoin yarn E to neck edge of left back sts and cast (bind) off first 4 sts, then k to end.
Dec one st at neck edge on next row. 23 [26: 28: 31] sts.
Work 2 rows without shaping.
Cast (bind) off all sts for shoulder edge.

Right front

With 3¾mm (US size 5) needles and yarn E, cast on 39 [43: 45: 49] sts and work as for back ribbing from ★★ to ★★.
Inc row (WS) Keeping rib correct, rib 4 [6: 2: 4], (work into front and back of next st, rib 9) 3 [3: 4: 4] times, work into front and back of next st, rib rem 4 [6: 2: 4] sts. 43 [47: 50: 54] sts.
Change to 4½mm (US size 7) needles.
Break off yarn E and change to yarn C.

Beg with a k row and using yarn C, work in st st until front measures 28 [29: 29: 30]cm/ 10¾ [11½: 11½: 11¾]in from beg, ending with a p row.
Break off yarn C and change to yarn E.
Beg with a k row and using yarn E, work 10 rows in st st, so ending with a p row.
Break off yarn E and change to yarn B.
Using yarn B, k one row.
Armhole shaping
Cont in st st throughout and still using yarn B, cast (bind) off 6 sts at beg of next row. 37 [41: 44: 48] sts.
Still using yarn B, work without shaping until front measures 48 [50: 51: 53]cm/18¾ [19¾: 20: 20¾]in from beg, ending at straight centre front edge after a p row.
Neck shaping
Still using yarn B, cast (bind) off 5 [6: 7: 8] sts at beg of next row (neck edge), 2 sts at same edge on next 3 alt rows, then dec one st at neck edge on next alt row.
Break off yarn B and change to yarn E.
Using yarn E for remainder of front, dec one st at neck edge on next 2 alt rows. 23 [26: 28: 31] sts.
Work 4 rows without shaping.
Cast (bind) off all sts for shoulder edge.

Left front

With 3¾mm (US size 5) needles and yarn E, cast on 39 [43: 45: 49] sts and work as for back ribbing from ★★ to ★★.
Inc row (WS) Keeping rib correct, rib 4 [6: 2: 4], (work into front and back of next st, rib 9) 3 [3: 4: 4] times, work into front and back of next st, rib rem 4 [6: 2: 4] sts. 43 [47: 50: 54] sts.
Change to 4½mm (US size 7) needles.
Break off yarn E and change to yarn A.
Beg with a k row and using yarn A, work in st st until front measures 20 [21: 21: 22]cm/ 7¾ [8¼: 8¼: 8½]in from beg, ending with a p row.
Break off yarn A and change to yarn E.
Beg with a k row and using yarn E, work 10 rows in st st, so ending with a p row.
Break off yarn E and change to yarn D.
Beg with a k row and using yarn D, work in st st until front measures 32 [33: 33: 34]cm/ 12¼ [13: 13: 13¼]in from beg, ending with p row.
Armhole shaping
Cont in st st throughout and still using yarn D, cast (bind) off 6 sts at beg of next row. 37 [41: 44: 48] sts.
Still using yarn D, work without shaping until front measures 48 [50: 51: 53]cm/18¾ [19¾: 20: 20¾]in from beg, ending at straight centre front edge after a k row.
Neck shaping
Still using yarn D, cast (bind) off 5 [6: 7: 8]

sts at beg of next row (neck edge), 2 sts at same edge on next 3 alt rows, then dec one st at neck edge on next alt row.
Break off yarn D and change to yarn E.
Using yarn E for remainder of front, dec one st at neck edge on next 2 alt rows. 23 [26: 28: 31] sts.
Work 4 rows without shaping.
Cast off all sts for shoulder edge.

Right sleeve

With 3¾mm (US size 5) needles and yarn E, cast on 43 [45: 45: 47] sts and work as for back ribbing from ★★ to ★★.
Inc row (WS) Keeping rib correct, rib 6 [7: 2: 3], (work into front and back of next st, rib 9) 3 [3: 4: 4] times, work into front and back of next st, rib rem 6 [7: 2: 3] sts. 47 [49: 50: 52] sts.
Change to 4½mm (US size 7) needles.
Break off yarn E and change to yarn A.
Beg with a k row, work in st st, inc one st at each end of every foll 6th row 8 [7: 6: 5] times, then on every foll 4th row 10 [12: 14: 16] times, **and at the same time** when sleeve measures 28cm/11in from beg, break off yarn A and work 10 rows in yarn E, then cont in yarn D. 83 [87: 90: 94] sts.
Cont in st st throughout and still using yarn D, work without shaping until sleeve measures 45 [46: 47: 48]cm/17¾ [18: 18½: 19]in from beg.
Work 10 rows in yarn E.
Cast (bind) off all sts.

Left sleeve

With 3¾mm (US size 5) needles and yarn E, cast on 43 [45: 45: 47] sts and work as for back ribbing from ★★ to ★★.
Inc row (WS) Keeping rib correct, rib 6 [7: 2: 3], (work into front and back of next st, rib 9) 3 [3: 4: 4] times, work into front and back of next st, rib rem 6 [7: 2: 3] sts. 47 [49: 50: 52] sts.
Change to 4½mm (US size 7) needles.
Break off yarn E and change to yarn B.
Beg with a k row, work in st st, inc one st at each end of every foll 6th row 8 [7: 6: 5] times, then on every foll 4th row 10 [12: 14: 16] times, **and at the same time** when sleeve measures 21cm/8¼in from beg, break off yarn A and work 10 rows in yarn E, then cont in yarn C. 83 [87: 90: 94] sts.
Cont in st st throughout and still using yarn C, work without shaping until sleeve measures 45 [46: 47: 48]cm/17¾ [18: 18½: 19]in from beg.
Work 10 rows in yarn E.
Cast (bind) off all sts.

Finishing and borders

Press lightly on WS with a cool iron, following instructions on yarn label and avoiding ribbing.
Join shoulder seams.
Neckband
With RS facing, 3¾mm (US size 5) needles and yarn E, pick up and k21 [22: 23: 24] sts evenly up right front neck edge, 35 [37: 39: 41] sts across back neck and 21 [22: 23: 24] sts down left front neck edge.
77 [81: 85: 89] sts.
Beg with 2nd rib row, work 8 rows in rib as on back.
Cast (bind) off loosely in rib.
Buttonhole band
With RS facing, 3¾mm (US size 5) needles and yarn E, pick up and k107 [111: 113: 117] sts evenly along straight centre front edge of right front, including edge of neckband.
Beg with 2nd rib row, work 3 rows in rib as on back, so ending with a WS row.
1st buttonhole row (RS) Beg at lower edge and keeping rib correct, rib 4 [3: 4: 3] sts, cast (bind) off 2, ★rib until there are 14 [15: 15: 16] sts on RH needle after buttonhole, cast off 2;★ rep from ★ to ★ 5 times more, rib to end.
2nd buttonhole row Work in rib, casting on 2 sts over each buttonhole.
Work 3 rows more in rib.
Cast (bind) off loosely in rib.
Button band
Work button band on left front as for buttonhole band (working 8 rows in rib), but omitting buttonholes.
Sew cast (bound) off edge of sleeves to sides of armholes and sew armhole cast (bind) off to last 8 rows on sides of sleeves.
Join side and sleeve seams.
Sew on the buttons to correspond with the buttonholes.

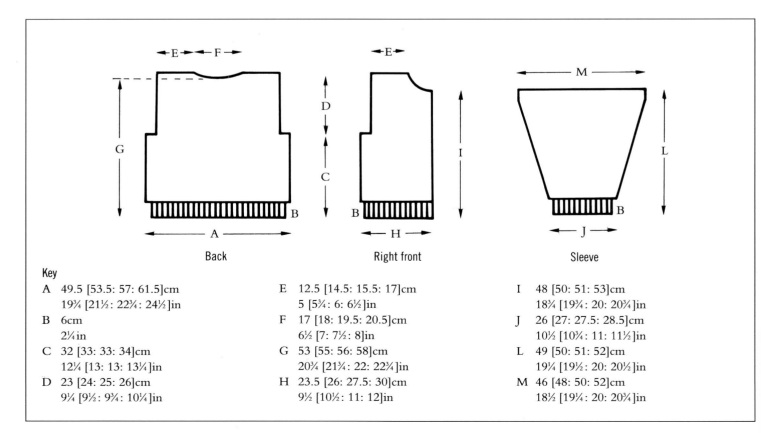

Back   Right front   Sleeve

Key
A 49.5 [53.5: 57: 61.5]cm
   19¾ [21½: 22¾: 24½]in
B 6cm
   2¼in
C 32 [33: 33: 34]cm
   12¼ [13: 13: 13¼]in
D 23 [24: 25: 26]cm
   9¼ [9½: 9¾: 10¼]in

E 12.5 [14.5: 15.5: 17]cm
   5 [5¾: 6: 6½]in
F 17 [18: 19.5: 20.5]cm
   6½ [7: 7½: 8]in
G 53 [55: 56: 58]cm
   20¾ [21¾: 22: 22¾]in
H 23.5 [26: 27.5: 30]cm
   9½ [10½: 11: 12]in

I 48 [50: 51: 53]cm
   18¾ [19¾: 20: 20¾]in
J 26 [27: 27.5: 28.5]cm
   10½ [10¾: 11: 11½]in
L 49 [50: 51: 52]cm
   19¼ [19½: 20: 20½]in
M 46 [48: 50: 52]cm
   18½ [19¼: 20: 20¾]in

BABY'S CIRCLES OUTFIT

IN ONDINE

✱✱

BABY'S SHORT-SLEEVED TOP

The short-sleeved top can be worked to go with the striped shorts or it can be worked on its own for a 2 year old child.

Sizes

To fit 3 months [6 months: 9 to 12 months: 18 months: 2 years]
Actual width around chest when completed 53 [55: 60: 64: 66]cm/21½ [22: 24: 25½: 26½]in
Directions for larger sizes are in brackets [ ]; if there is only one set of figures it applies to all sizes.

Materials

PINGOUIN Ondine:
2 [2: 2: 3: 3] balls Blanc No. 01 (A)
Small amount of Pacifique No. 25 (B)
Small amount of Citron No. 09 (C)
Small amount of Prairie No. 14 (D)
Small amount of Rouge No. 10 (E)
Pair each of 3mm and 3¾mm (US sizes 3 and 5) needles
3 small buttons

Tension (Gauge)

Worked with 3¾mm (US size 5) needles.
St st: 19 sts and 29 rows to 10cm/4in over st st; work a sample on 29 sts.
Note: For this design check number of rows to 10cm/4in carefully.

Stitches used

Special abbreviations

yo (yarn over) – to work a yo between 2 k sts, take yarn to front of work between two needles, then take yarn from front to back over top of RH needle to make a new loop on RH needle.

Colourwork pattern

The colourwork pattern on the front is worked in st st using the intarsia method. Use a separate small ball of yarn for each area of colour, twisting yarns when changing colours to avoid creating holes.
Follow chart for spot motifs, positioning them as directed in instructions.
The stripe pattern on the sleeves is worked in st st as directed in the instructions.

Instructions

Back

With 3mm (US size 3) needles and yarn A, cast on 51 [53: 57: 61: 63] sts and beg rib as foll:
1st rib row (RS) P1, ✱k1, p1; rep from ✱ to end.
2nd rib row K1, ✱p1, k1; rep from ✱ to end. Rep these 2 rows once more.✱✱
Change to 3¾mm (US size 5) needles.
Beg with a k row, work in st st until back measures 14 [15: 16: 17: 18]cm/5¼ [5¾: 6¼: 6½: 7]in from beg, ending with a p row.
Armhole shaping
Cont in st st throughout, cast (bind) off 4 [4: 4: 5: 5] sts at beg of next 2 rows. 43 [45: 49: 51: 53] sts.
Work 2 rows without shaping, so ending with a p row.
Divide for opening
Next row (RS) K21 [22: 24: 25: 26] sts and slip these sts onto a spare needle, cast (bind) off one st (centre st), k to end.
Cont with rem 21 [22: 24: 25: 26] sts only, for left back.
Work without shaping until back measures 24 [26: 28: 29: 31]cm/9¼ [10: 11: 11¼: 12]in from beg, ending at edge of centre opening after a p row.
Neck shaping
Cast (bind) off 6 [7: 8: 8: 9] sts at beg of next row (neck edge) and 4 sts at same edge on next alt row.
Work one row without shaping.
Cast (bind) off rem 11 [11: 12: 13: 13] sts for shoulder edge.
With WS facing, rejoin yarn to sts of right back and complete as for left back, reversing neck shaping.

Front

Work front exactly as given for back to ✱✱.
Change to 3¾mm (US size 5) needles.
Beg with a k row, work 2 [4: 2: 4: 6] rows in

st st, so ending with a p row.
Cont in st st throughout, beg working from chart (see page 104) on next row as foll:
1st chart row (RS) K8 [9: 11: 13: 14] A, join on C, k3 C, join on another ball of A, then k13 A, join on E, k3 E, join on A, then k13 A, join on B, k3 B, join on A, then k8 [9: 11: 13: 14] A.
2nd chart row Twisting yarns around each other when changing colours, p7 [8: 10: 12: 13] A, 5 B, 11 A, 5 E, 11 A, 5 C, then p7 [8: 10: 12: 13] A.
Cont in patt as now set, always twisting yarns when changing colours, until first row of 3 spots has been completed.
Break off spare yarns.
Using A only, work 6 [6: 8: 8: 8] rows.
Work 2nd row of 3 spots, but using colours shown on chart.
Cont in patt, using correct colours for spots and always working 6 [6: 8: 8: 8] rows in A between rows of spots, **and at the same time** when front measures 14 [15: 16: 17: 18]cm/5¼ [5¾: 6¼: 6½: 7]in from beg (ending with a p row) cast (bind) off 4 [4: 4: 5: 5] sts at beg of next 2 rows for armhole shaping, then cont on 43 [45: 49: 51: 53] sts without shaping and when last row of chart patt has been worked, cont in A only until front measures 21 [23: 24: 25: 26]cm/8¼ [9: 9½: 9¾: 10¼]in from beg, ending with a p row.
Neck shaping
Next row (RS) K17 [17: 19: 20: 21] sts and slip these sts onto a spare needle, cast (bind) off next 9 [11: 11: 11: 11] sts, k to end.
Cont with rem 17 [17: 19: 20: 21] sts only, for right front.
✱✱✱Dec one st at neck edge on next 4 rows, then on next 2 [2: 3: 3: 4] alt rows. 11 [11: 12: 13: 13] sts.
Work 3 [3: 4: 4: 5] rows without shaping.
Cast (bind) off all sts for shoulder edge.
With WS facing, rejoin yarn to neck edge of left front sts and complete as for right front from ✱✱✱ to end, reversing shaping.

Sleeves

The sleeves are worked sideways, beg at one side edge.
With 3¾mm (US size 5) needles and yarn C [A: A: A: A], cast on 12 [14: 15: 17: 18] sts (this is front edge of sleeve).
Work in stripe patt as foll:
First size only:
Working in st st and beg with a k row, work ✱2 rows C, 6 rows A, 2 rows B, 6 rows A, 2 rows D, 6 rows A, 2 rows E, 6 rows A;✱ rep from ✱ to ✱ once more, then work 2 rows C. Total of 66 rows.
2nd size only:
Working in st st and beg with a k row, work

2 rows A, ★2 rows C, 6 rows A, 2 rows B, 6 rows A, 2 rows D, 6 rows A, 2 rows E, 6 rows A;★ rep from ★ to ★ once more, then work 2 rows C, 2 rows A. Total of 70 rows.

3rd and 4th sizes only:
Working in st st and beg with a p row, work 5 rows A, ★2 rows C, 6 rows A, 2 rows B, 6 rows A, 2 rows D, 6 rows A, 2 rows E, 6 rows A;★ rep from ★ to ★ once more, then work 2 rows C, 5 rows A. Total of 76 rows.

5th size only:
Working in st st and beg with a k row, work 8 rows A, ★2 rows C, 6 rows A, 2 rows B, 6 rows A, 2 rows D, 6 rows A, 2 rows E, 6 rows A;★ rep from ★ to ★ once more, then work 2 rows C, 8 rows A. Total of 82 rows.

All sizes:
Cast (bind) off all sts.

Finishing and borders

Press lightly on WS with a cool iron, following instructions on yarn label and avoiding ribbing.
Join shoulder seams.
Neckband
With RS facing, 3mm (US size 3) needles and yarn A, pick up and k11 [12: 13: 13: 14] sts evenly across left back neck edge, 31 [33: 37: 37: 41] sts around front neck edge and 11 [12: 13: 13: 14] sts along right back neck. 53 [57: 63: 63: 69] sts.
Beg with 2nd rib row, work 3 rows in rib as on back.
Cast (bind) off loosely in rib.
Back buttonhole band
With RS facing, 3mm (US size 3) needles and yarn A, pick up and k23 [25: 27: 27: 29] sts evenly along right edge of back opening, including edge of neckband.
Work 2nd rib row as on back.
Make 3 buttonholes on next row as foll:
Buttonhole row (RS) Beg at upper edge and keeping rib correct, p1, k1, yo, k2tog, (rib 6 [6: 8: 8: 8], yo, k2tog) twice, rib rem 3 [5: 3: 3: 5] sts.
Work one row more in rib.
Cast (bind) off loosely in rib.
Back button band
On left edge of back opening pick up same number of sts as for buttonhole band.
Work 2nd rib row.
Cast (bind) off loosely in rib.
Sleeve borders
With RS facing, 3mm (US size 3) needles and yarn A, beg at cast-on edge of one sleeve and pick up and k43 [45: 49: 49: 55] sts along RH edge of sleeve.
Beg with 2nd rib row, work 3 rows in rib.

Cast (bind) off loosely in rib.
This completes border on left sleeve.
On right sleeve work border along opposite edge, beg at cast (bound) off edge.
Sew other side edge of each sleeve to sides of armholes, then sew armhole cast (bind) off to first 4 [4: 4: 5: 5] sts on cast-on and cast (bound) off edge of sleeves.
Join side and sleeve seams.
Lap back buttonhole band over button band and a little way over main part of left back.
Slip stitch lower edge in place.
Sew on buttons to left back edge on the pick-up row of band, to correspond with buttonholes.

BABY'S STRIPED SHORTS

The baby's striped shorts are worked in two pieces — back and front. Each piece is worked from side to side, and the waistband and leg borders are worked later.

Sizes

To fit 3 months [6 months: 9 to 12 months: 18 months]
Actual width around hips when completed 56 [60: 64: 68]cm/22 [24: 26: 27]in
Directions for larger sizes are in brackets [ ]; if there is only one set of figures it applies to all sizes.

Materials

PINGOUIN Ondine:
1 [1: 2: 2] balls Blanc No. 01 (A)
Small amount of Rouge No. 10 (B)
Small amount of Citron No. 09 (C)
Small amount of Pacifique No. 25 (D)
Small amount of Prairie No. 14 (E)
Pair each of 3mm and 3¾mm (US sizes 3 and 5) needles
Elastic thread for waistband

Tension (Gauge)

Worked with 3¾mm (US size 5) needles.
St st: 19 sts and 29 rows to 10cm/4in over st st; work a sample on 29 sts.

Stitches used

Stripe pattern

The simple stripe pattern is worked in st st as directed in the instructions.

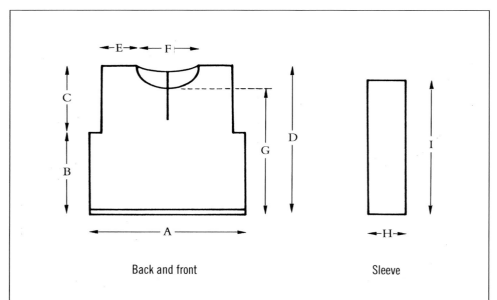

Back and front   Sleeve

Key
A   26.5 [27.5: 30: 32: 33]cm
    10¾ [11: 12: 12¾: 13¼]in
B   14 [15: 16: 17: 18]cm
    5¼ [5¾: 6¼: 6½: 7]in
C   11 [12: 13: 13: 14]cm
    4½ [4¾: 5¼: 5¼: 5½]in
D   25 [27: 29: 30: 32]cm
    9¾ [10½: 11½: 11¾: 12½]in
E   5.5 [5.5: 6: 6.5: 6.5]cm
    2 [2: 2¼: 2½: 2½]in

F   11 [12: 13: 13: 14]cm
    4¼ [4¾: 5: 5: 5½]in
G   21 [23: 24: 25: 26]cm
    8¼ [9: 9½: 9¾: 10¼]in
H   6 [7: 7.5: 9: 9.5]cm
    2½ [3: 3¼: 3½: 3¾]in
I   22.5 [24: 26: 26: 28]cm
    9 [9½: 10½: 10½: 11¼]in

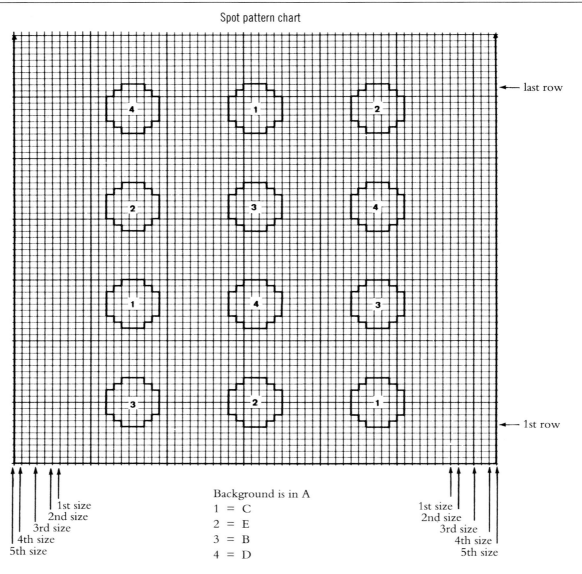

Spot pattern chart

Background is in A
1 = C
2 = E
3 = B
4 = D

Work 2 [4: 2: 4: 6] rows in A before beginning spot motifs, and work 6 [6: 8: 8: 8] rows
in A between the lines of spots.

Instructions

Back

The back is worked from side to side.

Right half back

With 3¾ mm (US size 5) needles and yarn A,
cast on 35 [38: 41: 44] sts and beg stripe patt
as foll:

1st size only:

Working in st st and beg with a k row, work
4 rows A, so ending with a p row.

2nd size only:

Working in st st and beg with a k row, work
6 rows A, so ending with a p row.

3rd size only:

Working in st st and beg with a k row, work
2 rows A, 2 rows E, work 6 rows A, so
ending with a p row.

4th size only:

Working in st st and beg with a k row, work

4 rows A, 2 rows E, work 6 rows A, so
ending with a p row.

All sizes:

Cont in st st throughout, work 2 rows B, 6
rows A, 2 rows C, 6 rows A, 2 rows D, 6
rows A, 2 rows E, 6 rows A, 2 rows B, 3
rows A, so ending with a k row.

Total of 41 [43: 47: 49] rows have been
worked to this point.

Crutch (crotch) shaping

Next row (WS) Using A, p17 [17: 18: 18]
sts, then turn leaving rem 18 [21: 23: 26] sts
on a spare needle.

Cont with these sts only, for leg section.

Using A, cast (bind) off 4 sts at beg of next
row, then p one row.

Using C, cast (bind) off 2 sts at beg of next
row, then p one row.

Using A, cast (bind) off 2 sts at beg of next
row and dec one st at beg of next alt row.

Using A, cast (bind) off rem 8 [8: 9: 9] sts.

This completes right half of back.

Left half of back

With 3¾ mm (US size 5) needles and yarn A,
cast on 8 [8: 8: 9: 9] sts for second leg.

1st row (WS) Using A, p to end.

2nd row Using A, cast on one st, k to end.

3rd row Using A, p to end.

4th row Using C, cast on 2 sts, k to end.

5th row Using C, p to end.

Cont in st st throughout and using A, cast on
2 sts at beg of next row and 4 sts at beg of
next alt row, so ending with a k row. 17 [17:
18: 18] sts.

Next row Using A, p17 [17: 18: 18], then
onto same needle p the 18 [21: 23: 26] sts
which were left on spare needle. 35 [38: 41:
44] sts.

Work 2 rows more in A, so ending with a
p row.

Complete this half without shaping, working
38 [40: 44: 46] rows as foll:

104

1st size only:
Work 2 rows C, 6 rows A, 2 rows D, 6 rows A, 2 rows E, 6 rows A, 2 rows B, 6 rows A, 2 rows C, 4 rows A.

2nd size only:
Work 2 rows C, 6 rows A, 2 rows D, 6 rows A, 2 rows E, 6 rows A, 2 rows B, 6 rows A, 2 rows C, 6 rows A.

3rd size only:
Work 2 rows C, 6 rows A, 2 rows D, 6 rows A, 2 rows E, 6 rows A, 2 rows B, 6 rows A, 2 rows C, 6 rows A, 2 rows D, 2 rows A.

4th size only:
Work 2 rows C, 6 rows A, 2 rows D, 6 rows A, 2 rows E, 6 rows A, 2 rows B, 6 rows A, 2 rows C, 6 rows A, 2 rows D, 4 rows A.

All sizes: Cast (bind) off all sts.

Front

Work front of shorts exactly as given for back of shorts.

Finishing and borders

Press lightly on WS with a cool iron, following instructions on yarn label.

Back waistband
With RS facing, 3mm (US size 3) needles and yarn A, pick up and k48 [50: 54: 56] sts evenly along upper edge of back.
Work 7 rows in k1, p1 rib.
Cast (bind) off loosely in rib.

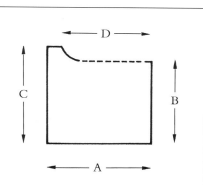

Right half back or Left half front

Key
A 18 [20: 21.5: 23]cm
   7¼ [8: 8½: 9¼]in
B 14 [15: 16: 17]cm
   5½ [6: 6½: 6¾]in
C 17 [17.5: 19: 19.5]cm
   6¾ [7: 7½: 7¾]in
D 14 [15.5: 16.5: 18]cm
   5½ [6¼: 6¾: 7¼]in

Front waistband
Work as for back waistband along upper edge of front.
Join side seams and waistband seams.

Leg border
With RS facing, 3mm (US size 3) needles and yarn A, pick up and k68 [72: 78: 82] sts evenly all around lower edge of one leg and work 4 rows in garter st (k every row).
Cast (bind) off loosely.
Work other leg border in same way.
Join centre back and front seams along shaped edges, then join inner leg seams.
Pass a row of elastic thread through WS of waistband on 2nd and 6th rib rows, securing ends in a seam.

BABY'S BOOTEES

The baby's bootees complete the circle and stripe outfit and the instructions are given for two sizes.

Sizes

To fit 3 months [6 months]
Directions for larger size are in brackets [ ]; if there is only one set of figures it applies to both sizes.

Materials

PINGOUIN Ondine:
1 ball Prairie No. 14 (A)
Small amount of Blanc No. 01 (B)
2 pairs of 3¼mm (US size 3) needles

Tension (Gauge)

Worked with 3¼mm (US size 3) needles.
Garter st: 20 sts and 38 rows to 10cm/4in over g st; work a sample on 30 sts.

Stitches used

The bootees are worked in garter stitch and k1, p1 ribbing.

Instructions

With 3¼mm (US size 3) needles and yarn yarn A, beg at back edge of sole, cast on 10 [12] sts.
Counting first row as RS, work in garter st for 6 [7]cm/2¼ [2¾]in, ending with a WS row. Break off yarn.

Mark centre of cast-on edge, then with RS facing, 3¼mm (US size 3) needles and yarn A, pick up and k4 [5] sts on second half of cast-on edge and 15 [17] sts along one side of sole; working sts of sole with 2nd needle, k4 [5], k2tog, k4 [5]; with 3rd needle pick up and k15 [17] sts along other side of sole and 4 [5] sts on first half of cast-on edge. 47 [55] sts.
Using 4th needle, work in rows of garter st for 3 [5] rows.
Break off yarn and slip off first 19 [22] sts onto another needle, rejoin yarn A and k next 9 [11] sts of toe, then turn leaving rem 19 [22] sts on another needle.
Cont on sole sts only.
Next row K2 [3], sl 1-k1-psso, k1, k2tog, k2 [3].
Cont in garter st and dec at each side of centre st on next 2 [3] alt rows.
K one row on rem 3 sts, then on foll row k these 3 sts tog.
Break off yarn and slip off 4 sts from those rem at each side onto same needle as the centre front st.
With RS facing and yarn B, cont on these 9 sts for instep as foll:
1st row Knit all sts.
2nd row (K1, p1) 4 times, k1.
3rd row (P1, k1) 4 times, p rem st tog with first st of those on needle at side, turn.
4th row (K1, p1) 4 times, k rem st tog with first st at this side, turn.
REp 3rd and 4th rows 7 [9] times more.
Break off yarn and place all rem 23 [25] sts onto one needle.
With RS facing, join on yarn A and work 2 rows in garter st.
Cast (bind) off loosely.
Join back seam neatly.
Work another bootee in same way.

STRIPED PULLOVER WITH CABLE IN FIL D'ECOSSE NO.4

❋❋

Sizes

To fit 81 [86: 91: 96: 102]cm/32 [34: 36: 38: 40]in bust

Actual width around bust when completed 98 [103: 108: 113: 118]cm/39 [41: 43: 45: 47]in

Directions for larger sizes are in brackets [ ]; if there is only one set of figures it applies to all sizes.

Materials

PINGOUIN Fil d'Ecosse No. 4:
5 [6: 6: 7: 7] balls Blanc No. 420 (A)
4 [5: 5: 6: 6] balls Bordeaux No. 441 (B)
Pair each of 3mm and 3¼mm (US sizes 2 and 3) needles
Cable needle (cn)

Tension (Gauge)

Worked with 3¼mm (US size 3) needles.
St st: 24 sts and 32 rows to 10cm/4in over st st; work a sample on 36 sts.

Stitches used

Striped pattern

The striped pattern repeat is worked over 12 rows as foll:
Beg with a k row, work in st st, working
6 rows B, 6 rows A; rep from * to *
throughout.
Note: The cable panel is worked separately and sewn to the front, see instructions.

Instructions

Back

With 3mm (US size 2) needles and yarn A, cast on 101 [107: 111: 117: 123] sts.

1st rib row (RS) P1, *k1, p1; rep from * to end.
2nd rib row K1, *p1, k1; rep from * to end.
Rep these 2 rows until work measures 8cm/ 3in from beg, ending with a first rib row.
Inc row (WS) Keeping rib correct, rib 8 [11: 3: 6: 9], work into front and back of next st, (rib 13 [13: 12: 12: 12], work into front and back of next st) 6 [6: 8: 8: 8] times, rib rem 8 [11: 3: 6: 9] sts. 108 [114: 120: 126: 132] sts.
Change to 3¼mm (US size 3) needles.
Beg with a k row, work in st st in striped patt (see Stitches Used), inc one st at each end of every foll 16th [16th: 16th: 18th: 18th] row 5 times. 118 [124: 130: 136: 142] sts.
Cont in stripe patt without shaping until back measures 38 [39: 40: 41: 42]cm/15 [15¼: 15¾: 16: 16½]in from beg, ending with a p row.
Make a note of the total number or rows worked in striped patt to this point.
Armhole shaping
Keeping stripe patt correct throughout, cast (bind) off 4 sts at beg of next 2 rows, 2 [2: 3: 3: 3] sts at beg of next 2 rows, 2 sts at beg of next 2 [4: 4: 6: 8] rows, then dec one st at beg of next 10 [8: 8: 6: 4] rows, so ending with a p row. 92 [96: 100: 104: 108] sts.★★
Work without shaping until back measures 59 [61: 63: 65: 67]cm/23¼ [24: 24¾: 25½: 26¼]in from beg, ending with a p row.
Shoulder and neck shaping
Cast (bind) off 9 [10: 10: 11: 11] sts at beg of next 2 rows.
Next row (RS) Cast (bind) off 9 [10: 10: 11: 11] sts, k until there are 14 [13: 14: 14: 15] sts on RH needle and leave these sts for right back, cast (bind) off next 28 [30: 32: 32: 34] sts, k to end.
Cont with 23 [23: 24: 25: 26] sts at end of needle only, for left back.
Cast (bind) off 9 [10: 10: 11: 11] sts at beg of next row and 4 sts at neck edge on foll row.
Cast (bind) off rem 10 [9: 10: 10: 11] sts to complete shoulder shaping.
With WS facing, rejoin yarn to neck edge of right back sts and cast (bind) off first 4 sts, p to end.
Cast (bind) off rem 10 [9: 10: 10: 11] sts.

Front

Work front exactly as given for back to ★★.
Neck shaping
Next row (RS) K46 [48: 50: 52: 54] sts, then turn leaving rem sts on a spare needle.
Cont on these sts only, for left front.
***Dec one st at neck edge on every alt row 11 [11: 11: 8: 8] times, then on every foll 3rd row 7 [8: 9: 12: 13] times.
28 [29: 30: 32: 33] sts.
Work without shaping until front is same length as back to beg of armhole shaping,

ending at armhole edge.
Shoulder shaping
Cast (bind) off 9 [10: 10: 11: 11] sts at beg of next row and next alt row.
Work one row without shaping.
Cast (bind) off rem 10 [9: 10: 10: 11] sts.
With RS facing, return to sts left unworked and rejoin correct colour to right front sts, then k to end.
Complete as for left front from *** to end, reversing all shapings.

Sleeves

With 3mm (US size 2) needles and yarn A, cast on 53 [55: 55: 55: 57] sts and work in rib as on back for 7 rows, so ending with a first rib row.
Inc row Keeping rib correct, (rib 12 [17: 13: 13: 13], work into front and back of next st) 3 [2: 3: 3: 3] times, rib rem 14 [19: 13: 13: 15] sts. 56 [57: 58: 58: 60] sts.
Change to 3¼mm (US size 3) needles.
Beg with a k row, work in st st in striped patt, inc one st at each end of every foll 6th row 18 [16: 13: 11: 8] times, then on every foll 4th row 1 [5: 10: 14: 19] times. 94 [99: 104: 108: 114] sts.
Work without shaping until 24 rows more have been worked than the total worked on back to armhole; the striped patt thus matches back at this point.
Top of sleeve shaping
Cast (bind) off 4 sts at beg of next 2 rows, 2 [2: 3: 3: 3] sts at beg of next 2 rows and 2 sts at beg of next 2 [4: 4: 6: 8] rows.
Dec one st at each end of every alt row 12 [12: 13: 14: 14] times.
Cast (bind) off 2 sts at beg of next 12 [12: 12: 10: 10] rows and 3 sts at beg of next 4 rows.
Cast (bind) off rem 18 [19: 20: 22: 24] sts.

Cable panel

With 3¼mm (US size 3) needles and yarn B, cast on 10 sts, then onto same needle cast on 10 sts using yarn A.
Beg cable panel as foll:
1st row (RS) With A, p1, p1, k8, twist B around A, with B, k8, p1, k1.
2nd row With B, k2, p8, twist A around B, with A, p8, k2.
3rd–18th rows Rep first and 2nd rows 8 times.
19th row With A, k1, p1, slip next 8 sts onto cn and hold at front of work, k next 8 sts in B, then with A, k8 from cn, p1, k1.
20th row With A, k2, p8, twist yarns, with B, p8, k2.
21st row With B, k1, p1, k8, twist yarns, with A, k8, p1, k1.
22nd–37th rows Rep 20th and 21st rows 8 times.

38th row As 20th row.

39th row With B, k1, p1, slip next 8 sts onto cn and hold at front of work, k next 8 sts in A, then with B, k8 from cn, p1, k1.

40th row As 2nd row.

These 40 rows form one patt repeat.

Cont in patt until panel measures 35 [36: 37: 38: 39]cm/14 [14¼: 14¾: 15: 15½]in from beg, ending with a RS row.

Divide for neck

Next row (WS) Using correct colour, k2, p8, turn leaving rem 10 sts on a st holder. Cont on these sts only.

Next row (RS) Cast on one st and k this st, k8, p1, k1. 11 sts.

Next row K2, p8, k1.

Next row K9, p1, k1.

Rep last 2 rows until this section fits up right front neck edge to top of shoulder and to centre back neck.

Break off yarn, leaving sufficient yarn for adjustment of length and place sts on a st holder.

Using correct colour for the other half of panel, cast on one st onto a 3¼mm (US size 3) needle and with this needle in right hand and with WS of rem sts facing, p8, k2.

Next row (RS) K1, p1, k9.

Next row K1, p8, k2.

Rep last 2 rows until this section is same length as first section.

Leave sts on a st holder.

Finishing

Press all pieces (except cable panel) lightly on WS with a cool iron, following instructions on yarn label and avoiding ribbing.
Join shoulder seams and sew in sleeves.
Join side and sleeve seams, matching stripes.
With WS of cable panel to RS of pullover, pin panel to centre of front, beg on first row of striped patt and ensuring that the row where sts were divided is level with first row of front neck shaping. Pin neck border sections along sides of front neck (having inner edges level), then pin them across back neck. Adjust length if necessary so that ends of these borders meet at centre back, then cast (bind) off tightly. Join these ends, then slip stitch panel and borders in place, taking small neat sts into the garter st edges.

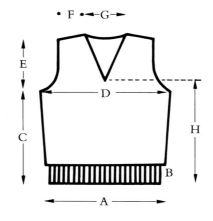

Back and front

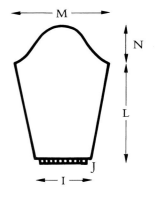

Sleeve

Key

A 45 [47.5: 50: 52.5: 55]cm
   18 [19: 20: 21: 22]in

B 8cm
   3in

C 35 [39: 40: 41: 42]cm
   15 [15¼: 15¾: 16: 16½]in

D 49 [51.5: 54: 56.5: 59]cm
   19½ [20½: 21½: 22½: 23½]in

E 21 [22: 23: 24: 25]cm
   8¼ [8¾: 9: 9½: 9¾]in

F 11.5 [12: 12.5: 13: 13.5]cm
   4½ [4¾: 5: 5: 5¼]in

G 15 [15.5: 16.5: 16.5: 17.5]cm
   5¾ [6: 6½: 6½: 6¾]in

H 43 [44: 45: 46: 47]cm
   17 [17¼: 17¾: 18: 18½]in

I 23 [23.5: 24: 24: 25]cm
   9¼ [9½: 9¾: 9¾: 10]in

J 2.5cm
   1in

L 40 [41: 42: 43: 44]cm
   15¾ [16: 16½: 17: 17¼]in

M 39 [41: 43: 45: 47.5]cm
   15½ [16½: 17¼: 18: 19]in

N 14 [15: 15.5: 16: 16.5]cm
   5½ [5¾: 6: 6¼: 6½]in

DIAMOND CARDIGAN
IN TEMPO

✳✳✳

Sizes

To fit 81 [86 to 91: 96: 102]cm/32 [34 to 36: 38: 40]in bust
Actual width around bust (buttoned) 99 [106.5: 113.5: 121]cm/39½ [42½: 45¼: 48¼]in
Directions for larger sizes are in brackets [ ]; if there is only one set of figures it applies to all sizes.

Materials

PINGOUIN Tempo:
8 [9: 10: 11] balls Noir No. 20 (A)
Small ball Blanc No. 01 (B)
1 ball Ble No. 264 (C)
1 ball Cardinal No. 66 (D)
1 ball Tropiques No. 72 (E)
Pair each of 3mm and 4mm (US sizes 3 and 6) needles
9 buttons

Tension (Gauge)

Worked with 4mm (US size 6) needles.
St st: 22 sts and 28 rows to 10cm/4in over st st; work a sample on 32 sts.

Stitches used

Colourwork pattern

The colourwork pattern on the fronts is worked in st st using the intarsia method. Use a separate small ball of yarn for each area of colour, twisting yarns when changing colours to avoid creating holes.
Follow the chart for the diamond motifs, positioning them as directed in the instructions.

Instructions

Back

With 3mm (US size 3) needles and yarn A, cast on 107 [115: 123: 131] sts and beg rib as foll:
★★1st rib row (RS) P1, ★k1, p1; rep from ★ to end.
2nd rib row K1, ★p1, k1; rep from ★ to end.
Rep these 2 rows until work measures 6 [7: 7: 8]cm/2¼ [2¾: 2¾: 3]in from beg, ending with a 2nd rib row.★★
Change to 4mm (US size 6) needles.
Beg with a k row and working in st st throughout, work without shaping until back measures 32 [33: 34: 35]cm/12½ [12¾: 13¼: 13½]in from beg, ending with a p row.
Armhole shaping
Cast (bind) off 6 [7: 7: 8] sts at beg of next 2 rows. 95 [101: 109: 115] sts.
Work without shaping until back measures 55 [57: 58: 60]cm/21½ [22¼: 22¾: 23½]in from beg, ending with a p row.
Neck shaping
Next row (RS) K32 [34: 37: 39] sts and slip these sts onto a spare needle, cast (bind) off next 31 [33: 35: 37] sts, k to end.
Cont with rem 32 [34: 37: 39] sts only, for left back.
Dec one st at neck edge on next 2 rows.
Cast (bind) off rem 30 [32: 35: 37] sts for shoulder edge.
With WS facing, rejoin yarn to neck edge of right back sts and dec one st, then p to end.
Dec one st at neck edge on next row.
Cast (bind) off rem 30 [32: 35: 37] sts for shoulder edge.

Right front

With 3mm (US size 3) needles and yarn A, cast on 53 [57: 61: 65] sts and work as for back ribbing from ★★ to ★★.
Change to 4mm (US size 6) needles.
Beg with a k row and working in st st throughout, beg patt from chart on next row as foll:
1st chart row (RS) K14 [16: 18: 20] sts, place a st marker on RH needle to indicate beg of chart patt, then working from chart k7 A, join on B, k5 B, 1 A, 5 B, then k7 A to complete chart, place another st marker on RH needle to indicate end of chart patt, k14 [16: 18: 20] A.
2nd chart row Twisting yarns around each other when changing colours, p14 [16: 18: 20] A, slip marker, then working from chart p7 A, 5 B, 1 A, 5 B, 7 A, slip marker, p14 [16: 18: 20] A.
Note: Slip markers on every row until patt is established when they can be removed.
3rd chart row K14 [16: 18: 20 A, then from

chart k8 A, 3 B, 3 A, 3 B, 8 A, then k14 [16: 18: 20] A.
Cont working from chart (joining on a ball of C on 7th row, then on 13th row joining on an extra ball of A for sts beyond diamond) until front is same length as back to beg of armhole shaping, but ending with a k row.
Armhole shaping
Cont to work from chart as set until chart is completed, cast (bind) off 6 [7: 7: 8] sts at beg of next row. 47 [50: 54: 57] sts.
Work without shaping until front measures 48 [50: 51: 53]cm/19 [19¾: 20¼: 21]in from beg, ending at straight centre front edge.
Neck shaping
Cast (bind) off 6 [7: 8: 9] sts at beg of next row (neck edge) and 2 sts at same edge on next 3 alt rows, then dec one st at neck edge on next 5 alt rows. 30 [32: 35: 37] sts.
Work without shaping until front is same length as back to shoulder edge.
Cast (bind) off all sts.

Left front

Work left front as given for right front, but reversing all shapings.

Sleeves

With 3mm (US size 3) needles and yarn A, cast on 51 [53: 53: 55] sts and work as for back ribbing from ★★ to ★★, but ending with a first (RS) rib row.
Inc row (WS) Keeping rib correct, rib 4 [5: 5: 3], (work into front and back of next st, rib 6) 6 [6: 6: 7] times, work into front and back of next st, rib rem 4 [5: 5: 2] sts. 58 [60: 60: 63] sts.
Change to 4mm (US size 6) needles.
Beg with a k row, work in st st, inc one st at each end of every foll 4th row 22 [19: 22: 19] times, then on every foll 3rd row 2 [6: 3: 7] times. 106 [110: 110: 115] sts.
Cont in st st without shaping until sleeve measures 49 [50: 51: 52]cm/19¼ [19½: 20: 20½]in from beg.
Cast (bind) off all sts.

Finishing and borders

Press lightly on WS with a cool iron, following instructions on yarn label and avoiding ribbing.
Join shoulder seams.
Neckband
With RS facing, 3mm (US size 3) needles and yarn A, pick up and k26 [27: 28: 29] sts evenly up right front neck edge, 37 [39: 41: 43] sts across back neck and 26 [27: 28: 29] sts down left front neck edge. 89 [93: 97: 101] sts.

Beg with 2nd rib row, work 8 rows in rib as on back.
Cast (bind) off loosely in rib.

Buttonhole band
With RS facing, 3mm (US size 5) needles and yarn A, pick up and k131 [137: 139: 145] sts evenly along straight centre front edge of right front, including edge of neckband.
Beg with 2nd rib row, work 3 rows in rib as on back, so ending with a WS row.

1st buttonhole row (RS) Beg at lower edge and keeping rib correct, rib 5 [4: 5: 4] sts, cast (bind) off 2, ★rib until there are 13 [14: 14: 15] sts on RH needle after buttonhole, cast off 2;★ rep from ★ to ★ 7 times more, rib to end.

2nd buttonhole row Work in rib, casting on 2 sts over each buttonhole.
Work 3 rows more in rib.
Cast (bind) off loosely in rib.

Button band
Work button band on left front as for buttonhole band (working 8 rows in rib), but omitting buttonholes.
Sew cast (bound) off edge of sleeves to sides of armholes and sew armhole cast (bind) off to last 7 [8: 8: 10] rows on sides of sleeves.
Join side and sleeve seams.
Sew on the buttons to correspond with the buttonholes.

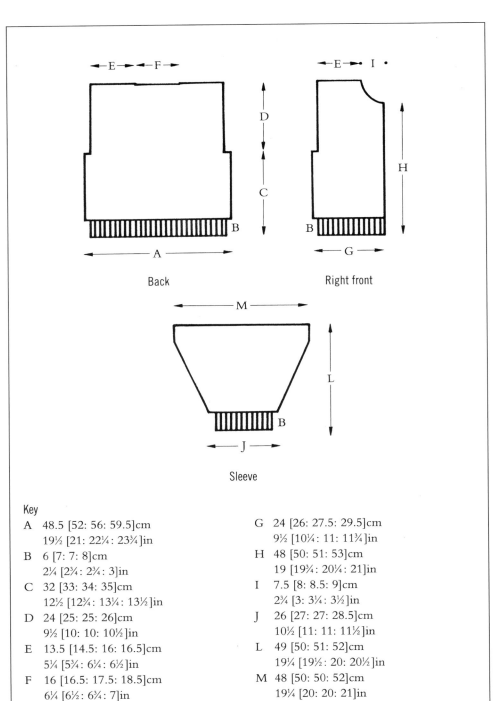

Back

Right front

Sleeve

Key

A 48.5 [52: 56: 59.5]cm
    19½ [21: 22¼: 23¾]in
B 6 [7: 7: 8]cm
    2¼ [2¾: 2¾: 3]in
C 32 [33: 34: 35]cm
    12½ [12¾: 13¼: 13½]in
D 24 [25: 25: 26]cm
    9½ [10: 10: 10½]in
E 13.5 [14.5: 16: 16.5]cm
    5¼ [5¾: 6¼: 6½]in
F 16 [16.5: 17.5: 18.5]cm
    6¼ [6½: 6¾: 7]in

G 24 [26: 27.5: 29.5]cm
    9½ [10¼: 11: 11¾]in
H 48 [50: 51: 53]cm
    19 [19¾: 20¼: 21]in
I 7.5 [8: 8.5: 9]cm
    2¾ [3: 3¼: 3½]in
J 26 [27: 27: 28.5]cm
    10½ [11: 11: 11½]in
L 49 [50: 51: 52]cm
    19¼ [19½: 20: 20½]in
M 48 [50: 50: 52]cm
    19¼ [20: 20: 21]in

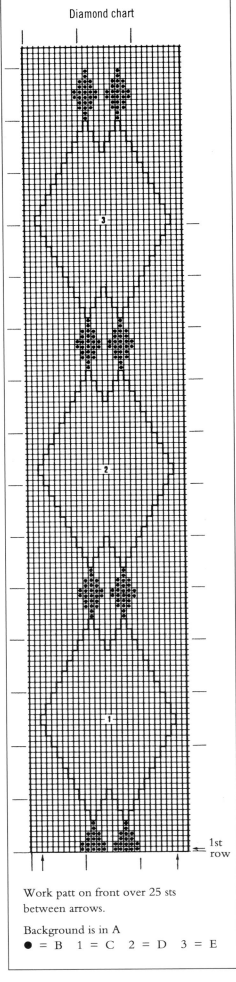

Diamond chart

1st row

Work patt on front over 25 sts between arrows.

Background is in A
● = B   1 = C   2 = D   3 = E

CHILD'S STRIPED PULLOVER IN CORRIDA 4

*

Sizes

To fit ages 6 [8: 10: 12: 14] years or 63 [68: 72: 76: 81]cm/25 [27: 28½: 30: 32]in chest
Actual width around chest when completed 79 [83: 89: 93: 99]cm/31½ [33: 35½: 37: 39½]in
Directions for larger sizes are in brackets [ ]; if there is only one set of figures it applies to all sizes.

Materials

PINGOUIN Corrida 4:
5 [6: 7: 7: 8] balls Blanc No. 501 (A)
2 balls Indigo No. 559 (B)
Pair each of 3¼mm and 4mm (US sizes 3 and 6) needles
Cable needle (cn)

Tension (Gauge)

Worked with 4mm (US size 6) needles.
St st: 20 sts and 28 rows to 10cm/4in over st st; work a sample on 28 sts.

Stitches used

The pullover is worked in st-st stripes with k1, p1 ribbing. The directions for these stitches are given in the instructions.

Instructions

Back

With 3¼mm (US size 3) needles and yarn B, cast on 75 [79: 85: 89: 95] sts and beg rib as foll:
1st rib row (RS) P1, *k1, p1; rep from * to end.
2nd rib row K1, *p1, k1; rep from * to end.
Rep these 2 rows once more.

Change to 4mm (US size 6) needles and yarn A.
Beg with a k row, work in st st, working 10 rows A, 4 rows B and 9 rows A, so ending with a k row.
Now complete side openings as foll:
Break off yarn and onto free needle cast on 2 sts using A, take needle in right hand and p sts of main part, then cast on 2 sts at end of needle. 79 [83: 89: 93: 99] sts.
Cont in st st, work (4 rows B, 10 rows A) 3 times, then work 4 rows B.
This completes striped panel.
Break off B and cont in A only.
Work in st st without shaping until back measures 36 [39: 42: 44: 47]cm/14 [15¼: 16½: 17¼: 18½]in from beg, ending with a p row.
Change to 3¼mm (US size 3) needles.
Work 3 rows in rib as at beg of back.
Cast (bind) off loosely in rib.

Front

Work front of pullover exactly as given for back of pullover.

Yokes

The yoke is worked in 3 sections: one back yoke which goes from shoulder to shoulder and two front yokes which go from shoulder to neck edge.
Back yoke
With 3¼mm (US size 3) needles and yarn A, cast on 21 [21: 21: 25: 25] sts and work in k1, p1 rib as on back until this section fits across upper edge of back.
Cast (bind) off loosely in rib.
Left front yoke
With 3¼mm (US size 3) needles and yarn A, cast on 21 [21: 21: 25: 25] sts and work in k1, p1 rib as on back for 13 [13.5: 15: 15.5: 16.5]cm/5 [5¼: 5¾: 6: 6½]in.
Cast off loosely in rib.
Right front yoke
Work right front yoke as for left front yoke.

Sleeves

With 3¼mm (US size 3) needles and yarn B, cast on 39 [41: 43: 45: 47] sts and work in rib as on back for 4 rows, inc one st at centre of last row and so ending with a 2nd rib row. 40 [42: 44: 46: 48] sts.
Change to 4mm (US size 6) needles and yarn A.
Beg with a k row and working in st st throughout, (work 10 rows A, 4 rows B) 4 times, then cont in A for remainder of sleeve, **and at the same time** inc one st at each end of every foll 6th row 3 [6: 9: 12: 15] times, then on every foll 4th row 13 [11: 9: 7: 5]

times. 72 [76: 80: 84: 88] sts.
Work without shaping until sleeve measures
29 [33: 37: 41: 45]cm/11½ [13: 14½: 16:
17¾]in from beg.
Cast (bind) off all sts.

Finishing and side borders

Press lightly on WS with a cool iron,
following instructions on yarn label and
avoiding ribbing.
Sew one side edge of back yoke to upper
edge of back, stitching underneath the ribbed
border. Pin front yokes to upper edge of
front underneath the ribbed border, having
cast-on edge of each yoke level with outer
edge and leaving approx 13 [14: 15: 16:
17]cm/5 [5½: 5¾: 6¼: 6½]in free at centre
for neckline. Sew these yokes in place.
Side borders
With RS facing, 3¼mm (US size 3) needles
and yarn B, pick up and k27 sts along one
side edge of back as far as the row where 2 sts
were cast on. Beg with 2nd rib row, work 3
rows in rib as on back.
Cast off loosely in rib.
Work a similar border on other side of back
and on both sides of front. Then sew upper
edges of these borders to cast-on edges.
Join upper edges of front yokes to upper edge
of back yoke for shoulder seams, leaving
neckline free.
On each side edge, mark a point 18 [19: 20:
21: 22]cm/7¼ [7½: 8: 8¼: 8¾]in below
shoulder seam for armholes and sew cast
(bound) off edge of sleeves between markers,
catching in sides of upper border on front
and back in these seams.
Join side and sleeve seams, matching stripes
and leaving side borders at lower edges of
back and front open.

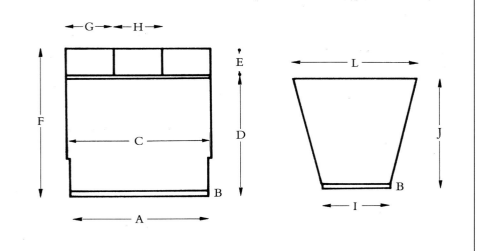

Back and front   Sleeve

Key

A   37.5 [39.5: 42.5: 44.5: 47.5]cm
    15 [15¾: 17: 17¾: 19]in
B   1.5cm
    ½in
C   39.5 [41.5: 44.5: 46.5: 49.5]cm
    15¾ [16½: 17¾: 18½: 19¾]in
D   36 [39: 42: 44: 47]cm
    14 [15¼: 16½: 17¼: 18½]in
E   8 [8: 8: 9: 9]cm
    3 [3: 3: 3½: 3½]in
F   44 [47: 50: 53: 56]cm
    17 [18¼: 19½: 20¾: 22]in

G   13 [13.5: 15: 15.5: 16.5]cm
    5 [5¼: 5¾: 6: 6½]in
H   13 [14: 15: 16: 17]cm
    5 [5½: 5¾: 6¼: 6½]in
I   20 [21: 22: 23: 24]cm
    8 [8½: 8¾: 9¼: 9½]in
J   29 [33: 37: 41: 45]cm
    11½ [13: 14½: 16: 17¾]in
L   36 [38: 40: 42: 44]cm
    14½ [15¼: 16: 16¾: 17½]in

DIAMOND AND ZIGZAG PULLOVER

IN TEMPO

✳✳

Sizes

To fit 81 to 86 [91: 96]cm/32 to 34 [36: 38]in bust

Actual width around bust when pullover has been completed 103 [108: 114]cm/41 [43: 45½]in

Directions for larger sizes are in brackets [ ]; if there is only one set of figures it applies to all sizes.

Materials

PINGOUIN Tempo:
8 [9: 10] balls Noir No. 20 (A)
2 balls Bourgogne No. 23 (B)
1 ball Ble No. 264 (C)
1 ball Bouteille No. 24 (D)
1 ball Cobalt No. 55 (E)
Pair each of 3¼mm and 4mm (US sizes 3 and 6) needles

Tension (Gauge)

Worked with 4mm (US size 6) needles.
St st: 22 sts and 28 rows to 10cm/4in over st st; work a sample on 32 sts.

Stitches used

Colourwork pattern

The colourwork pattern on the back and front is worked in st st using the intarsia method.
Use a separate small ball of yarn for each area of colour, twisting yarns when changing colours to avoid creating holes.
Follow the instructions for the first band of colour and follow the chart for the remainder of the colourwork pattern.

Instructions

Back

With 3¼mm (US size 3) needles and yarn A, cast on 113 [119: 125] sts and beg rib as foll:
1st rib row (RS) P1, *k1, p1; rep from * to end.
2nd rib row K1, *p1, k1; rep from * to end.
Rep these 2 rows twice more, so ending with a WS row.
Change to 4mm (US size 6) needles.
Beg with a k row, work in st st for 4 [6: 8] rows, so ending with a p row.
Break off yarn A.
Using 3 small balls of yarn B and 2 small balls of yarn D, beg first band of colour on next row as foll:
1st row (RS) Join on B, k22 [25: 25] in B, join on D, k23 [23: 25] D, join on B, k23 [23: 25] B, join on D, k23 [23: 25] D, join on B, k22 [25: 25] B.
2nd row P22 [25: 25] B, 23 [23: 25] D, 23 [23: 25] B, 23 [23: 25] D, 22 [25: 25] B.
3rd-10th rows Rep first and 2nd rows 4 times more.
Break off balls of yarn.
Using yarn A and beg with a k row, work 8 [8: 10] rows in st st.
Joining on colours as required, beg working patt from chart on next row as foll:
1st chart row (RS) K8 [11: 14] A, *join on C, k1 C, 15 A;* rep from * to * 5 times more, join on C, k1 C, 8 [11: 14] A.
2nd chart row P7 [10: 13] A, *3 C, then 13 A;* rep from * to * 5 times more, p3 C, then p7 [10: 13] A.
Cont in st st throughout, work in patt as now set until diamonds are completed on 26th chart row.
27th-30th chart rows Work 4 rows in st st in A only.
31st chart row K 0 [1: 4], 3 [5: 5] E, *11 A, 5 E;* rep from * to * 5 times more, k11 A, 3 [5: 5] E, 0 [1: 4] A.
32nd-36th rows Work in patt as set, foll chart.
37th-40th chart rows Work 4 rows in A only.
41st chart row K8 [11: 14] A, *1 B, 15 A;* rep from * to * 5 times more, k1 B, 8 [11: 14] A.
42nd chart row P7 [10: 13] A, *3B, 13A;* rep from * to * 5 times more, p3 B, 7 [10: 13] A.
Cont working from chart as now set until 51st chart row has been completed.
52-62nd chart rows Work 11 rows in B only.
Break off B and change to A for remainder of back.
Work without shaping until back measures 54 [56: 58]cm/21¼ [22: 22¾]in from beg, ending with a p row.

Neck shaping
Beg neck shaping on next row as foll:
Next row (RS) K41 [43: 45] sts and slip these sts onto a spare needle, cast (bind) off next 31 [33: 35] sts, k to end.
Cont with these rem 41 [43: 45] sts only, for left back.
P one row.
Cast (bind) off 5 sts at beg of next row (neck edge), then dec one st at neck edge on next 2 rows. 34 [36: 38] sts.
Work one row without shaping.
Cast (bind) off all sts for shoulder edge.
With WS facing, rejoin yarn to neck edge of right back sts and cast (bind) off first 5 sts, p to end.
Dec one st at neck edge on next 2 rows. 34 [36: 38] sts.
Work 2 rows without shaping.
Cast (bind) off all sts for shoulder edge.

Front

Work as given for back until front measures 49 [51: 53]cm/19¼ [20: 20¾]in from beg, ending with a p row.
Neck shaping
Beg neck shaping on next row as foll:
Next row (RS) K48 [50: 52] sts and slip these sts onto a spare needle, cast (bind) off next 17 [19: 21] sts, k to end.
Cont with these rem 48 [50: 52] sts only, for right front.
P one row.
Cast (bind) off 4 sts at beg of next row (neck edge) and 2 sts at same edge on next 3 alt rows, then dec one st at neck edge on next 4 alt rows. 34 [36: 38] sts.
Work 3 rows without shaping.
Cast (bind) off all sts for shoulder edge.
With WS facing, rejoin yarn to neck edge of left front sts and cont as for right front from ** to **.
Work 4 rows without shaping.
Cast (bind) off all sts for shoulder edge to complete front.

Sleeves

With 3¼mm (US size 3) needles and yarn A, cast on 51 [55: 57] sts and work 6 rows in rib as on back, but inc one st at centre of last row for first size only, so ending with a WS row. 52 [55: 57] sts.
Change to 4mm (US size 6) needles.
Beg with a k row, work in st st, inc one st at each end of every foll 4th row 27 [28: 29] times. 106 [111: 115] sts.
Work in st st without shaping until sleeve measures 45 [46: 47]cm/17¾ [18: 18½]in from beg.
Cast (bind) off all sts.

Finishing and neckband

Press lightly on WS with a cool iron, following instructions on yarn label and avoiding ribbing.
Join right shoulder seam.

Neckband

With RS facing, 3¼mm (US size 3) needles and yarn A, pick up and k61 [63: 65] sts evenly around front neck edge and 48 [50: 52] sts across back neck. 109 [113: 117] sts. Beg with a 2nd row, work 8 rows in rib as on back.
Cast (bind) off loosely in rib.
Join left shoulder seam and neckband seam. Sew cast (bound) off edge of sleeves to sides of the section worked in A after last row of chart. Join side and sleeve seams.

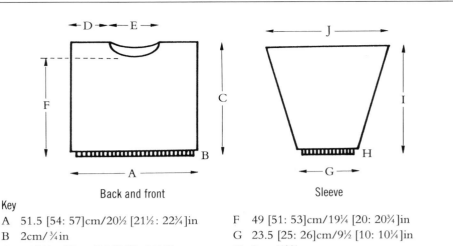

Back and front

Sleeve

Key

A	51.5 [54: 57]cm/20½ [21½: 22¾]in
B	2cm/¾in
C	56 [58: 60]cm/22 [22¾: 23½]in
D	15.5 [16.5: 17]cm/6¼ [6½: 7]in
E	20.5 [21: 23]cm/8 [8½: 8¾]in

F	49 [51: 53]cm/19¼ [20: 20¾]in
G	23.5 [25: 26]cm/9½ [10: 10¼]in
H	3cm/1¼in
I	45 [46: 47]cm/17¾ [18: 18½]in
J	48 [50.5: 52]cm/19¼ [20: 21]in

Pattern chart

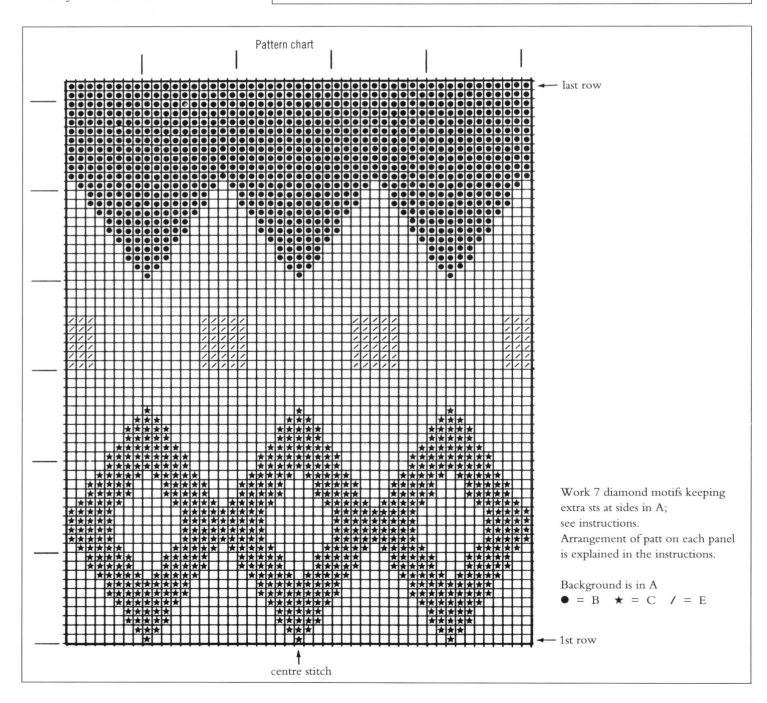

last row

1st row

centre stitch

Work 7 diamond motifs keeping extra sts at sides in A;
see instructions.
Arrangement of patt on each panel is explained in the instructions.

Background is in A
● = B   ★ = C   / = E

COUNTRY
CLASSICS

These last six designs are perfect for winter sport and would make treasured Christmas presents. The man's cable and stripe crewneck and all three women's sweaters suit all age groups – from teens to the over eighties. Especially eye-catching are the woman's bobble and cable Aran pullover and the child's Aran cardigan, both inspired by traditional Irish fishermen's sweaters. Designers continue to find endless variations for those delightful Aran textures.

SIMPLE RIBBED TURTLENECK IN SOFT'HAIR

*

Sizes

To fit 81 [86 to 91: 96: 102: 107 to 112]cm/ 32 [34 to 36: 38: 40: 42 to 44]in bust
Actual width around bust when completed 102 [109: 113: 121: 128]cm/40½ [44: 45: 48: 51½]in

Directions for larger sizes are in brackets [ ]; if there is only one set of figures it applies to all sizes.

Materials

PINGOUIN Soft'Hair:
5 [5: 5: 6: 6] balls Ecru No. 21 or Amande No. 28 (A)
5 [5: 5: 6: 6] balls Vison No. 37 (B)
3 balls Tempete No. 49 (C)
Pair each of 3¾mm, 4mm and 4½mm (US sizes 5, 6 and 7) needles
4.00mm (US size F/5) crochet hook

Tension (Gauge)

Worked with 4½mm (US size 7) needles.
Rib patt: 21 sts and 30 rows to 10cm/4in over rib patt; work a sample on 31 sts as foll:
On first row work (p3, k1) 7 times, p3, to form a foundation row, then work in patt beg with a 2nd rib patt row.

Stitches used

Special abbreviations

k1 below – insert RH needle from front to back through st below next st on LH needle and knit this st, allowing st above to drop off LH needle as st is completed.

Rib pattern

Work the rib pattern over a multiple of 4 sts plus 3 extra sts as foll:

1st row (RS) P3, ★k1 below, p3;★ rep from ★ to ★.
2nd row ★K3, p1;★ rep from ★ to ★, ending k3.
These 2 rows form one patt repeat.
Note: During shapings do not k below on st which comes at side edge. Always work cast (bind) offs in patt and when casting (binding) off in patt on a RS row, work k1 normally instead of k1 below during cast (bind) off.

Instructions

Back

With 3¾mm (US size 5) needles and yarn C, cast on 107 [115: 119: 127: 135] sts and beg k1, p1 rib as foll:
1st rib row (RS) P1, ★k1, p1; rep from ★ to end.
2nd rib row K1, ★p1, k1; rep from ★ to end.
Rep these 2 rows until work measures 8cm/ 3in from beg, ending with a 2nd rib row.
Change to 4½mm (US size 7) needles.
Work in rib patt (see Stitches Used) until back measures 18 [19: 20: 21: 22]cm/7 [7½: 7¾: 8¼: 8½]in from beg, ending with a 2nd (WS) patt row.
Break off yarn C and change to yarn B.
K one row (RS).
Beg with a 2nd patt row, cont in patt until back measures 44 [45: 46: 47: 48]cm/17¼ [17¾: 18: 18½: 18¾]in, ending with a 2nd (WS) patt row.
Break off yarn B and change to yarn A.
K one row (RS).
Beg with a 2nd patt row, cont in patt until back measures 64 [66: 67: 69: 71]cm/25 [26: 26½: 27: 27¾]in from beg, ending with a 2nd (WS) patt row.
Shoulder and neck shaping
Keeping patt correct as set throughout, cast (bind) off 8 [9: 9: 10: 11] sts at beg of next 2 rows.
Beg neck shaping on next row as foll:
Next row (RS) Cast (bind) off 8 [9: 9: 10: 11] sts, work in patt until there are 24 [25: 27: 28: 29] sts on RH needle and leave these sts for right back, cast (bind) off next 27 [29: 29: 31: 33] sts, work in patt to end.
Cont with 32 [34: 36: 38: 40] sts at end of needle only, for left back.
Cast (bind) off 8 [9: 9: 10: 11] sts at beg of next row and 4 sts at neck edge on foll row; rep last 2 rows again.
Cast (bind) off rem 8 [8: 10: 10: 10] sts to complete shoulder shaping.
With WS facing, rejoin yarn to neck edge of right back sts and cast (bind) off first 4 sts, then work in patt to end.
Cast (bind) off 8 [9: 9: 10: 11] sts at beg of next row and 4 sts at neck edge on foll row.
Cast (bind) off rem 8 [8: 10: 10: 10] sts.

Front

Work as given for back until front measures 57 [59: 60: 61: 63]cm/22¼ [23¼: 23¾: 24: 24¾]in from beg, ending with a 2nd (WS) patt row.
Neck shaping
Beg neck shaping on next row as foll:
Next row (RS) Work 44 [47: 49: 53: 56] sts sts in patt, then turn leaving rem sts on a spare needle.
Cont on these sts only, for left front.
★★Cast (bind) off 3 sts at beg of next row (neck edge) and 2 sts at same edge on next 2 alt rows, then dec one st at neck edge on next 5 [5: 5: 6: 6] alt rows. 32 [35: 37: 40: 43] sts.
Work without shaping until front is same length as back to beg of shoulder shaping, ending at armhole edge.
Shoulder shaping
Cast (bind) off 8 [9: 9: 10: 11] sts at beg of next row and next 2 alt rows.
Work one row without shaping.
Cast (bind) off rem 8 [8: 10: 10: 10] sts.
With RS facing, return to sts left unworked and slip first 19 [21: 21: 21: 23] sts (centre front sts) onto a st holder, rejoin yarn to rem 44 [47: 49: 53: 56] sts of right front and complete as for left front from ★★ to end, reversing shapings.

Sleeves

With 3¾mm (US size 5) needles and yarn C, cast on 53 [55: 55: 57: 59] sts and work in k1, p1 rib as on back, beg with a 2nd [first: first: 2nd: first] rib row, for 3cm/1¼in, ending with a first [2nd: 2nd: first: 2nd] rib row.
Change to 4½mm (US size 7) needles.
Beg rib patt on next row as foll:
1st row (RS) P2 [3: 3: 2: 3], rep from ★ to ★ in first rib patt row, ending k1 below, p2 [3: 3: 2: 3].
2nd row K2 [3: 3: 2: 3], p1, rep from ★ to ★ in 2nd rib patt row, ending k2 [3: 3: 2: 3].
Cont in patt as now set for 3 [1: 3: 1: 1] rows more.
Working extra sts into patt, cont in patt, inc one st at each end of next row, then on every foll 4th row 27 [29: 29: 30: 31] times, **and at the same time** cont in yarn C until sleeve measures 18 [19: 20: 21: 22]cm/7 [7½: 7¾: 8¼: 8½]in from beg (ending with a WS row), change to yarn B and k one row (RS), then cont in patt.
When incs are completed, work in patt without shaping on 109 [115: 115: 119: 123] sts until sleeve measures 45 [46: 47: 48: 49]cm/17¾ [18: 18½: 18¾: 19¼]in from beg, ending with a RS row.
Cast (bind) off all sts in patt.

Finishing and collar

Do not press. Collar is made in two sections before shoulder seams are joined.

Front collar

With RS facing, 4mm (US size 6) needles and yarn A, pick up and k20 [20: 21: 25: 25] sts evenly down left front neck edge, work in patt across 19 [21: 21: 21: 23] sts from st holder, then pick up and k20 [20: 21: 25: 25] sts up right front neck. 59 [61: 63: 71: 73] sts. Beg rib patt on next row as foll:

Next row (WS) P0 [1: 0: 0: 1], *k3, p1;* rep from * to *, ending k3 [0: 3: 3: 0].

Next row (RS) K0 [1: 0: 0: 1], p3, *k1 below, p3;* rep from * to *, ending k0 [1: 0: 0: 1].

The last 2 rows set the rib patt which coincides with rib patt on centre sts of front. Cont in patt as now set for 5cm/2in, ending with a 2nd (WS) patt row.

Now beg rib patt again with another 2nd (WS) patt row to reverse patt and cont for 8cm/3in, then change to 4½mm (US size 7) needles and cont in patt until collar measures 25cm/10in from beg, ending with a first (RS) patt row.

Cast (bind) off loosely in patt.

Back collar

With RS facing, 4mm (US size 6) needles and yarn A, pick up and k43 [45: 45: 47: 49] sts evenly across back neck, taking care to pick up and k one st in every cast (bound) off st.

Beg rib patt on next row as foll:

Next row (WS) K3 [0: 2: 3: 0], p1, *k3, p1;* rep from * to *, ending k3 [0: 2: 3: 0].

Next row (RS) K0 [1: 0: 0: 1], p3 [3: 2: 3: 3], *k1 below, p3;* rep from * to *, ending k1 below, p3 for first size only [k1 for 2nd size only: k1 below, p2 for 3rd size only: k1 below, p3 for 4th size only: k1 for 5th size only].

Keeping patt correct as now set, work as for front collar.

Join shoulder seams, matching patt and cont seams along sides of collar for 5cm/2in, then join remainder of collar seams on reverse side.

On each side edge of back and front mark a point 26 [27: 27: 28: 29]cm/10¼ [11: 11: 11¼: 11¾]in below shoulder seams for armholes and sew cast (bound) off edge of sleeves between these points.

Join side and sleeve seams.

Fringe

Cut lengths of yarn A, approx 22cm/9in long and form fringe in last row worked in B on back as foll:

Hold 4 strands tog and fold them in half, then insert the crochet hook under first k rib on back, draw centre of the strands a little way through the k rib and pass the ends through the loop on the hook, then tighten the knot.

Make a knot in same way in every alt k rib across this row on back and across same row of front; then form fringe along upper edge of sleeves again working into every alt k rib. Trim fringe evenly.

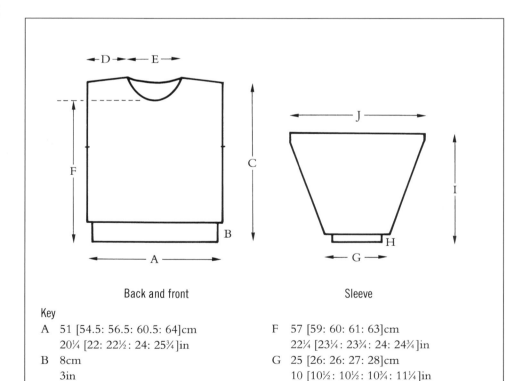

Back and front

Sleeve

Key

A 51 [54.5: 56.5: 60.5: 64]cm
    20¼ [22: 22½: 24: 25¾]in
B 8cm
    3in
C 64 [66: 67: 69: 71]cm
    25 [26: 26½: 27¾]in
D 15 [16.5: 17.5: 19: 20.5]cm
    6 [6½: 6¾: 7½: 8]in
E 20.5 [21: 21: 22: 23]cm
    8 [8¼: 8¼: 8½: 9]in

F 57 [59: 60: 61: 63]cm
    22¼ [23¼: 23¾: 24: 24¾]in
G 25 [26: 26: 27: 28]cm
    10 [10½: 10½: 10¾: 11¼]in
H 3cm
    1¼in
I 45 [46: 47: 48: 49]cm
    17¾ [18: 18½: 18¾: 19¼]in
J 52 [54.5: 54.5: 56.5: 58.5]cm
    20¾ [22: 22: 22½: 23½]in

MAN'S CABLE AND STRIPE CREWNECK

IN STAR + OR PURE LAINE No.5

✳✳✳

Sizes

To fit 86 to 91 [96 to 102]cm/34 to 36 [38 to 40]in chest
Actual width around chest when completed 106 [118]cm/42½ [47]in
Directions for larger size are in brackets [ ]; if there is only one set of figures it applies to both sizes.

Materials

Either PINGOUIN Star +:
8 [9] balls Bleu Metal No. 94 (A)
6 balls Marron Glace No. 28 ((B)
7 [8] balls Marengo No. 66 (C)
Pair each of 3¾ mm and 4½ mm (US sizes 5 and 7) needles
Cable needle (cn)
Or PINGOUIN Pure Laine No. 5:
7 [8] balls Noir No. 24 (A)
5 balls Noisette No. 335 ((B)
6 [7] balls Marengo No. 26 (C)
Pair each of 4mm and 5mm (US sizes 6 and 8) needles
Cable needle (cn)

Tension (Gauge)

Worked with 4½ mm (US size 7) needles for Star + or 5mm (US size 8) for Pure Laine No. 5.
Trellis patt: 24 sts and 24 rows to 10cm/4in over trellis patt; work a sample on 44 sts.
Diamond and cable patt: tension (gauge) over diamond and cable patt is the same; it is not necessary to work another sample if tension (gauge) over trellis patt is correct.
Striped panels: each measure 4cm/1½in in depth.
Note: An inc row is worked at beg of each

patt panel and a dec row at end before working striped panel.

Stitches used

Special abbreviations

kfb – knit into front and back of next st.
pfb – purl into front and back of next st.
cable 6 back – slip next 3 sts onto cn and hold at back of work, k3, then k3 from cn.
cable 4 back – slip next 2 sts onto cn and hold at back of work, k2, then k2 from cn.
C4R (cross 4 right) – slip next st onto cn and hold at back of work, k3, then p1 from cn.
C4L (cross 4 left) – slip next 3 sts onto cn and hold at front of work, p1, then k3 from cn.

Striped panel No. 1

Work the striped panel No. 1 over 14 rows as foll:
Work 4 rows in garter st in yarn C.
Work 2 rows garter st in yarn B.
Work 2 rows st st in yarn A.
Work 2 rows garter st in yarn B.
Work 4 rows garter st in yarn C.

Striped panel No. 2

Work the striped panel No. 2 over 14 rows as foll:
Work 4 rows in garter st in yarn A.
Work 2 rows garter st in yarn C.
Work 2 rows st st in yarn B.
Work 2 rows garter st in yarn C.
Work 4 rows garter st in yarn A.

Trellis pattern

Work trellis patt over a multiple of 14 sts plus 2 extra sts as foll:
1st row (RS) P5, *cable 6 back, p8;* rep from * to *, ending cable 6 back, p5.
2nd row K5, *p6, k8;* rep from * to *, ending p6, k5.
3rd row P4, *C4R, C4L, p6;* rep from * to *, ending C4R, C4L, p4.
4th row K4, *p3, k2, p3, k6;* rep from * to *, ending p3, k2, p3, k4.
5th row P3, *C4R, p2, C4L, p4;* rep from * to *, ending C4R, p2, C4L, p3.
6th row K3, *p3, k4;* rep from * to *, ending p3, k3.
7th row P2, *C4R, p4, C4L, p2;* rep from * to *.
8th row K2, *p3, k6, p3, k2;* rep from * to *.
9th row P1, *C4R, p6, C4L;* rep from * to *, ending p1.
10th row K1, p3, *k8, p6;* rep from * to *, ending k8, p3, k1.

11th row P1, k3, *p8, cable 6 back;* rep from * to *, ending p8, k3, p1.
12th row As 10th row.
13th row P1, *C4L, p6, C4R;* rep from * to *, ending p1.
14th row As 8th row.
15th row P2, *C4L, p4, C4R, p2;* rep from * to *.
16th row As 6th row.
17th row P3, *C4L, p2, C4R, p4;* rep from * to *, ending C4L, p2, C4R, p3.
18th row As 4th row.
19th row P4, *C4L, C4R, p6;* rep from * to *, ending C4L, C4R, p4.
20th row As 2nd row.
These 20 rows form one patt repeat.

Diamond panel

Work diamond panel over 16 sts as foll:
1st row (RS) P5, cable 6 back, p5.
2nd row K5, p6, k5.
3rd row P4, C4R, C4L, p4.
4th row K4, p3, k2, p3, k4.
5th row P3, C4R, p2, C4L, p3.
6th row K3, p3, k4, p3, k3.
7th row P2, C4R, p4, C4L, p2.
8th row K2, p3, k1, p4, k1, p3, k2.
9th row P1, C4R, p1, cable 4 back, p1, C4L, p1.
10th row K1, p3, k2, p4, k2, p3, k1.
11th row C4R, p2, cable 4 back, p2, C4L.
12th row P3, k3, p4, k3, p3.
13th row C4L, p2, cable 4 back, p2, C4R.
14th row As 10th row.
15th row P1, C4L, p1, cable 4 back, p1, C4R, p1.
16th row As 8th row.
17th row P2, C4L, p4, C4R, p2.
18th row As 6th row.
19th row P3, C4L, p2, C4R, p3.
20th row As 4th row.
21st row P4, C4L, C4R, p4.
22nd row As 2nd row.
These 22 rows form one patt repeat.

Single cable

Work single cable pattern over 6 sts as foll:
1st row (RS) K6.
2nd row P6.
3rd and 4th rows As first and 2nd rows.
5th row Cable 6 back.
6th row As 2nd row.
7th and 8th rows As first and 2nd rows.
These 8 rows form one patt repeat.

Instructions

Back

With smaller needles and yarn A, cast on 99 [111] sts and beg rib as foll:

1st rib row (RS) P1, *k1, p1; rep from * to end.

2nd rib row K1, *p1, k1; rep from * to end.
Rep these 2 rows until work measures 8 [9]cm/3 [3½]in from beg, ending with a 2nd rib row.

Inc row (RS) P1, pfb, p2, *kfb 3 times, p8;* rep from * to * 7 [8] times more, kfb 3 times, then for first size only p2, pfb, p1 [for 2nd size only p5]. 128 [142] sts.
Change to larger needles.
Work foundation row for trellis patt as foll:

Foundation row (WS) K5, (p6, k8) 8 [9] times, p6, k5.
Now still using yarn A, work in trellis patt (see Stitches Used) until first patt row of 3rd patt repeat has been completed, so ending with a RS row.

Dec row (WS) K5, *p2tog 3 times, k8;* rep from * to * 7 [8] times more, p2tog 3 times, k5. 101 [112] sts.
Now work striped panel No. 1 over next 14 rows, so ending with a WS row.
Change to yarn B for next section.

Inc row (RS) K5, *kfb 3 times, k8;* rep from * to * 7 [8] times more, kfb 3 times, k5. 128 [142] sts.
Now work the foundation row in same way as for previous trellis patt section.
Work in trellis patt until 10th patt row of 2nd patt repeat has been completed, so ending with a WS row.

Armhole shaping
Keeping trellis patt correct, cast (bind) off 5 sts at beg of next row.

Dec row (WS) Cast (bind) off first 5 sts, k until there are 7 sts on RH needle, *p2tog 3 times, k8;* rep from * to * 6 [7] times more, p2tog 3 times, k7. 94 [105] sts.
Now work striped panel No. 2 over next 14 rows, so ending with a WS row.
Change to yarn C for next section.

First size only:
Inc row (RS) K5, (kfb, k2) 28 times, k5. 122 sts.

2nd size only:
Inc row (RS) K7, (kfb, k2, kfb, k3) 13 times, kfb, k6. 132 sts.

Both sizes:
Foundation row (WS) K6 [7], *p6, k7 [8];* rep from * to * 7 times more, p6, k6 [7].
Now beg diamond and cable patt on next row as foll:

1st row (RS) P1 [2], *work first row of diamond panel over next 16 sts, p2 [3], work first row of single cable over next 6 sts, p2 [3];* rep from * to * 3 times more, work first row of diamond panel over next 16 sts, p1 [2].
Cont in diamond and cable patt as now set until the back measures 26 [28]cm/10¼ [11]in from the base of the armholes, ending with a WS patt row.

Make a note of the number of rows worked in this section of patt.

Shoulder and neck shaping
Keeping patt correct as set throughout, cast (bind) off 9 [10] sts at beg of next 2 rows.

Next row (RS) Cast (bind) off 9 [10] sts, work in patt until there are 27 [28] sts on RH needle and leave these sts for right back, cast (bind) off next 32 [36] sts, work in patt to end.
Cont with 36 [38] sts at end of needle only, for left back.
Cast (bind) off 9 [10] sts at beg of next row and 4 sts at neck edge on foll row; rep last 2 rows again.
Cast (bind) off rem 10 sts to complete shoulder shaping.
With WS facing, rejoin yarn to neck edge of right back sts and cast (bind) off first 4 sts, then work in patt to end.
Cast (bind) off 9 [10] sts at beg of next row and 4 sts at neck edge on foll row.
Cast (bind) off rem 10 sts.

Front

Work front as given for back until 16 rows fewer than on back to beg of shoulder shaping have been worked, so ending with a WS row.

Neck shaping
Beg neck shaping on next row as foll:

Next row (RS) Work 53 [56] sts in patt and slip these sts onto a spare needle, cast (bind) off next 16 [20] sts, work in patt to end.
Cont with 53 [56] sts only, for right front.
Work one row without shaping.
**Cast (bind) off 4 sts at beg of next row (neck edge) and next alt row, 2 sts at same edge on next 2 alt rows, then dec one st at neck edge on next 4 alt rows. 37 [40] sts.

Shoulder shaping
Keeping neck edge straight, cast (bind) off 9 [10] sts at beg of next row and next 2 alt rows.
Work one row without shaping.
Cast (bind) off rem 10 sts.
With WS facing, rejoin yarn to neck edge of left front sts and complete as for right front from ** to end.

Sleeves

With smaller needles and yarn A, cast on 51 [55] sts and work in rib as on back for 7 [8]cm/2¾ [3] in, ending with a 2nd rib row.

Inc row (RS) P0 [1], pfb, p1 [2], *kfb 3 times, p8;* rep from * to * 3 times more, kfb 3 times, p1 [2], pfb, p0 [1]. 68 [72] sts.
Change to larger needles.

Foundation row (WS) K3 [5] (p6, k8) 4 times, p6, k3 [5].
Now still using yarn A, work in trellis patt

beg trellis patt on next row as foll:

1st row (RS) P3 [5], rep from ★ to ★ in first patt row of trellis patt 4 times, cable 6 back, p3 [5].

Cont in trellis patt as now set, but inc one st at each end of 3rd and 7th patt rows of first patt repeat, then on every foll 6th row 4 times, keeping extra sts at sides in rev st st. 80 [84] sts.

Work in trellis patt without shaping until first row of 3rd patt repeat has been completed, so ending with a RS row.

Dec row (WS) K9 [11], ★p2tog 3 times, k8;★ rep from ★ to ★ 3 times more, p2tog 3 times, k9 [11]. 65 [69] sts.

Work striped panel No. 1 over next 14 rows, but inc one st at each end of 6th and 12th rows of this panel, so ending with a WS row. 69 [73] sts.

Change to yarn B for next section.

Inc row (RS) K3 [5], ★kfb 3 times, k3, kfb, k3;★ rep from ★ to ★ 5 times more, kfb 3 times, k3 [5]. 96 [100] sts.

Now work the foundation row in same way as for previous trellis patt section, arranging patt as before, then work in trellis patt, inc one st at each end of 3rd row of patt, then every foll 4th row 5 times more, keeping extra sts in rev st st. 108 [112] sts.

Work without shaping until 11th patt row of 3rd patt repeat has been completed, so ending with a RS row.

Dec row (WS) K5 [7], p3, ★k8, p2tog 3 times;★ rep from ★ to ★ 5 times more, k8, p3, k5 [7]. 90 [94] sts.

Work striped panel No. 2 over next 14 rows, but inc one st at each end of 6th and 12th rows of this panel, so ending with a WS row. 94 [98] sts.

Change to yarn C for next section.

First size only:

Inc row (RS) K3, (kfb, k3, kfb, k2) 13 times. 120 sts.

2nd size only:

Inc row (RS) K5, (kfb, k2) 30 times, k3. 128 sts.

Both sizes:

Foundation row (WS) K5, ★p6, k7 [8];★ rep from ★ to ★ 7 times more, p6, k5.

Now beg diamond and cable patt on next row as foll:

1st row (RS) ★Work first row of diamond panel over next 16 sts, p2 [3], work first row of single cable over next 6 sts, p2 [3];★ rep from ★ to ★ 3 times more, work first row of diamond panel over next 16 sts.

Cont in diamond and cable patt as now set, inc one st at each end of every foll 4th row 3 times, keeping extra sts in rev st st. 126 [134] sts.

Work in patt without shaping until sleeve measures 54 [56]cm/21¼ [22]in from beg. Cast (bind) off all sts.

Do not press. Join right shoulder seam, matching patt.

Neckband

With RS facing, smaller needles and yarn C, pick up and k59 [63] sts evenly around front neck edge and 42 [46] sts across back neck. 101 [109] sts.

Beg with 2nd rib row, work in rib as on back for 11cm/4¼in.

Cast (bind) off very loosely in rib.

Join left shoulder seam and neckband seam. Then fold neckband in half to WS and slip stitch cast (bound) off edge to WS of picked-up sts.

Sew cast (bound) off edge of sleeves to sides of armholes, then sew armhole cast (bind) off to last 6 rows on sides of sleeves.

Join side and sleeve seams.

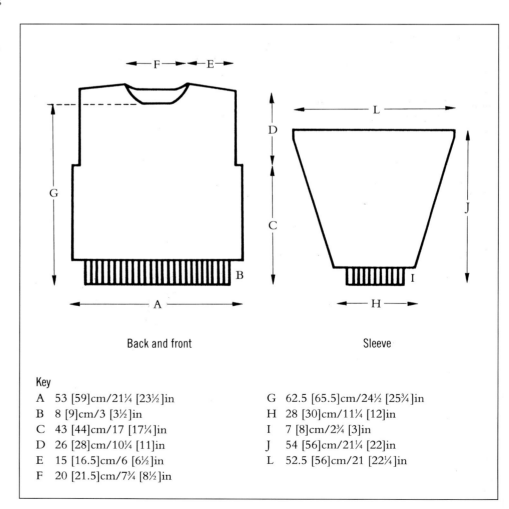

Back and front · Sleeve

Key

A 53 [59]cm/21¼ [23½]in
B 8 [9]cm/3 [3½]in
C 43 [44]cm/17 [17¼]in
D 26 [28]cm/10¼ [11]in
E 15 [16.5]cm/6 [6½]in
F 20 [21.5]cm/7¾ [8½]in

G 62.5 [65.5]cm/24½ [25¾]in
H 28 [30]cm/11¼ [12]in
I 7 [8]cm/2¾ [3]in
J 54 [56]cm/21¼ [22]in
L 52.5 [56]cm/21 [22¼]in

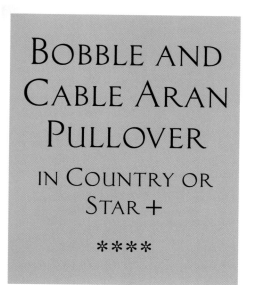

BOBBLE AND CABLE ARAN PULLOVER

IN COUNTRY OR STAR +

✱✱✱✱

Sizes

To fit 86 to 94 [99 to 107]cm/34 to 37 [39 to 42]in bust
Actual width around bust when completed 105 [117]cm/42 [47]in
Directions for larger size are in brackets [ ]; if there is only one set of figures it applies to both sizes.

Materials

Either PINGOUIN Country:
15 [18] balls Bleu Grise No. 02
Or PINGOUIN Star +:
16 [19] balls Bleu Cendre No. 49
Pair each of 3¾mm, 4mm and 4½mm (US sizes 5, 6 and 7) needles
2 cable needles (cn)

Tension (Gauge)

Worked with 4½mm (US size 7) needles.
St st: 18 sts and 24 rows to 10cm/4in over st st; work a sample on 27 sts.
Overall patt: 26 sts and 24 rows to 10cm/4in over overall patt; it is not necessary to work a sample provided the tension (gauge) over st st is correct.
Note: Unless you are experienced with Aran-type designs it is advisable to practise some of the patts first.

Stitches used

Special abbreviations

pfb – purl into front and back of next st.
k loop – insert LH needle from front to back under horizontal loop between needles, then k through back of it.

MB (make bobble) – into next st (k into front, then into back) twice, turn, p these 4 sts, turn, k4, turn, p4, turn, k these 4 sts tog through back.
T2 (twist 2) – pass RH needle behind first st on LH needle and k into back of 2nd st leaving it on LH needle, then k into front of first st and slip both sts off LH needle.
cable 4 back – slip next 2 sts onto cn and hold at back of work, k next 2 sts, then k2 from cn.
cable 4 front – slip next 2 sts onto cn and hold at front of work, k next 2 sts, then k2 from cn.
C4L (cross 4 left) – slip next 2 sts onto cn and leave at front of work, p2, then k2 from cn.
C4R (cross 4 right) – slip next 2 sts onto cn and leave at back of work, k2, then p2 from cn.
C5L (cross 5 left) – slip next 4 sts onto cn and leave at front of work, p1, then k4 from cn.
C5R (cross 5 right) – slip next st onto cn and leave at back of work, k4, then p1 from cn.
C6L (cross 6 left) – slip next 2 sts onto a cn and leave at front of work, slip next 2 sts onto 2nd cn and leave at back of work, k2, now p2 from back cn, then k2 from front cn.
C6R (cross 6 right) – slip next 4 sts onto cn and leave at back of work, k2, now pass the 2 p sts from other end of cn back onto LH needle, bring cn to front, p2 from LH needle, then k2 from cn.
C9L (cross 9 left) – slip next 4 sts onto a cn and leave at front of work, slip next st onto 2nd cn and leave at back of work, k4, now p1 from back cn, then k4 from front cn.
C12L (cross 12 left) – slip next 4 sts onto a cn and leave at front of work, slip next 4 sts onto 2nd cn and leave at back of work, k4, now k4 from back cn, then k4 from front cn.
C12R (cross 12 right) – slip next 8 sts onto cn and leave at back of work, k4, now pass the 4 sts from other end of cn back onto LH needle, bring cn to front, k4 from LH needle, then k4 from cn.

Zigzag panel No. 1

Work zigzag panel No. 1 over 14 sts as foll:
1st row (RS) P2, C4L, p8.
2nd row K8, p2, k4.
3rd row P4, C4L, p6.
4th row K6, p2, k6.
5th row P6, C4L, p4.
6th row K4, p2, k8.
7th row P8, C4L, p2.
8th row K2, p2, k10.
9th row P8, C4R, p2.
10th row As 6th row.
11th row P6, C4R, p4.
12th row As 4th row.

13th row P4, C4R, p6.
14th row As 2nd row.
15th row P2, C4R, p8.
16th row K10, p2, k2.
17th-23rd rows As first-7th rows.
This completes zigzag panel No. 1 which is worked in back and front lower bands (panel on collar is slightly different).

Zigzag panel No. 2

Work zigzag panel No. 2 over 14 sts as foll:
1st row (RS) P8, C4R, p2.
2nd row K4, p2, k8.
3rd row P6, C4R, p4.
4th row K6, p2, k6.
5th row P4, C4R, p6.
6th row K8, p2, k4.
7th row P2, C4R, p8.
8th row K10, p2, k2.
9th row P2, C4L, p8.
10th row As 6th row.
11th row P4, C4L, p6.
12th row As 4th row.
13th row P6, C4L, p4.
14th row As 2nd row.
15th row P8, C4L, p2.
16th row K2, p2, k10.
17th-23rd rows As first-7th rows.
This completes zigzag panel No. 2 which is worked in back and front lower bands.

Woven rib panel

Work woven rib panel over 14 sts as foll:
1st row (RS) (K2, p2) 3 times, k2.
2nd and all WS rows (P2, k2) 3 times, p2.
3rd row C6L, p2, C6L.
5th row and 7th rows As first row.
9th row K2, p2, C6R, p2, k2.
11th row As first row.
12th row As 2nd row.
These 12 rows form one patt repeat.

Honeycomb pattern panel

Work honeycomb patt panel over 16 [24] sts as foll:
1st row (RS) K2, (p4, k4) once [twice], p4, k2.
2nd row P2, (k4, p4) once [twice], k4, p2.
3rd row (C4L, C4R) 2 [3] times.
4th row K2, (p4, k4) once [twice], p4, k2.
5th row P2, (k4, p4) once [twice], k4, p2.
6th row As 4th row.
7th row (C4R, C4L) 2 [3] times.
8th row As 2nd row.
These 8 rows form one patt repeat.

Centre panel

Work centre panel over 53 sts as foll:
1st row (RS) P3, k4, p3, (k4, p2) twice, k4,

p1, k4, (p2, k4) twice, p3, k4, p3.

2nd row K3, p4, k3, (p4, k2) twice, p4, k1, p4, (k2, p4) twice, k3, p4, k3.

3rd row P3, cable 4 front, p3, k4, p2, cable 4 front, p2, k4, p1, k4, p2, cable 4 back, p2, k4, p3, cable 4 back, p3.

4th row As 2nd row.

5th and 6th rows As first and 2nd rows.

7th row P3, cable 4 front, p3, k4, p2, cable 4 front, p2, C9L, p2, cable 4 back, p2, k4, p3, cable 4 back, p3.

8th row As 2nd row.

9th and 10th rows As first and 2nd rows.

11th row P3, cable 4 front, p3, C5L, p1, cable 4 front, p1, C5R, p1, C5L, p1, cable 4 back, p1, C5R, p3, cable 4 back, p3.

12th row K3, p4, k4, (p4, k1) twice, p4, k3, (p4, k1) twice, p4, k4, p4, k3.

13th row P3, k4, p4, C5L, k4, C5R, p3, C5L, k4, C5R, p4, k4, p3.

14th row K3, p4, (k5, p12) twice, k5, p4, k3.

15th row P3, cable 4 front, p5, k4, cable 4 front, k4, p5, k4, cable 4 back, k4, p5, cable 4 back, p3.

16th row As 14th row.

17th row P3, k4, p2, MB, p2, C12R, p5, C12L, p2, MB, p2, k4, p3.

18th and 19th rows As 14th and 15th rows.

20th row As 14th row.

21st row P3, k4, p4, C5R, k4, C5L, p3, C5R, k4, C5L, p4, k4, p3.

22nd row As 12th row.

23rd row P3, cable 4 front, p3, C5R, p1, cable 4 front, p1, C5L, p1, C5R, p1, cable 4 back, p1, C5L, p3, cable 4 back, p3.

24th row As 2nd row.

25th and 26th rows As first and 2nd rows.

27th row As 7th row.

28th row As 2nd row.

These 28 rows form one patt repeat for the centre panel.

Instructions

Back

With 3¾mm (US size 5) needles, cast on 114 [122] sts and beg double rib as foll:

1st rib row (RS) P2, ★k2, p2; rep from ★ to end.

2nd rib row K2, ★p2, k2; rep from ★ to end.

Rep these 2 rows once more, so ending with a WS row.

Beg lower border on next row as foll:

First size only:

1st row (RS) (Work first row of zigzag panel No. 1 over next 14 sts, T2, p2, T2) 3 times, (work first row of zigzag panel No. 2 over next 14 sts, T2, p2, T2) twice, work first row of zigzag panel No. 2 over last 14 sts.

2nd row (Work 2nd row of zigzag panel No. 2 over next 14 sts, k2, p2, k2) twice, work 2nd row of zigzag panel No. 2 over next 14 sts, (p2, k2, p2, work 2nd row of zigzag panel No. 1 over next 14 sts) 3 times.

2nd size only:

1st row (RS) P2, T2, (work first row of zigzag panel No. 1 over next 14 sts, T2, p2, T2) 3 times, (work first row of zigzag panel No. 2 over next 14 sts, T2, p2, T2) twice, work first row of zigzag panel No. 2 over next 14 sts, T2, p2.

2nd row K2, p2, (work 2nd row of zigzag panel No. 2 over next 14 sts, k2, p2, k2) twice, work 2nd row of zigzag panel No. 2 over next 14 sts, (p2, k2, p2, work 2nd row of zigzag panel No. 1 over next 14 sts) 3 times, p2, k2.

Both sizes:

Cont in patt as now set, always working the twist rib patt as on last 2 rows, until zigzag panels have been completed, so ending with a RS row.

First size only:

Inc row (WS) P4, (pfb, p3) 9 times, k1, k2tog, k1, p4, (k2, pfb twice) twice, k2tog, (pfb twice, k2) twice, p4, k1, k2tog, k1, (p3, pfb) 9 times, p4. 137 sts.

2nd size only:

Inc row (WS) P5, (pfb, p2) 13 times, k1, k2tog, k1, p4, (k2, pfb twice) twice, k2tog, (pfb twice, k2) twice, p4, k1, k2tog, k1, (p2, pfb) 13 times, p5. 153 sts.

Both sizes:

Change to 4½mm (US size 7) needles.

Beg main patt on next row as foll:

1st row (RS) K6, p3, work first row of woven rib panel over next 14 sts, p3, work first row of honeycomb patt panel over next 16 [24] sts, work first row of centre panel over next 53 sts, work first row of honeycomb patt panel over next 16 [24] sts, p3, work first row of woven rib panel over next 14 sts, p3, k6.

Cont in patt as now set, keeping the 6 sts at each end in st st and the groups of 3 sts in rev st st (and making a bobble on the group of 3 sts between woven rib panel and honeycomb patt panel on centre st each time 17th row of centre panel is worked) until back measures 41 [43]cm/16 [17]in from beg, ending with a WS row.

Armhole shaping

Keeping patt correct throughout, cast (bind) off 4 [6] sts at beg of next 2 rows. 129 [141] sts.

Work without shaping until back measures 65 [68]cm/25½ [26¾]in from beg, ending with a WS row.

Shoulder and neck shaping

Cast (bind) off 12 [14] sts at beg of next 2 rows.

Next row (RS) Cast (bind) off 12 [14] sts, work in patt until there are 22 [24] sts on RH needle and leave these sts for right

back, cast (bind) off next 37 sts, work in patt to end.

Cont with 34 [38] sts at end of needle only, for left back.

Cast (bind) off 12 [14] sts at beg of next row and 10 sts at neck edge on foll row.

Cast (bind) off rem 12 [14] sts to complete shoulder shaping.

With WS facing, rejoin yarn to neck edge of right back sts and cast (bind) off first 10 sts, then work in patt to end.

Cast (bind) off rem 12 [14] sts.

Front

Work front as given for back until front measures 60 [63]cm/23½ [24¾]in from beg, ending with a WS row.

Neck shaping

Next row (RS) Work 52 [58] sts in patt and slip these sts onto a spare needle, cast (bind) off next 25 sts, work in patt to end.

Cont with 52 [58] sts only, for right front.

Work one row without shaping.

★★Cast (bind) off 6 sts at beg of next row (neck edge), 4 st at same edge on next alt row, 2 sts on next 2 alt rows, then dec one st at neck edge on next 2 alt rows. 36 [42] sts.

Shoulder shaping

Keeping neck edge straight, cast (bind) off 12 [14] sts at beg of next row and next alt row.

Work one row without shaping.

Cast (bind) off rem 12 [14] sts.

With WS facing, rejoin yarn to neck edge of left front sts and complete as for right front from ★★ to end.

Sleeves

With 3¾mm (US size 5) needles, cast on 50 [54] sts and beg double rib as foll:

1st rib row (RS) K0 [2], (p2, k2) 12 times, p2, k0 [2].

2nd rib row P0 [2], (k2, p2) 12 times, k2, p0 [2].

Rep these 2 rows once more, so ending with a WS row.

Beg lower border on next row as foll:

1st row (RS) P2 [4], T2, p2, T2, work first row of zigzag panel No. 1 over next 14 sts, T2, p2, T2, work first row of zigzag panel No. 2 over next 14 sts, T2, p2, T2, p2 [4].

Cont in patt as now set until zigzag panels have been completed, so ending with a RS row.

Inc row (WS) P1 [3], pfb 7 times, k1, k2tog, k1, p4, (k2, pfb twice) twice, k2tog, (pfb twice, k2) twice, p4, k1, k2tog, k1, pfb 7 times, p1 [3]. 69 [73] sts.

Change to 4½mm (US size 7) needles.

Beg main patt on next row as foll:

1st row (RS) K2 [4], p4, k2, forming part of honeycomb patt panel, work first row of

centre panel over next 53 sts, then k2, p4, k2 [4], forming part of honeycomb patt panel.
Cont in patt as now set for 2 rows more.
Cont in patt, inc one st at each end of next row, then on every foll 4th row 11 [7] times, then on every foll 3rd row 11 [17] times, **and at the same time** work extra sts into patt as foll:
The first 8 [14] sts added at each side will complete the honeycomb patt panel, the next 3 sts should be worked in rev st st and the rem 12 [8] sts at each side in st st.
115 [123] sts.
Work in patt without shaping until sleeve measures 49 [52]cm/19¼ [20½]in from beg.
Cast (bind) off all sts.

Collar

The collar for both of the sizes is the same.
With 3¾mm (US size 5) needles, cast on 114 sts and work in double rib as on back for 3 rows.
Inc row (WS) Keeping rib correct, rib 20, (k1, k loop, k1, rib 34) twice, k1, k loop, k1, rib 20. 117 sts.
Change to 4½mm (US size 7) needles.
Beg patt on next row as foll:
1st row (RS) (P2, T2) twice, ★p8, C4R, p3, C4L, p8;★ (T2, p2) twice, T2, rep from ★ to ★ once, (T2, p2) twice, T2, rep from ★ to ★ once, (T2, p2) twice.
2nd row (K2, p2) twice, ★k8, p2, k7, p2, k8;★ (p2, k2) twice, p2, rep from ★ to ★ once, (p2, k2) twice, p2, rep from ★ to ★ once, (p2, k2) twice.
Cont keeping panels of twist rib correct.
3rd row Rib 8, ★p6, C4R, p7, C4L, p6;★ (rib 10, rep from ★ to ★ once) twice, rib 8.
4th row Rib 8, ★k6, p2, k11, p2, k6;★ (rib 10, rep from ★ to ★ once) twice, rib 8.
5th row Rib 8, ★p4, C4R, p11, C4L, p4;★ (rib 10, rep from ★ to ★ once) twice, rib 8.
6th row Rib 8, ★k4, p2, k15, p2, k4;★ (rib 10, rep from ★ to ★ once) twice, rib 8.
7th row Rib 8, ★p4, C4L, p5, MB, p5, C4R, p4;★ (rib 10, rep from ★ to ★ once) twice, rib 8.
8th row As 4th row.
9th row Rib 8, ★p6, C4L, p7, C4R, p6;★ (rib 10, rep from ★ to ★ once) twice, rib 8.
10th row As 2nd row.
11th row Rib 8, ★p8, C4L, p3, C4R, p8;★ (rib 10, rep from ★ to ★ once) twice, rib 8.
12th row Rib 8, ★k10, p2, k3, p2, k10;★ (rib 10, rep from ★ to ★ once) twice, rib 8.
These 12 rows form one patt repeat.
Work 6 rows more in patt.
Change to 4mm (US size 6) needles.
Cont in patt until 7th patt row of 3rd patt repeat has been completed.
On next row work k2tog over each bobble.
Cast (bind) off all sts.

Finishing

Do not press. Join shoulder seams, matching all cable patts.
Sew cast (bound) off edge of sleeves to sides of armholes and sew armhole cast (bind) off to last 5 [8] rows on sides of sleeves.
Join side and sleeve seams.
Join collar seam.
With RS of collar to WS of pullover and placing seam at centre back, sew cast (bound) off edge of collar to neck edges with a flat seam. Fold collar out onto RS.

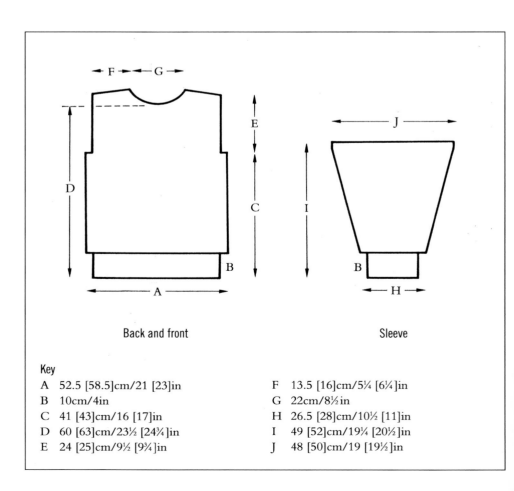

Back and front   Sleeve

Key
A 52.5 [58.5]cm/21 [23]in   F 13.5 [16]cm/5¼ [6¼]in
B 10cm/4in   G 22cm/8½in
C 41 [43]cm/16 [17]in   H 26.5 [28]cm/10½ [11]in
D 60 [63]cm/23½ [24¾]in   I 49 [52]cm/19¼ [20½]in
E 24 [25]cm/9½ [9¾]in   J 48 [50]cm/19 [19½]in

Child's Aran Cardigan

in Star +

✳✳✳

Sizes

To fit ages 6 [8: 10: 12: 14] years or 63 [68: 72: 76: 81]cm/25 [27: 28½: 30: 32]in chest
Actual width around chest (buttoned) 82.5 [87: 91: 95: 98.5]cm/32¼ [34¼: 35½: 37¼: 38¾]in

Directions for larger sizes are in brackets [ ]; if there is only one set of figures it applies to all sizes.

Materials

PINGOUIN Star +:
10 [11: 12: 13: 14] balls Ecru No. 17
Pair each of 4mm and 4½mm (US sizes 6 and 7) needles
4mm (US size 6) circular needle for centre front bands
Cable needle (cn)
5 buttons

Tension (Gauge)

Worked with 4½mm (US size 7) needles.
Rev st st: 18 sts and 24 rows to 10cm/4in over rev st st; work a sample on 27 sts.
Single cable panel: measures 2cm/¾in in width.
Double cable panel: measures 7cm/2¾in in width; work a sample on 30 sts, working 2 sts in rev st st at each end of row.
Fishbone patt panel: measures 5cm/2in in width; work a sample on 18 sts, working 2 sts in rev st st at each end of row.

Stitches used

Special abbreviations

cable 6 back – slip next 3 sts onto cn and hold at back of work, k3, then k3 from cn.
cable 6 front – slip next 3 sts onto cn and hold at front of work, k3, then k3 from cn.
cable 4 back – slip next 2 sts onto cn and hold at back of work, k2, then k2 from cn.
C2R (cross 2 right) – slip next st onto cn and hold at back of work, k1, then p1 from cn.
C2L (cross 2 left) – slip next st onto cn and hold at front of work, p1, then k1 from cn.

Cable panel No. 1

Work cable panel No. 1 over 6 sts as foll:
1st row (RS) K6.
2nd row P6.
3rd row Cable 6 back.
4th row P6.
These 4 rows form one patt repeat for cable panel No. 1.

Cable panel No. 2

Work cable panel No. 2 over 6 sts as foll:
1st row (RS) K6.
2nd row P6.
3rd row Cable 6 front.
4th row P6.
These 4 rows form one patt repeat for cable panel No. 2.

Double cable panel

Work double cable panel over 26 sts as foll:
1st row (RS) K6, (p2, k4) twice, p2, k6.
2nd row P6, k2, (p4, k2) twice, p6.
3rd row Cable 6 back, (p2, k4) twice, p2, cable 6 front.
4th row As 2nd row.
5th-8th rows As first-4th rows.
9th and 10th rows As first and 2nd rows.
11th row Slip 8 sts onto cn and hold at back of work, k4, then working sts from cn k2, p2, k4; p next 2 sts; slip next 4 sts onto cn and hold at front of work, k4, p2, k2, then k sts from cn.
12th row As 2nd row.
13th-16th rows As first-4th rows.
These 16 rows form one patt repeat for double cable panel.

Fishbone pattern

Work fishbone patt over 14 sts as foll:
1st row (RS) (K1, p1) twice, k6, (p1, k1) twice.
2nd row (P1, k1) twice, p6, (k1, p1) twice.
3rd row K1, C2R twice, cable 4 back, C2L twice, k1.
4th row P2, k1, p1, k1, p4, k1, p1, k1, p2.
5th row C2R twice, k6, C2L twice.
6th row As 2nd row.
Rep 3rd-6th rows inclusive to form patt (first and 2nd rows are foundation rows and are not worked again).

Instructions

Back

With 4mm (US size 6) needles, cast on 98 [102: 106: 110: 114] sts and beg double rib.
1st rib row (RS) K2, *p2, k2; rep from * to end.
2nd rib row P2, *k2, p2; rep from * to end.
Rep these 2 rows twice more, then first row again, so ending with a RS row.
Inc row (WS) Keeping rib correct, rib 4 [6: 8: 2: 4], work into front and back of next st, (rib 5 [5: 5: 6: 6], work into front and back of next st) 15 times, rib rem 3 [5: 7: 2: 4] sts. 114 [118: 122: 126: 130] sts.
Change to 4½mm (US size 7) needles.
1st patt row (RS) P4 [5: 5: 5: 7], work first row of cable panel No. 1 (see Stitches Used) over next 6 sts, *p3 [3: 4: 5: 5], work first row of double cable panel over next 26 sts, p3 [3: 4: 5: 5];* work first row of fishbone patt over next 14 sts, p2 [4: 4: 4: 4], work first row of fishbone patt over next 14 sts; rep from * to * once, work first row of cable panel No. 2 over next 6 sts, p4 [5: 5: 5: 7].
Cont in patt as now set, keeping all patts correct and working sts between panels and at sides in rev st st, until back measures 27 [29: 31: 33: 35]cm/10¾ [11½: 12: 13: 13¾]in from beg, ending with a WS row.
Armhole shaping
Keeping patt correct as set throughout, cast (bind) off 3 sts at beg of next 2 rows. 108 [112: 116: 120: 124] sts.
Work without shaping until back measures 44 [47: 50: 53: 56]cm/17¼ [18½: 19½: 20¾: 22]in from beg, ending with a WS row.
Shoulder and neck shaping
Next row (RS) Cast (bind) off 11 [11: 11: 12: 12] sts, work in patt until there are 31 [32: 33: 34: 35] sts on RH needle and leave these sts for right back, cast (bind) off next 24 [26: 28: 28: 30] sts, work in patt to end.
Cont with 42 [43: 44: 46: 47] sts at end of needle only, for left back.
Cast (bind) off 11 [11: 11: 12: 12] sts at beg of next row and 5 sts at neck edge on foll row; rep last 2 rows again.
Cast (bind) off rem 10 [11: 12: 12: 13] sts to complete shoulder shaping.
With WS facing, rejoin yarn to neck edge of right back sts and complete as for left back, reversing shaping.

Right front

With 4mm (US size 6) needles, cast on 46 [50: 50: 54: 54] sts and work 7 rows in double rib as on back, so ending with a RS row.
Inc row (WS) Keeping rib correct, rib 3 [5: 5: 3: 2], work into front and back of next st,

(rib 3 [4: 3: 5: 4], work into front and back of next st) 10 [8: 10: 8: 10] times, rib rem 2 [4: 4: 2: 1] sts. 57 [59: 61: 63: 65] sts.★★
Change to 4½mm (US size 7) needles.
1st patt row (RS) P1 [2: 2: 2: 2], work first row of fishbone patt over next 14 sts, p3 [3: 4: 5: 5], work first row of double cable panel over next 26 sts, p3 [3: 4: 5: 5], work first row of cable panel No. 2 over next 6 sts, p4 [5: 5: 5: 7].
Cont in patt as now set until front is same length as back to beg of armhole shaping, ending with a WS row.
Front and armhole shaping
Beg front and armhole shaping as foll:
Keeping patt correct as set throughout, dec one st at beg of next row for front shaping, then on foll row cast (bind) off 3 sts at beg of row (armhole edge) and dec one st at end (centre front edge) of same row.
★★★Work one row without shaping, then dec one st at front edge on next 2 rows; rep last 3 rows 6 [6: 6: 4: 4] times more, then dec one st at front edge on every alt row 6 [7: 8: 12: 13] times. 32 [33: 34: 36: 37] sts.
Work without shaping until front is same length as back to beg of shoulder shaping, ending at armhole edge.
Shoulder shaping
Cast (bind) off 11 [11: 11: 12: 12] sts at beg of next row and next alt row.
Work one row without shaping.
Cast (bind) off rem 10 [11: 12: 12: 13] sts.

Left front

Work as given for right front to ★★.
Change to 4½mm (US size 7) needles.
Beg patt on next row as foll:
1st patt row (RS) P4 [5: 5: 5: 7], work first row of cable panel No. 1 over next 6 sts, p3 [3: 4: 5: 5], work first row of double cable panel over next 26 sts, p3 [3: 4: 5: 5], work first row of fishbone patt over next 14 sts, p1 [2: 2: 2: 2].
Cont in patt as now set until front is same length as back to beg of armhole shaping, ending with a WS row.
Front and armhole shaping
Keeping patt correct as set throughout, cast (bind) off 3 sts at beg of next row (armhole edge) and dec one st at end of same row (centre front edge).
Dec one st at front edge on next row.
Complete as for right front from ★★★ to end, reversing shapings.

Sleeves

With 4mm (US size 6) needles, cast on 42 [42: 46: 46: 46] sts and work 7 rows in double rib as on back, so ending with a RS row.
Inc row (WS) Keeping rib correct, rib 4 [2: 6: 4: 2], work into front and back of next st, (rib 1, work into front and back of next st) 17 [19: 17: 19: 21] times, rib rem 3 [1: 5:

3: 1] sts. 60 [62: 64: 66: 68] sts.
Change to 4½mm (US size 7) needles.
1st patt row (RS) P0 [1: 1: 1: 2], work first row of fishbone patt over next 14 sts, p3 [3: 4: 5: 5], work first row of double cable panel over next 26 sts, p3 [3: 4: 5: 5], work first row of fishbone patt over next 14 sts, p0 [1: 1: 1: 2].
Cont in patt as now set for 2 [4: 4: 4: 4] rows more.
Work in patt, inc one st at each end of next row, then on every foll 6th row 4 [4: 7: 9: 12] times, then on every foll 4th row 7 [8: 6: 5: 3] times, working all extra sts in rev st st. 84 [88: 92: 96: 100] sts.
Work in patt without shaping until sleeve measures 31 [34: 38: 42: 46]cm/12¼ [13¼: 15: 16½: 18] in from beg. Cast (bind) off.

Finishing and front bands

Do not press. Join shoulder seams.
Front bands
With RS facing and 4mm (US size 6) circular needle, pick up and k62 [67: 71: 76: 81] sts up straight centre front edge of right front, 42 [44: 46: 48: 50] sts up sloping edge to shoulder, 34 [36: 40: 42: 44] sts across back neck, 42 [44: 46: 48: 50] sts down sloping edge of left front and 62 [67: 71: 76: 81] sts down straight front edge. 242 [258: 274: 290: 306] sts.
Working back and forth in rows on circular needle and beg with a 2nd rib row, work 3 rows in double rib as on back, so ending with a WS row.
Beg buttonholes on next row as foll:
For girl's version only:
1st buttonhole row (RS) Keeping rib correct, rib 5 [6: 6: 3: 4], cast (bind) off 2, ★rib until there are 11 [12: 13: 15: 16] sts on RH needle after previous buttonhole, cast (bind) off 2;★ rep from ★ to ★ 3 times more, rib to end.
For boy's version only:
1st buttonhole row (RS) Keeping rib correct, rib to last 59 [64: 68: 73: 78] sts, cast (bind) off 2, ★rib until there are 11 [12: 13: 15: 16] sts on RH needle after previous buttonhole, cast (bind) off 2;★ rep from ★ to ★ 3 times more, rib to end.
Both versions:
2nd buttonhole row Work in rib, casting on 2 sts over each buttonhole.
Work 2 rows more in rib, so ending with a WS row.
P one row (RS). Cast (bind) off knitwise.
Sew cast (bound) off edge of sleeves to sides of armholes and sew armhole cast (bind) off to last 4 rows on sides of sleeves. Join side and sleeve seams. Sew on the buttons to correspond with the buttonholes.

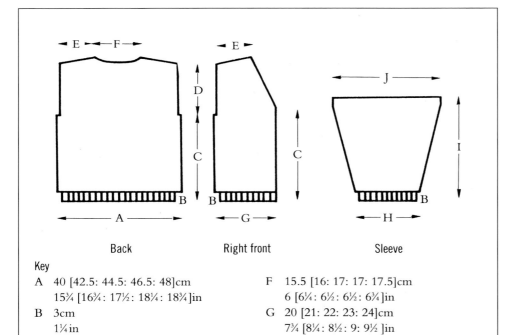

Back   Right front   Sleeve

Key
A 40 [42.5: 44.5: 46.5: 48]cm
   15¾ [16¾: 17½: 18¼: 18¾]in
B 3cm
   1¼in
C 27 [29: 31: 33: 35]cm
   10¾ [11½: 12: 13: 13¾]in
D 17 [18: 19: 20: 21]cm
   6½ [7: 7½: 7¾: 8¼]in
E 11 [11.5: 12: 12.5: 13]cm
   4¼ [4½: 4¾: 5: 5¼]in

F 15.5 [16: 17: 17: 17.5]cm
   6 [6¼: 6½: 6½: 6¾]in
G 20 [21: 22: 23: 24]cm
   7¾ [8¼: 8½: 9: 9½]in
H 21 [22: 22.5: 23.5: 24]cm
   8¼ [8½: 8¾: 9¼: 9½]in
I 31 [34: 38: 42: 46]cm
   12¼ [13¼: 15: 16½: 18]in
J 34 [36: 38: 40: 42]cm
   13¼ [14: 15: 15¾: 16½]in

GIRL'S SAMPLER SWEATER

IN STAR + AND FRANCE +

*

Sizes

To fit ages 4 [6: 8: 10: 12] years or 58 [63: 68: 72: 76]cm/23 [25: 27: 28½: 30]in chest
Actual width around chest when completed 73 [80: 84: 90: 96]cm/29½ [32: 33½: 36: 38¼]in
Directions for larger sizes are in brackets [ ]; if there is only one set of figures it applies to all sizes.

Materials

PINGOUIN Star +:
5 [6: 7: 8: 9] balls Ecru No. 17 (A)
1 ball or part-ball Jade No. 50 (B)
PINGOUIN France +:
1 ball or part-ball Ble No. 91 (C)
1 ball or part-ball Ficelle No. 53 (D)
Pair each of 3¾mm and 4mm (US sizes 5 and 6) needles
4mm (US size F/5) crochet hook for edging

Tension (Gauge)

Worked with 4mm (US size 6) needles.
St st: 19 sts and 26 rows to 10cm/4in over st st; work a sample on 28 sts.
Neckband patt: 28 sts to 10cm/4in and 8 rows to 3cm/1¼in over neckband patt; it is not necessary to work a sample of this patt.

Stitches used

The sweater is worked with in one colour in plain st st with a twisted stitch neckband. The motifs and letters are embroidered on after the knitting has been completed. The 7-row lower borders (across the front and around the cuffs) are embroidered in Swiss darning (duplicate st) and the sampler section is embroidered either in Swiss darning or cross stitch, as preferred.

Special abbreviations

C2L (cross 2 left) – pass RH needle behind first st on LH needle and k into back of 2nd st leaving it on LH needle, then k into front of first st and slip both sts off LH needle.
C2R (cross 2 right) – pass RH needle in front of first st on LH needle and lift up 2nd st and k it leaving it on LH needle, then k first st and slip both sts off LH needle.
dc (US sc) – double crochet (US single crochet).
rev dc (US rev sc) – reverse double crochet (US reverse single crochet) is worked as dc (sc) but from left to right instead of right to left, to form a rounded raised edge.

Instructions

Back

With 4mm (US size 6) needles and yarn A, cast on 70 [76: 80: 86: 92] sts.
Beg with a k row, work in st st until back measures 23 [25: 27: 29: 31]cm/9 [9¾: 10½: 11¼: 12¼]in from beg, ending with a p row.
Armhole shaping
Working in st st throughout, cast (bind) off 3 [4: 4: 5: 5] sts at beg of next 2 rows. 64 [68: 72: 76: 82] sts.
Work without shaping until back measures 40 [43: 46: 49: 52]cm/15¾ [17: 18: 19¼: 20¾]in from beg, ending with a p row.
Shoulder and neck shaping
Next row (RS) Cast (bind) off 6 [6: 7: 7: 8] sts, k until there are 19 [20: 20: 21: 22] sts on RH needle and leave these sts for right back, cast (bind) off next 14 [16: 18: 20: 22] sts, k to end.
Cont with 25 [26: 27: 28: 30] sts at end of needle only, for left back.
Cast (bind) off 6 [6: 7: 7: 8] sts at beg of next row and 3 sts at neck edge on foll row; rep last 2 rows again.
Cast (bind) off rem 7 [8: 7: 8: 8] sts to complete shoulder shaping.
With WS facing, rejoin yarn to neck edge of right back sts and cast (bind) off first 3 sts, then p to end.
Cast (bind) off 6 [6: 7: 7: 8] sts at beg of next row and 3 sts at neck edge on foll row.
Cast (bind) off rem 7 [8: 7: 8: 8] sts.

Front

Work as given for back until front measures 35 [38: 41: 43: 46]cm/13¾ [15: 16: 17: 18]in from beg, ending with a p row.

Neck shaping
Next row (RS) K28 [29: 30: 32: 34] sts and slip these sts onto a spare needle, cast (bind) off next 8 [10: 12: 12: 14] sts, k to end.
Cont with rem 28 [29: 30: 32: 34] sts only, for right front.
P one row.
**Cast (bind) off 3 sts at beg of next row (neck edge), 2 sts at same edge on next alt row, then dec one st at neck edge on next 4 [4: 4: 5: 5] alt rows. 19 [20: 21: 22: 24] sts.
Work 2 rows without shaping, so ending at armhole edge.
Shoulder shaping
Cast (bind) off 6 [6: 7: 7: 8] sts at beg of next row and foll alt row.
Work one row without shaping.
Cast (bind) off rem 7 [8: 7: 8: 8] sts.
With WS facing, rejoin yarn to neck edge of left front sts and complete as for right front from ** to end.

Sleeves

With 4mm (US size 6) needles and yarn A, cast on 33 [35: 37: 39: 41] sts.
Beg with a k row, work in st st, inc one st at each end of every foll 6th row 0 [2: 4: 6: 8] times, then on every foll 4th row 16 [15: 14: 13: 12] times. 65 [69: 73: 77: 81] sts.
Work without shaping in st st until sleeve measures 29 [33: 36: 40: 43]cm/11½ [13: 14: 15¾: 17]in from beg.
Cast (bind) off all sts.

Finishing and borders

Press lightly on WS with a cool iron, following instructions on yarn label.
Embroidery on front
The colour in Star + (B) is used single for the embroidery and the two colours in France + (C and D) are each used double.
Beg on 4th [6th: 10th: 12th: 16th] row of front and using a tapestry needle, work in Swiss darning (duplicate st) across the row using C for first row of patt.
Now beg and ending at positions indicated, work next 5 rows from chart, then work next row entirely in C.
Note: Next section of patt (which forms sampler) can also be worked in Swiss darning or in cross stitch, as preferred.
Miss next 4 rows after the row in C, then on foll row miss 9 [12: 14: 17: 20] sts from RH edge; (work in D on next 3 sts, miss one st) 12 times, work in D on next 3 sts, miss rem 10 [13: 15: 18: 21] sts.
Work remainder of sampler as now set, following chart.
Embroidery on sleeves
Beg on 4th [6th: 8th: 10th: 12th] row, work

across row in Swiss darning, using C for first row of patt.

On foll row, work centre 3 sts in D, then following chart work remainder of patt on each side of these sts.

Work next 5 rows in patt, then work one row in C.

Neckband

Join right shoulder seam.

With RS facing, 4mm (US size 6) needles and yarn A, pick up and k52 [56: 60: 66: 70] sts evenly around front neck edge and 36 [38: 40: 42: 44] sts across back neck. 88 [94: 100: 108: 114] sts.

Beg neckband patt on next row as foll:

1st row (WS) Purl.

2nd row K1, ★C2L;★ rep from ★ to ★, ending k1.

3rd row Purl.

4th row K1, ★C2R;★ rep from ★ to ★, ending k1.

Rep first, 2nd and 3rd rows once more.

Change to 3¾mm (US size 5) needles.

Rep 4th row.

Cast (bind) off tightly.

Join left shoulder seam and neckband seam. Sew cast (bound) off edge of sleeves to sides of armholes and sew armhole cast (bind) off to last 4 [5: 5: 7: 7] rows on sides of sleeves. Join side and sleeve seams.

Edging

With RS facing and crochet hook, join yarn A at base of right side seam, work one chain, then work evenly in dc (US sc) from right to left around lower edge of sweater, join with a slip stitch to chain at beg of row; do not turn. Still with RS facing, work one row of rev dc (US rev sc) from left to right (again around lower edge), then join with a slip stitch to beg of row. Fasten off.

Work a similar edging around lower edge of each sleeve.

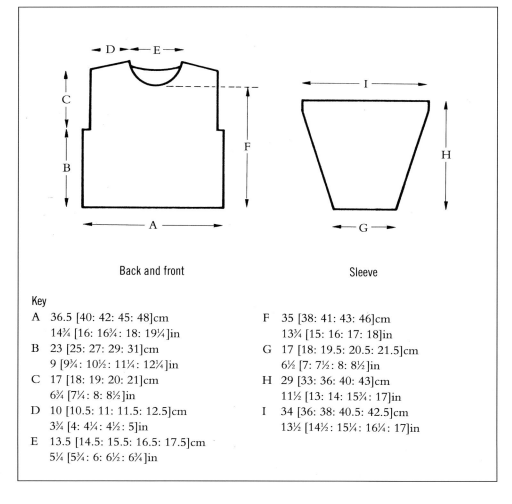

Back and front

Sleeve

Key

A 36.5 [40: 42: 45: 48]cm
   14¾ [16: 16¾: 18: 19¼]in
B 23 [25: 27: 29: 31]cm
   9 [9¾: 10½: 11¼: 12¼]in
C 17 [18: 19: 20: 21]cm
   6¾ [7¼: 8: 8½]in
D 10 [10.5: 11: 11.5: 12.5]cm
   3¾ [4: 4¼: 4½: 5]in
E 13.5 [14.5: 15.5: 16.5: 17.5]cm
   5¼ [5¾: 6: 6½: 6¾]in

F 35 [38: 41: 43: 46]cm
   13¾ [15: 16: 17: 18]in
G 17 [18: 19.5: 20.5: 21.5]cm
   6½ [7: 7½: 8: 8½]in
H 29 [33: 36: 40: 43]cm
   11½ [13: 14: 15¾: 17]in
I 34 [36: 38: 40.5: 42.5]cm
   13½ [14½: 15¼: 16¼: 17]in

Embroidery chart

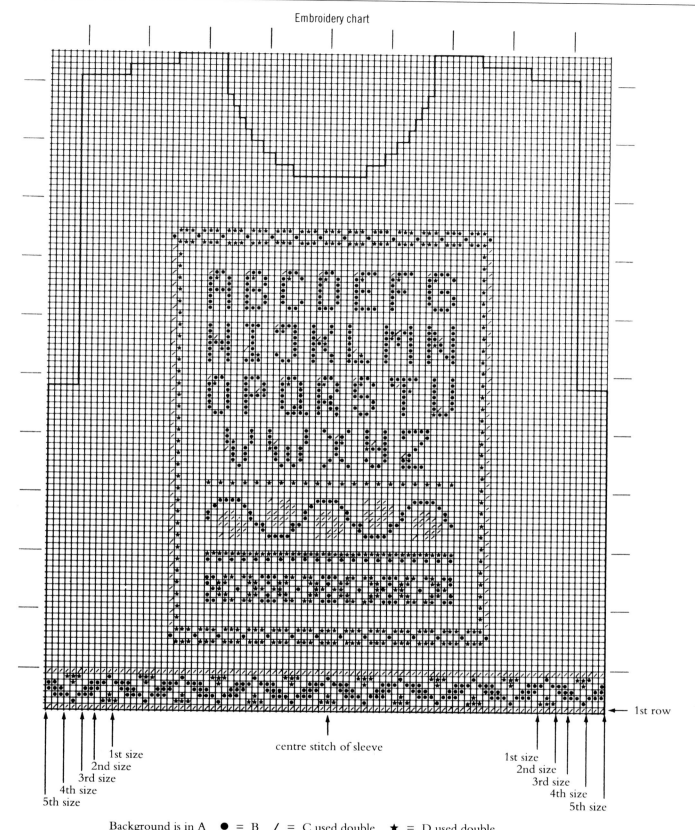

1st row

1st size
2nd size
3rd size
4th size
5th size

centre stitch of sleeve

1st size
2nd size
3rd size
4th size
5th size

Background is in A   ● = B   / = C used double   ★ = D used double

Front: Work sts between arrows according to size for the first 7 chart rows, using Swiss darning (duplicate st). Section forming sampler can either be worked in Swiss darning or in cross stitch. See instructions for exact position of both sections.

Sleeves: Work only the first 7 chart rows in Swiss darning (duplicate st); see instructions for exact position of these 7 rows.

Note: Armhole, neck and shoulder shapings are fully explained in the instructions; they vary according to size and should not be worked from this chart.

Embroidered Pullover in Soft'Hair and Angora 70

✱✱

Sizes

To fit 81 to 86 [91: 96: 102 to 107: 112]cm/32 to 34 [36: 38: 40 to 42: 44]in bust
Actual width around bust when completed 103 [109: 115: 121: 127]cm/41 [43½: 46: 48: 51]in
Directions for larger sizes are in brackets [ ]; if there is only one set of figures it applies to all sizes.

Materials

PINGOUIN Soft'Hair:
10 [11: 12: 13: 14] balls Amande No. 28 (A)
3 [3: 3: 4: 4] balls Loden No. 27 **or** Vison No. 37 (B)
PINGOUIN Angora 70:
2 balls Ecru No. 108 (C)
Pair each of 3¼mm and 4mm (US sizes 3 and 6) needles
6 buttons

Tension (Gauge)

Worked with 4mm (US size 6) needles.
St st: 20 sts and 27 rows to 10cm/4in over st st; work a sample on 30 sts.

Stitches used

The pullover is worked in st st with k1, p1 ribbing. The motifs are embroidered in Swiss darning (duplicate st) on the back and front after the knitting has been completed.

Instructions

Back

With 3¼mm (US size 3) needles and yarn B, cast on 99 [105: 111: 117: 123] sts and beg rib as foll:
1st rib row (RS) P1, *k1, p1; rep from * to end.
2nd rib row K1, *p1, k1; rep from * to end.
Rep these 2 rows twice more, so ending with a 2nd rib row.
Change to 4mm (US size 6) needles.
Beg with a k row, work 36 rows in st st, so ending with a p row.
Cont in st st throughout, inc one st at each end of next row.
Work 13 rows more in yarn B (50 rows in st st in B in total), so ending with a WS row.
Break off yarn B and change to yarn A.
Work 22 rows without shaping.
Inc one st at each end of next row. 103 [109: 115: 121: 127] sts.
Work without shaping until back measures 39 [40: 41: 42: 43]cm/15¼ [15¾: 16: 16½: 17]in from beg, ending with a p row.
Armhole shaping
Place a marker loop in a contrasting yarn at each end of last row to indicate beg of shaping.
Cast (bind) off one st at beg of next 2 rows and 2 sts at beg of next 2 rows; rep these 4 rows again.
Cast (bind) off one st at beg of next 4 rows. 87 [93: 99: 105: 111] sts.
Work without shaping until back measures 64 [66: 68: 70: 72]cm/25 [26: 26¾: 27½: 28¼]in from beg, ending with a p row.
Shoulder and neck shaping
Cast (bind) off 6 [7: 7: 8: 8] sts at beg of next 2 rows.
Next row (RS) Cast (bind) off 6 [7: 7: 8: 8] sts, k until there are 22 [22: 24: 24: 26] sts on RH needle and leave these sts for right back, cast (bind) off next 19 [21: 23: 25: 27] sts, k to end.
Cont with 28 [29: 31: 32: 34] sts at end of needle only, for left back.
Cast (bind) off 6 [7: 7: 8: 8] sts at beg of next row and 4 sts at neck edge on foll row; rep last 2 rows again.
Cast (bind) off rem 8 [7: 9: 8: 10] sts to complete shoulder shaping.
With WS facing, rejoin yarn to neck edge of right back sts and cast (bind) off first 4 sts, then p to end.
Cast (bind) off 6 [7: 7: 8: 8] sts at beg of next row and 4 sts at neck edge on foll row.
Cast (bind) off rem 8 [7: 9: 8: 10] sts.

Front

Work as given for back until front measures 58 [60: 62: 64: 66]cm/22¾ [23½: 24½: 25: 26]in from beg, ending with a p row.
Neck shaping
Next row (RS) K37 [39: 41: 43: 45] sts and slip these sts onto a spare needle, cast (bind) off next 13 [15: 17: 19: 21] sts, k to end.
Cont with rem 37 [39: 41: 43: 45] sts only, for right front (leaving rem sts for later).
P one row.
Cast (bind) off 3 sts at beg of next row (neck edge) and 2 sts at same edge on next 2 alt rows, then dec one st at neck edge on next 4 alt rows. 26 [28: 30: 32: 34] sts.
Work 2 rows more without shaping, so ending at armhole edge.
Shoulder shaping
Cast (bind) off 6 [7: 7: 8: 8] sts at beg of next row and next 2 alt rows.
Work one row without shaping.
Cast (bind) off rem 8 [7: 9: 8: 10] sts.
With WS facing, rejoin yarn to neck edge of left front sts and cont as for right front from ** to **, then work shoulder shaping as on right front, beg on foll row.
Note: Left front shoulder is 3 rows lower than right front to allow space for shoulder border to be worked later.

Sleeves

With 3¼mm (US size 3) needles and yarn A, cast on 47 [49: 51: 53: 55] sts and work 6 rows in rib as on back, but inc one st at centre of last row. 48 [50: 52: 54: 56] sts.
Change to 4mm (US size 6) needles.
Beg with a k row, work in st st, inc one st at each end of every foll 6th row 3 [2: 1: 1: 0] times, then on every foll 4th row 23 [25: 27: 28: 30] times. 100 [104: 108: 112: 116] sts.
Work without shaping until sleeve measures 45 [46: 47: 48: 49]cm/17¾ [18: 18½: 18¾: 19¼]in from beg, ending with a p row.
Top of sleeve shaping
Place a marker loop in a contrasting yarn at each end of last row to indicate beg of shaping.
Cast (bind) off one st at beg of next 2 rows and 2 sts at beg of next 2 rows; rep these 4 rows again.
Cast (bind) off one st at beg of next 4 rows.
Cast (bind) off rem 84 [88: 92: 96: 100] sts.

Finishing and collar

Press lightly on WS with a cool iron, following instructions on yarn label and avoiding ribbing.
Embroidery
Using yarn C and a tapestry needle, work motifs on back and front in Swiss darning (duplicate st), following chart.
Collar
Join right shoulder seam.
With RS facing, 3¼mm (US size 3) needles and yarn A, pick up and k66 [68: 70: 72: 74] sts evenly around front neck edge and 41 [43: 45: 47: 49] sts across back neck. 107 [111: 115: 119: 123] sts.
Beg with a first rib row (this will be RS of

collar), work in rib as on back for 22cm/
8½in.
Cast (bind) off loosely in rib.

Shoulder buttonhole band

With RS facing, 3¼mm (US size 3) needles
and yarn C, pick up and k28 [30: 32: 34: 36]
sts evenly across left front shoulder edge and
13 sts along the first 5cm/2in of collar. 41
[43: 45: 47: 49] sts.
Rep 2nd rib row, then make buttonholes on
next row as foll:

1st buttonhole row (RS) Keeping rib
correct and beg at shoulder edge, rib 4 [4: 5:
4: 4], cast (bind) off 2, ★rib until there are 8
[9: 9: 10: 11] sts on RH needle after
buttonhole, cast (bind) off 2;★ rep from ★ to
★ twice more, rib to end.

2nd buttonhole row Work in rib, casting
on 2 sts over each buttonhole.
Work one row more in rib.
Cast (bind) off loosely in rib.

Shoulder button band

Work button band on left back shoulder as
for buttonhole band, but beg with the sts
picked up on collar section and omitting
buttonholes.

Collar borders

With RS of collar facing, 3¼mm (US size 3)
needles and yarn C, pick up and k45 sts
evenly along the rem 17cm/6½in on front
edge of collar.
Beg with a 2nd rib row, work 4 rows in rib.
Cast (bind) off loosely in rib.
Work a similar border on back edge of collar.
Neatly join inner edges of borders on collar.
Lap front shoulder band over back band and
sew in place at outer edge.
Matching markers, sew shaped top edges of
sleeves to armholes, stitching through double
thickness on shoulder bands.
Remove markers.
Join side and sleeve seams.
Sew 4 buttons to button band to correspond
with buttonholes, then sew rem 2 buttons
to front section of collar on RS as ornament
(see photo).

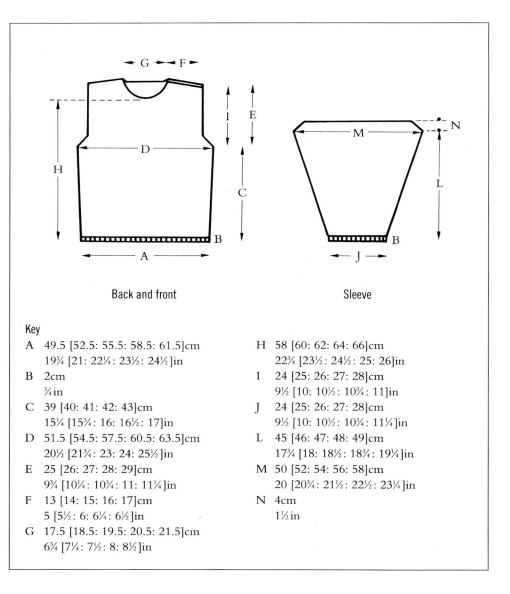

Back and front   Sleeve

Key

A	49.5 [52.5: 55.5: 58.5: 61.5]cm	
	19¾ [21: 22¼: 23½: 24½]in	
B	2cm	
	¾in	
C	39 [40: 41: 42: 43]cm	
	15¼ [15¾: 16: 16½: 17]in	
D	51.5 [54.5: 57.5: 60.5: 63.5]cm	
	20½ [21¾: 23: 24: 25½]in	
E	25 [26: 27: 28: 29]cm	
	9¾ [10¼: 10¾: 11: 11¼]in	
F	13 [14: 15: 16: 17]cm	
	5 [5½: 6: 6¼: 6½]in	
G	17.5 [18.5: 19.5: 20.5: 21.5]cm	
	6¾ [7¼: 7½: 8: 8½]in	
H	58 [60: 62: 64: 66]cm	
	22¾ [23½: 24½: 25: 26]in	
I	24 [25: 26: 27: 28]cm	
	9½ [10: 10½: 10¾: 11]in	
J	24 [25: 26: 27: 28]cm	
	9½ [10: 10½: 10¾: 11¼]in	
L	45 [46: 47: 48: 49]cm	
	17¾ [18: 18½: 18¾: 19¼]in	
M	50 [52: 54: 56: 58]cm	
	20 [20¾: 21½: 22½: 23¼]in	
N	4cm	
	1½in	

Embroidery chart

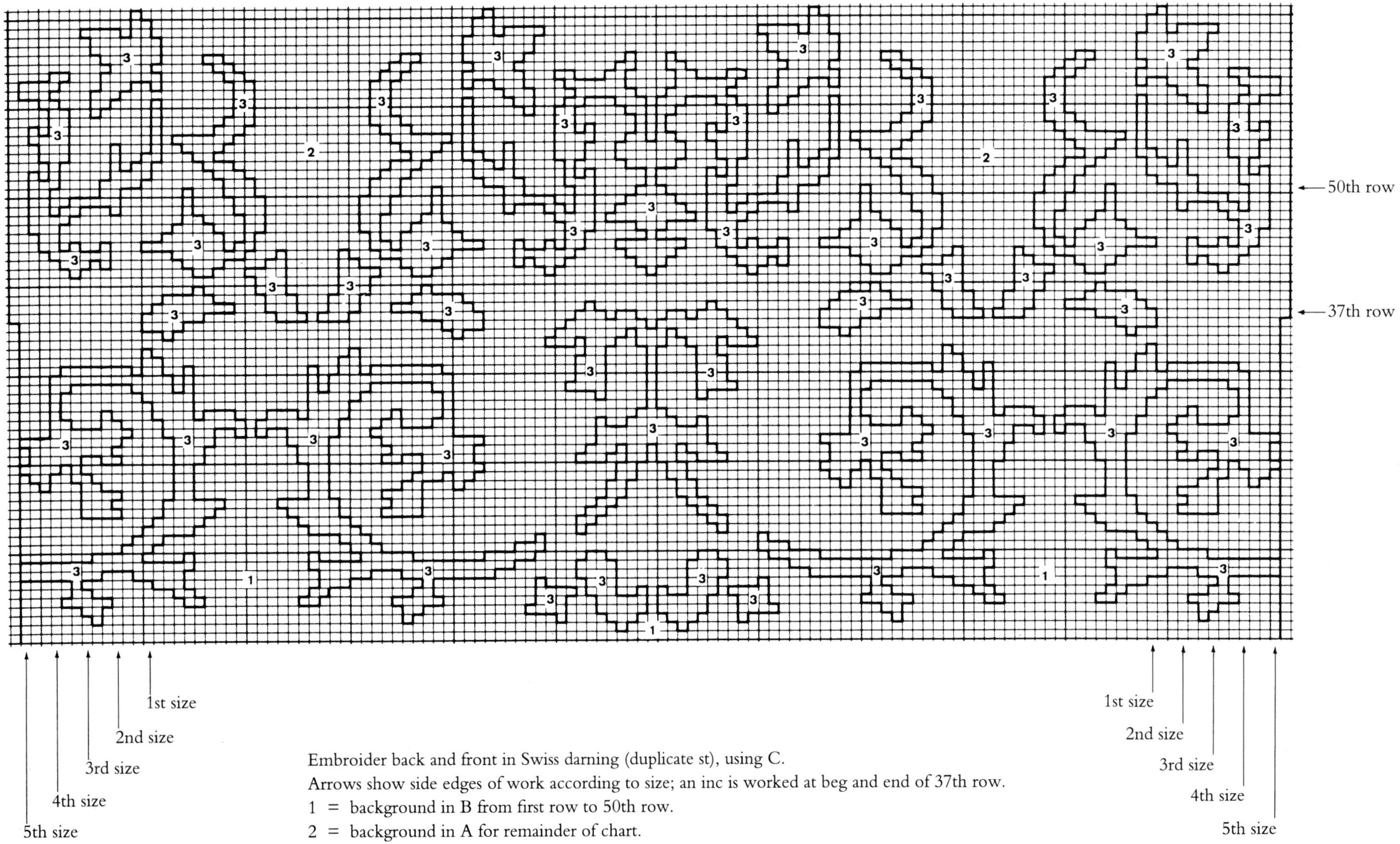

50th row
37th row

1st size
2nd size
3rd size
4th size
5th size

1st size
2nd size
3rd size
4th size
5th size

Embroider back and front in Swiss darning (duplicate st), using C.
Arrows show side edges of work according to size; an inc is worked at beg and end of 37th row.
1 = background in B from first row to 50th row.
2 = background in A for remainder of chart.
3 = embroider in C.

KNITTING PATTERN INFORMATION

Knitting skill levels

Each of the knitting patterns is graded according to the knitting skill required to make the sweater. The levels are as follows:

∗   easy knitting
∗∗   for average knitter
∗∗∗   for experienced knitter
∗∗∗∗ challenging knitting

UK and US knitting terminology

UK and US knitting terminology are almost identical, but where they differ, the US term is given in parentheses, i.e. cast (bind) off, tension (gauge), etc.

Tension (Gauge)

Always knit a sample as instructed before beginning your sweater. Then, if necessary, change needle size to achieve the correct number of stitches and rows to 10cm/4in. Remember – **to save time, take time to check tension (gauge)**.

Knitting needle conversion chart

USA	Old UK	Metric
0	14	2mm
1	13	2¼mm★
		2½mm★★
2	12	2¾mm★
	11	3mm
3	10	3¼mm★
4		3½mm★★
5	9	3¾mm★
	8	4mm
6		
7	7	4½mm
8	6	5mm
9	5	5½mm
10	4	6mm
10½	3	6½mm
	2	7mm
	1	7½mm
11	0	8mm
13	00	9mm

★   UK size only
★★ Continental European size only

Knitting abbreviations

The following abbreviations have been used in the knitting patterns. Any abbreviations which require special instructions are given at the beginning of the patterns under the heading Stitches Used.

alt alternate
approx approximately
beg begin(ning)
cm centimetre(s)
cn cable needle
cont continu(e)(ing)
dec decreas(e)(ing)
foll follow(s)(ing)
g gramme(s)
g st garter st
in inch(es)
inc increas(e)(ing)
k knit
LH left hand
m metre(s)
mm millimetre(s)
oz ounce(s)
p purl
patt(s) pattern(s)
psso pass slip stitch over
rem remain(s)(ing)
rep repeat(s)(ing)
rev st st reverse st st
RH right hand
RS right side(s)
sl slip
st(s) stitch(es)
st st stocking (US stockinette) stitch
tbl through back of loop(s)
tog together
WS wrong side(s)
yd yard(s)
yo yarn over RH needle to make a new st
★ work the instructions after or between asterisks as many times as instructed
( ) work the instructions inside the parentheses as many times as instructed

YARN INFORMATION

Buying yarn

It is always best to buy the specific yarn recommended in a knitting pattern. But if you wish to buy a alternative yarn, be sure to buy a substitute which is the same type of yarn; i.e. buy another cotton yarn for a cotton, or a mohair for a mohair, etc. Detailed descriptions for PINGOUIN yarns are given below. These descriptions should be used as a guide if you are choosing a substitute yarn. Also remember that if you change yarns, you must calculate the amount of yarn required by metrage (yardage) and not by ball weight. Ask your yarn shop for assistance if you are in doubt.

Note: The quantities of yarn stated in the PINGOUIN knitting patterns are based on average requirements and are approximate.

Pingouin yarn descriptions

The following PINGOUIN yarns have been used for knitting patterns in this book.

Andes
Generic weight: medium weight yarn
Fibre content: 40% wool, 30% alpaca and 30% acrylic
Ball size: 50g/1¾oz; approx 110m/122yd per ball
Recommended needle size for st st: 3½mm (US size 4)
Tension (gauge) over 10cm/4in st st: 24 sts and 32 rows

Angora 70
Generic weight: lightweight yarn
Fibre content: 70% angora and 30% lambswool
Ball size: 25g/1oz; approx 90m/99yd per ball
Recommended needle size for st st: 3½mm (US size 4)
Tension (gauge) over 10cm/4in st st: 26 sts and 33 rows

Corrida 3
Generic weight: lightweight yarn
Fibre content: 60% cotton and 40% acrylic
Ball size: 50g/1¾oz; approx 210m/230yd per ball
Recommended needle size for st st: 3mm (US size 3)
Tension (gauge) over 10cm/4in st st: 28 sts and 37 rows

Corrida 4
Generic weight: medium weight yarn
Fibre content: 60% cotton and 40% acrylic
Ball size: 50g/1¾oz; approx 110m/120yd per ball
Recommended needle size for st st: 4mm (US size 6)
Tension (gauge) over 10cm/4in st st: 21 sts and 28 rows

Country
Generic weight: medium-heavy weight yarn
Fibre content: 40% acrylic, 30% wool and 30% mohair
Ball size: 50g/1¾oz; approx 96m/106yd per ball
Recommended needle size for st st: 4mm (US size 6)
Tension (gauge) over 10cm/4in st st: 20 sts and 28 rows

Fil d'Ecosse No. 4
Generic weight: medium weight yarn
Fibre content: 100% cotton
Ball size: 50g/1¾oz; approx 100m/110yd per ball
Recommended needle size for st st: 4mm (US size 6)
Tension (gauge) over 10cm/4in st st: 24 sts and 29 rows

France +
Generic weight: medium weight yarn
Fibre content: 50% wool and 50% acrylic
Ball size: 50g/1¾oz; approx 115m/126yd per ball
Recommended needle size for st st: 3½mm (US size 4)
Tension (gauge) over 10cm/4in st st: 23 sts and 30 rows

Ondine
Generic weight: medium-heavy weight yarn
Fibre content: 97% cotton and 3% polyamide
Ball size: 50g/1¾oz; approx 100m/110yd per ball
Recommended needle size for st st: 4mm (US size 6)
Tension (gauge) over 10cm/4in st st: 19 sts and 33 rows

Pingolaine
Generic weight: fine weight yarn
Fibre content: 100% pure new wool
Ball size: 50g/1¾oz; approx 200m/220yd per ball
Recommended needle size for st st: 3mm (US size 3)
Tension (gauge) over 10cm/4in st st: 30 sts and 40 rows

Pure Laine No. 5
Generic weight: medium-heavy weight yarn
Fibre content: 100% wool
Ball size: 50g/1¾oz; approx 92m/101yd per ball
Recommended needle size for st st: 5mm (US size 8)
Tension (gauge) over 10cm/4in st st: 19 sts and 25 rows

Soft'Hair
Generic weight: medium-heavy weight yarn
Fibre content: 50% mohair, 25% wool and 25% acrylic
Ball size: 50g/1¾oz; approx 110m/121yd per ball
Recommended needle size for st st: 4½mm (US size 7)
Tension (gauge) over 10cm/4in st st: 19 sts and 23 rows

Star +
Generic weight: medium-heavy weight yarn
Fibre content: 50% wool and 50% acrylic
Ball size: 50g/1¾oz; approx 85m/93yd per ball
Recommended needle size for st st: 4½mm (US size 7)
Tension (gauge) over 10cm/4in st st: 18 sts and 24 rows

Sweet'Hair
Generic weight: medium weight yarn
Fibre content: 50% mohair, 25% wool and 25% acrylic
Ball size: 50g/1¾oz; approx 150m/165yd per ball
Recommended needle size for st st: 4mm (US size 6)
Tension (gauge) over 10cm/4in st st: 22 sts and 28 rows

Tempo
Generic weight: medium weight yarn
Fibre content: 85% acrylic and 15% wool
Ball size: 50g/1¾oz; approx 115m/126yd per ball
Recommended needle size for st st: 4mm (US size 6)
Tension (gauge) over 10cm/4in st st: 22 sts and 32 rows

Pingouin yarn addresses

PINGOUIN yarns are widely available in yarn shops and department stores. To find a stockist/retailer near you contact one of the following distributors.

Australia
Handicrafts Australia Pty Ltd,
173 Burwood Road, Burwood NSW 2134.
Tel: 02747/5788. Fax: 02747/5654.

Austria
Pingouin SA, Agent: M J Grassl,
Per Albin Hansson Strasse 42, A 1100 Vienna.
Tel: 0222/688224. Fax: 0222/6882244.

Brazil
Paramount Lanul SA,
Rua Alexandre Dumas 1901, 04717 Sao Paulo.
Tel: 11 548 5200. Telex: 11 55465 Lans BR.

Belgium–Luxembourg
Agent Pingouin, JC Tex BVBA MJ Carton, rue du Poirier 6, 7191 Ecaussinnes.
Tel: 67 44 22 87. Fax: 67 44 22 87.

Canada
Promafil Canada Ltd, 300 Bd Laurentien,
Suite 100, Saint Laurent, QE H4M 2L4.
Tel: 514 747 2938. Fax: 514 748 9358.

Cyprus
Zaco Ltd, 170 Ledra Street, PO Box 1860,
Nicosia. Tel: 2 465115. Fax: 2 461849.

Finland
Oy Nordia Produkter Vilppulante 20A,
00700 Helsinki. Tel: 345 33 61. Fax: 353 597.

Germany
Freidr Ackermann GmbH & Co,
Neckargartacher Str 111, 7100 Heilbronn.
Tel: 07131/4710. Fax: 07131/471149.
Konrad Tiedt GmbH & Co, Goseriede 4,
3000 Hannover 1.
Tel: 0511/14155. Fax: 0511/13385.

Greece
Zachariades, 21 rue Voulis, Athens 105 63.
Tel: 1 32 24 296. Fax: 1 32 36 638.

Holland
Pako Handwerken BV, Postbus 60,
Flevolaan 25A, 1382 Jx Weesp.
Tel: 2940 15070. Fax: 2940 15099.

Italy
Aries, Via Pico Della Mirandola 8/B,
20151 Milan. Tel: 238 010 380.

Japan
Nichifutsu Boeki KK, DF, Building 8 Go,
2, 2 Chome Minami Aoyama Minato Ku,
Toyko. Tel 33 403 0330. Fax 33 404 4472.

Mauritius
Omarjee et Cie, 35 rue Mere Barthelemy,
Port Louis. Tel: 240 1312. Fax: 212 0940.

Mexico
Exclusivas Eva SA de CV,
Boulevard Miguel Hidalgo No. 1616,
Fracc. La Presa y la Reforma, CP 43660,
Tulancingo Hidalgo.

Reunion
Omarjee, BP 64, 192 rue du Mal Leclerc,
97462 Saint Denis. Tel: 21 46 30.

St Pierre & Miquelon
12 rue des Francais libres, BP 1014,
97500 St Pierre & Miquelon.
Tel: 41 37 30. Fax: 41 46 63.

South Africa
Saprotex International Pty Ltd, PO Box 1293,
5200 East London.
Tel: 403 631 551. Fax: 403 631 169.

Spain
Pingouin SA, 9 av Sarria,08029 Barcelona.
Tel: 3 410 60 00. Fax: 3 410 75 94.

Sweden
Nordiska Trend Garn, PO Box 5015,
44851 Tollered.
Tel: 302 327 30. Fax: 302 328 47.

Switzerland
Pingouin SA, Case Postale no. 87,
12 route de Meyrin, 1211 Geneva 7.
Tel: 227 337 626. Fax 227 332 787.

UK
Pingouin UK, Shaftesbury Centre, Percy Street,
Swindon, Wilts SN2 2AZ.
Tel: 79 35 14055. Fax: 79 34 36679.

USA
Laninter U.S.A., PO Box 1542,
476 Longpoint Road, Mount Pleasant,
SC 29465.
Tel: 803 881 1277. Fax: 803 881 2025.

Acknowledgements

The publisher and the editor would like to thank Florence Joubert at Pingouin in Paris, Philippa Wolledge and Anne Foy for their valuable help.